RELATIONSHIP THERAPY

2 BOOKS IN 1:
ANXIETY IN RELATIONSHIP AND COUPLE THERAPY.
MANAGE ANXIETY IN LOVE IN 7 SIMPLE STEPS, CHANGE YOUR BAD HABITS AND IMPROVE YOUR MARRIAGE, RESCUE BROKEN EMOTIONAL TIES.

By Michelle Miller

MICHELLE MILLER

THIS BOOK INCLUDES

BOOK 1:

ANXIETY IN RELATIONSHIP:

The 7 Simple Steps To Manage Anxiety In Relationship And Fight Fear Of Abandonment. Avoid Attachment To Your Partner, Codependency, Jealousy And All Kind Of Negativity.

BOOK 2:

COUPLE THERAPY:

Change Your Bad Habits in Love Following This Effective Couples Therapy Guide. You Can Easily Improve Your Marriage, Rescue Broken Relationship, Solve Most Common Conflicts.

MICHELLE MILLER

© Copyright 2020 - All rights reserved.

The content contained within this book may not be reproduced, duplicated or transmitted without direct written permission from the author or the publisher.

Under no circumstances will any blame or legal responsibility be held against the publisher, or author, for any damages, reparation, or monetary loss due to the information contained within this book. Either directly or indirectly.

Legal Notice:

This book is copyright protected. This book is only for personal use. You cannot amend, distribute, sell, use, quote or paraphrase any part, or the content within this book, without the consent of the author or publisher.

Disclaimer Notice:

Please note the information contained within this document is for educational and entertainment purposes only. All effort has been executed to present accurate, up to date, and reliable, complete information. No warranties of any kind are declared or implied. Readers acknowledge that the author is not engaging in the rendering of legal, financial, medical or professional advice. The content within this book has been derived from various sources. Please consult a licensed professional before attempting any techniques outlined in this book.

By reading this document, the reader agrees that under no circumstances is the author responsible for any losses, direct or indirect, which are incurred as a result of the use of information contained within this document, including, but not limited to, — errors, omissions, or inaccuracies.

RELATIONSHIP THERAPY

Table of Contents

Introduction 12

Chapter 1: General Preface On Anxiety 20

Chapter 2: Fear Of Abandonment 28

Chapter 3: Jealousy...34

Chapter 4: Insecurity 40

Chapter 5: Attachment 48

Chapter 6: Negative Thinking 56

Chapter 7: How To Solve All Problems In 7 Steps And Change Habits. 62

Chapter 8: Some Exercise To Control Anxiety (Muscle Relaxation And Breathing) 70

Chapter 9: Advice For Couples...76

Chapter 10: How To End Anxiety 82

Chapter 11: The Areas That Most Impact Anxiety................. 88

Chapter 12: Self-Evaluation Of Anxiety In A Relationship 96

Chapter 13: How To Improve Your Mood 104

Chapter 14: The Diamond Inside Anxiety 112

Chapter 15: How To Master Your Emotions......................... 116

Chapter 16: Toxic Relationship 122

Chapter 17: Know Your Partner 130

Chapter 18: Therapy And Treatment For Anxiety 136

Chapter 19: Conflicts In Relationship 142

Chapter 20: Anxiety And Miscommunication 150

Chapter 21: Build A Healthy, Long-Lasting And Loving Relationship 156

Chapter 22: Wrong Mental Habits **164**

Chapter 23: Repair Your Relationships When Dealing With Anxiety And Depression **170**

Chapter 24: Helping Your Partner Deal With Anxiety **176**

Chapter 25: Put Anxiety In The Past **186**

Chapter 26: Working It Out **192**

Chapter 27: 10 Habits That Can Make Your Partner's Anxiety Worse **198**

Chapter 28: *Road To Healing* **204**

Conclusion **212**

COUPLE THERAPY

Table Of Contents

Introduction	220
Chapter 1: Understand Each Partners Inner World	226
Chapter 2: Strengthen Friendship And Intimacy	232
Chapter 3: Finding Each Other In New Ways	240
Chapter 4: Facing The Future Together	242
Chapter 5: How Emotions Affect Your Partner	248
Chapter 6: Fighting Less And Feeling Better	256
Chapter 7: Protecting Your Relationship From Affairs	266
Chapter 8: Rescue Broken Relationship	272
Chapter 9: Some Example Of Conversation And Dialogue In Different Day Moments	276
Chapter 10: Significant Habits Of Good Relationships	282
Chapter 11: Cultivating New And Healthy Relationships	290
Chapter 12: How Do We Work Together	298
Chapter 13: Practice Empathy...	304
Chapter 14: Couples And Compromise...............................	310
Chapter 15: Know Your Partner	316
Chapter 16: Couples Therapy Exercises For Improving Communication	320
Chapter 17: Steps To Set Relationship Goals	326
Chapter 18: The Importance Of Having Fun To Couples	332
Chapter 19: Learn How To Apologize	340
Chapter 20: Accepting And Sharing Opinions	346
Chapter 21: How Couples Therapy Helps	352
Chapter 22: Things You Should Do Before Marriage	358

Chapter 23: Creating A Higher Sense Of Intimacy With Your Partner 362

Chapter 24: Marriage Secrets 368

Chapter 25: Dealing With Temptations 374

Chapter 26: How To Live A Happy Relationship 382

Chapter 27: Overcoming Negative Thinking 390

Chapter 28: Tips And Strategies To Maintain Your Emotional Wellbeing 398

Chapter 29: How And Why To Protect Each Other 406

Chapter 30: Love 414

Conclusion 420

MICHELLE MILLER

ANXIETY IN RELATIONSHIP:

The 7 Simple Steps To Manage Anxiety In Relationship And Fight Fear Of Abandonment. Avoid Attachment To Your Partner, Codependency, Jealousy And All Kind Of Negativity.

By Michelle Miller

MICHELLE MILLER

Introduction

All pairs experience anxiety. Occasionally stress and anxiety originate from troubles at the office or with household and or friends that we carry over into our partnerships. Stress and anxiety can likewise arise from the couple's issues, such as an argument, distinctions in wants or requires, or sensation ignored.

Anxiety Can Negatively Influence Relationships.

Although tension prevails, it can be harmful to relationships. Usually, individuals suppress or keep their anxiety to themselves, which makes it tough for their companions to comprehend what they are undergoing and to supply assistance.

Not managing stress can develop a negative cycle where partners "catch" each other's weight. This happens because tension is transmittable-- when our partners are stressed out, we become worried. Think back to a debate that escalated rapidly. You could have "caught" each other's stress and anxiety during the discussion, which made you both feel even more frazzled and made you say things you would not have or else stated. Pairs obtain embedded this unfavorable cycle as well as may be too stressed out to take care of the underlying issue(s).

The Key to Tension Is Just How Couples Handle It.

Couples need to determine as well as speak about what creates their anxiety and what they require when they feel stressed. Although it could be tough to talk about what is producing tension, especially if it is brought on by something within the partnership, it is helpful for companions to speak about their needs and also for partners to supply assistance. Those couples that are most effective in dealing with stress tackle it together. They produce a sensation like they remain in it with each other as well as are a team.

What Can You Do?

Check-in with each other and also pay attention first before you supply options. Ask your partner(s) what you can do to help as well as to make their day smoother. Hug more frequently. It appears weird but embracing for at the very least 30 secs after work each day can assist your bodies to line up and calm each other down. Keep attached throughout tension. Discussing your stress and also having a supportive companion to see you through it makes you as well as your partnership is stronger. Most of us have demanding experiences from time to time because tension can come from numerous sources. Funds. Household stress. Work. Relationships.

And it can have a genuinely distorting effect on our practices. It can make us feel genuinely reduced and also not want to speak to people - with a propensity to close ourselves away and also keep our feelings on the inside.

As well as it can be tough to be self-aware when it pertains to your feedback to tension, very commonly, it can seem like these means of expression are a little outside of your control. Many people find themselves avoiding speaking with others as well as becoming taken out without somewhat knowing they're doing it or unexpected themselves by becoming all of a sudden snappy, cranky and unreasonable.

To offer a little viewpoint on this, our coping mechanisms in these kinds of circumstances are frequently affected by what we experienced maturing. If our parents didn't reveal treatment quickly, we might have become rather experienced at looking after ourselves - indeed, we might have needed to - and so this reaction can kick back in instantly as an adult. Likewise, we commonly duplicate the practices of our moms and dads and also their responses to tension when we're younger.

Just how tension can impact connections.

It's not difficult to see why either of these behaviors would affect your relationship adversely. If you're ending up being withdrawn, your partner is most likely to feel pressed away. And also, if you get stylish, they may feel injured or come to be defensive. What can be truly bothersome, though, is that they may intend to help, as well as think that their efforts are being rebuffed. This can feel like an actual rejection, as well as can result in them becoming withdrawn or snappy themselves. Thus, the problems of stress can snowball as one companion begins to act in an adverse or unconstructive method, so may the various other.

Additional including in this is the truth that they may not become aware of why you're functioning as you are. It might not be quickly evident that it's a tension that's causing you to state unkind points or be unresponsive when talked with. They may feel it's something they have done. This can undoubtedly be mad and also annoying - both for the hurt created and also complication about why it's happening.

Without some type of intervention, the void caused by this kind of circumstance can get bigger and also more significant. And the more you seem like your partner - that, once more, may just wish to assist - gives tension themselves, the much less likely you'll want to try to close that space.

Commonly, the most effective method to proceed in situations such as this is by utilizing a strategy that enables the person experiencing the stress to remain in fee of how much they claim. Very frequently, the very best first step is to say: 'Exactly how can I help simply?' These places firm strongly with experiencing individual problems and are much less likely to make them feel under.

And if your companion is open to talking, then the very same emphasis - on them, and their firm - ought to continue to use. Once more, there can be a lure to right away begin to provide remedies or to get them to 'attempt to see the silver lining' - yet, in a feeling, these can be demanding feedbacks in themselves. They can seem like reasoning's, or as if you're disregarding their experience as one that's quickly fixable. Sometimes, this is precisely the feedback that the cagey person was afraid: one that demands they accede to it, as opposed to one that correctly absorbs precisely how they're feeling, and what they believe.

Instead, it can be a lot more practical to sympathize and also to ask inquiries simply. Very frequently, when we're discovering something challenging, what we want isn't a solution, but just a person to be there with us and provide emotional support. Providing this - even if it implies sitting silently together or simply embracing - might be all they require to begin to seem like the scenario is in control.

Tension can be useful.

Experiencing tension doesn't always indicate your relationship is going to suffer. Instead, your assumption of stress and anxiety-- such as seeing it as a challenge that you can overcome-- is necessary. By watching pressure as a chance to share as well as open with each other, relationships end up being more potent since pairs find out how to browse tension and construct resources to much better deal with future stress and anxiety. Partners discover what they need from each various other and reveal one another that they are looked after, valued, and understood. Having a partner who is always there for you as well as reacts to your needs aids your body to manage stress and anxiety better and also makes anxiety feel much less extreme.

Stress

Does that word define your life today? If so, you're not the only one. Most of us experience stress and anxiety. It might be something significant: a new relocation, a health and wellness worry, a harmful partnership. Yet frequently it is something small: a hectic week at work, a youngster house ill on a day loaded with meetings, the post-work/school thrill to put supper on the moment, the last-minute demand from an employer. These tiny everyday inconveniences can add up and also have huge repercussions overtime for our partnerships. Why? Tension in other areas of our life's spills over right into our connections. The work-life problem is a leading source of stress today. Also, research has revealed over and over again that we bring anxiety and even pressure from work and other parts of our lives home with us, hurting our partnerships.

When people are stressed out, they end up being more taken out and also sidetracked, and even less caring. They likewise have much less time for recreation, which leads to the alienation between partners. Stress and anxiety additionally draw out people's worst attributes, which may influence their partners to take out as well, because who wishes to be around someone when they are acting their worst? Gradually, the relationship comes to be more superficial (less we-ness as well as participation in each other's lives), and also couples happen to be a lot more withdrawn, experiencing more problems, distress, and alienation in the partnership.

Stress and anxiety likewise influence our physical as well as psychological health as well as areas extra strain on the relationship. Stress can specifically be bad for couples who remain in rocky relationships since these couples tend to be a lot more strongly affected by daily occasions (good as well as bad) than couples in more steady relationships. However, also for healthy and balanced, stable relationships, tension can create people to see troubles in their relationships that aren't there.

A pair who usually connects well might see their communication break down over an especially challenging week, and also, as a result of the tension as well as sapped sources, they feel like there are real interaction troubles in their relationships. Likewise, a pair which is usually caring may have little love when stressed and also, therefore, pertained to believe that they have an issue with respect as well as time together, instead of identifying it is just the anxiety. These misperceptions can create discontentment with otherwise healthy connections as well as lead people to try to solve the incorrect trouble (interaction, affection) rather than identifying as well as resolving the actual source of the concern (stress).

How to Reduce High Couple Conflicts

The problem belongs to all connections. In an intimate partnership, where the risks are top, as well as sensations, run deep, the problem is unavoidable. Nonetheless, the problem can wear at the fabric of a connection if it is regular or if it crowds out love, love, and also support.

The best study on the dispute in couples was done by John Gottman, the master pairs' study. In one research study, Gottman took an example of high conflict pairs as well as separated them right into two therapy groups. One team discovered problem resolution skills as well as the other group focused on enhancing what he calls the "marital friendship." Pairs in this 2Nd group worked on structure trust, goodwill, and also compassion in their relationships. Gottman found that couples who reinforced their relationship reduced the problem to a much better degree than those who discovered dispute resolution skills.

So, what is the message from these two sets of research? If you want to reduce disputes in your partnership, focus on increasing the favorable instead of lowering the negative. Look for opportunities to improve your relationship with your partner. Look for methods to reveal affection and support. Search for chances to produce goodwill and also depend on it. Be kind. Be empathic.

MICHELLE MILLER

CHAPTER 1:

General Preface on Anxiety

The American Psychological Association (APA) specifies anxiousness as "a feeling characterized by sensations of stress, stressed ideas and physical modifications like enhanced blood pressure."

Understanding the difference between normal sensations of anxiety and an anxiety disorder calling for clinical attention can assist an individual in identifying and treating the problem. Everybody feels distressed now and then. It's a common emotion. As an example, you may contact worried when faced with trouble at the office, before taking a test, or before making a vital choice.

Stress and anxiety conditions are different, though. They are a group of mental diseases, as well as the distress they trigger can maintain you from carrying on with your life regularly. For individuals who have one, worry and anxiety are constant as well as frustrating and can be disabling. However, with therapy, many individuals can take care of those sensations and get back to a satisfying life. When an individual encounters possibly harmful or distressing triggers, feelings of stress and anxiety are not just typical but necessary for survival.

Since the earliest days of humankind, the method of predators and also incoming threat triggers alarms in the body and also permits incredibly elusive activity. These alarm systems become noticeable in the form of an elevated heartbeat, sweating, as well as boosted level of sensitivity to environments. The risk causes a rush of adrenalin, a hormone, and chemical messenger in mind, which consequently triggers these anxious responses in a procedure called the "fight-or-flight" reaction. This prepares people to physically confront or leave any type of potential hazards to safety and security.

For many individuals, ranging from bigger pets as well as an impending threat is a much less significant issue than it would have been for very early human beings. Stress and anxieties currently revolve around the job, cash, domesticity, wellness, and also other important issues that demand a person's focus without always calling for the 'fight-or-flight' response.

The anxious sensation before an important life occasion or throughout a difficult situation is an all-natural echo of the initial 'fight-or-flight' reaction. It can still be essential to survival-- anxiety about being struck by a car when crossing the street, for example, means that an individual will naturally look at both methods to avoid the threat.

Stress and anxiety is your body's all-natural action to stress and anxiety. It's a sensation of concern or worry concerning what will be ahead. The first day of the institution, going to a job interview, or providing a speech might trigger many people to feel scared and worried. Yet if your feelings of stress and anxiety are severe, last for longer than six months, as well as are hindering your life, you might have an anxiety condition.

Anxiety disorders

The period or extent of a distressed feeling can, in some cases, be out of proportion to the original trigger, or stress factor. Physical signs and symptoms, such as raised blood pressure as well as queasiness, may also develop. These responses move beyond stress and anxiety and they might get into a stress and anxiety condition. The APA defines a person with an anxiety disorder as "having persisting invasive thoughts or problems." As soon as stress and anxiety get to the stage of a disease, it can hinder daily function.

It's typical to feel distressed about transferring to a brand-new area, beginning a brand-new job, or taking a test. This type of anxiousness is unpleasant, but it may inspire you to function more difficult and to do a much better job. Ordinary anxiety is a sensation that reoccurs constantly; however, it does not interfere with your everyday life. When it comes to an anxiousness condition, the feeling of fear may be with you at all times. It is intense and often crippling.

This kind of anxiety may trigger you to stop doing things you appreciate. In extreme cases, it might prevent you from going into an elevator, going across the street, or even leaving your home. If left neglected, the anxiety will undoubtedly keep getting worse. Anxiety problems are one of the most usual types of mental illness as well as can influence any person at any kind of age. According to the American Psychiatric Organization, females are more likely than men to be identified with an anxiousness problem.

Types of Anxiety Disorder

Generalized Anxiety Disorder

Generalized Anxiety Disorder, GAD, is an anxiety problem defined by chronic anxiousness, overstated worry, as well as tension, even when there is little or nothing to prompt it.

Generalized Anxiety Disorder (GAD) is identified by relentless as well as extreme stress over many different things. Individuals with GAD may expect catastrophe as well as maybe excessively worried about money, wellness, family, job, or various other concerns. People with GAD discover it hard to control their fear. They may worry higher than seems called for regarding actual occasions or might anticipate the most awful also when there is no obvious factor for concern.

GAD is diagnosed when a person locates it tough to manage worry on more days than not for at the very least six months and has three or more symptoms. Learn more concerning signs. This sets apart GAD from worry that may be specific to a fixed stress factor or for a lot more limited time.

GAD affects 6.8 million grownups, or 3.1% of the U.S. populace, in any kind of provided year. Females are twofold as most likely to be influenced than male. The problem begins slowly and can start across the life cycle, though the risk is most significant between childhood years as well as middle age. Although the exact root cause of GAD is unknown, there is evidence that organic aspects, family members' history, as well as life experiences, explicitly demanding ones, might contribute.

In some cases, just the idea of making it through the day creates anxiousness. Individuals with GAD don't understand just how to stop the worry cycle and feel it is past their control. However, they typically assume that their stress and anxiety is more extreme than the circumstance warrants. All anxiousness problems might relate to trouble enduring uncertainty, and therefore many individuals with GAD attempt to prepare or control circumstances. Lots of people believe concern avoids poor things from occurring, so they see it is high-risk to give up interest. Sometimes, people can fight with physical signs such as stomachaches and also migraines.

When their anxiety level is moderate or with treatment, individuals with GAD can operate socially, have full as well as significant lives, as well as be gainfully utilized. Lots of GAD may prevent circumstances since they have the disorder, or they may not capitalize on possibilities due to their fear (social situations, travel, promos, etc.). Some individuals can have difficulty performing the most comfortable daily activities when their stress and anxiety is severe.

Obsessive-Compulsive Disorder (OCD).

Obsessive-Compulsive Disorder is a stress and anxiety disorder and also is identified by reoccurring, unwanted thoughts, or repeated actions. Recurring habits such as hand cleaning, counting, examining, or cleaning are typically made with the hope of stopping compulsive ideas or making them go away. Executing these supposed "rituals," however, offers just short-lived alleviation, and also not performing them markedly raises anxiety.

Obsessive-- the necessary condition is a mental illness in which an individual really feels the demand to perform specific regimens consistently, or has certain thoughts always. The individual is unable to control either the ideas or tasks for higher than a short time. Common compulsions include hand cleaning, checking off points, and inspecting to see if a door is locked. Some may have trouble throwing points out. These tasks strike such a degree that the person's life is negatively affected, usually occupying greater than an hour a day. Most grownups recognize that the behaviors do not make sense. The problem is related to tics, anxiousness problems, and also a raised danger of suicide.

The cause is unknown. There seem some hereditary components with both identical twins regularly impacted than both non-identical doubles. Threat aspects include a background of child misuse or another stress-inducing event. Some instances have been recorded to take place following infections. The medical diagnosis is based upon the signs and symptoms as well as requires eliminating other medication necessary or preventive reasons. Rating scales such as the Yale-- Brownish Compulsive Uncontrollable Scale can be made use of to assess the severity. Other problems with comparable symptoms include anxiety problems, major depressive disorder, eating conditions, tic problems, and obsessive-compulsive personality disorder.

The therapy involved is cognitive-behavioral therapy, and occasionally antidepressants such as discerning serotonin reuptake inhibitors or clomipramine. CBT for OCD entails boosting exposure to what creates the problems while not permitting the repeated behavior to occur. While clomipramine appears to function along with SSRIs, it has more significant adverse effects, so it is commonly reserved as a 2ND line treatment. Atypical antipsychotics may serve when used in addition to an SSRI in treatment-resistant cases, yet are likewise associated with an enhanced danger of side effects. Without therapy, the problem often lasts years.

Obsessive-- uncontrollable condition influences regarding 2.3% of people at some time in their life. Percentages throughout a provided year are about 1.2%, and also it takes place worldwide. It is uncommon for symptoms to start after the age of 35, and half of the individuals create troubles before 20. Males and also ladies are influenced equally. The phrase compulsive-- uncontrollable is often made use of in a casual manner unrelated to OCD to explain a person as being excessively careful, perfectionistic, soaked up, or otherwise infatuated.

Panic Disorder.

A panic attack is an anxiousness condition as well as is characterized by unexpected and repeated episodes of intense anxiety accompanied by physical signs that might include chest discomfort, heart palpitations, and shortness of breath, dizziness, or stomach distress.

Panic disorder is a stress and anxiety condition defined by returning unexpected panic attacks. Anxiety attack is sudden durations of intense anxiety that might consist of palpitations, sweating, shaking, shortness of breath, feeling numb, or a sensation that something awful is most likely to occur. The optimum level of signs occurs within minutes. There might be continuous worries about having additionally struck as well as avoidance of locations where attacks have happened in the past.

The cause of the panic attack is unknown. Panic disorder typically runs in the family members. Threat factors consist of smoking, emotional stress, as well as a background of youngster abuse. Medical diagnosis entails dismissing various other possible reasons for anxiety, including various other mental illnesses, clinical problems such as heart disease or hyperthyroidism, and also substance abuse. Evaluating the condition may be done by using a survey.

A panic attack is usually treated with counselling as well as medications. The kind of therapy made use of is typically cognitive behavioral therapy, which works in over half of people. Pills made use of consist of antidepressants and also sometimes benzodiazepines or beta-blockers. Following stopping treatment, as much as 30% of individuals have a reappearance.

Panic disorder influences 2.5% of people at some point in their life. It usually starts throughout adolescence or very early the adult years, but any type of age can be affected. It is less usual for youngsters and also older people. Women are more frequently affected than males.

MICHELLE MILLER

CHAPTER 2:

Fear of Abandonment

Although it stems from your childhood, abandonment anxiety can be projected on any romantic relationships you develop as an adult. When faced with the idea of losing a loved one, it can trigger your attachment style. Sometimes, people with abandonment issues will behave in ways that they push their partners to leave them. This is one of the techniques of coping with abandonment. Unconsciously, they speed up the process so their fear will be gone.

This behavior is unhelpful and deepens the fear, making it more intense and is placing the suffering person in a vicious cycle of anxiety. Once the alarm is present, the person who suffers from abandonment anxiety will behave in such ways that affirm his fears, and he will never be able to get out of the loop. In order to be able to break away from this anxiety, you must understand your behaviors, why they appear, and how to change them. Some acts of abandonment anxiety are the following:

1. Sabotaging relationships, purposefully pushing the partner away, so you do not get hurt once he leaves you.

2. Having numerous shallow relationships. Mainly due to an inability to bond with your partner on a deeper level. When a partnership begins, the person suffering from abandonment anxiety will feel it is time to break up. The idea behind this

behavior is that if you do not build a stable connection with your partner, it will not hurt once he leaves.

3. Clinging to bad relationships. Some people with abandonment anxiety might stay in unhealthy relationships at any cost because their fear of being alone is stronger than the need for security.

4. Need for constant reassurance. Need for your partner to affirm repeatedly that he loves you and that he will never leave. Even with this continuous reassurance, you are still unable to trust them enough to gain relief from anxiety.

5. Separation anxiety. Believed only happens to children, it has been observed in adults too. Some people feel extreme anxiety symptoms when left alone, without a partner for short or long periods.

6. Panic is a common symptom of abandonment anxiety. When you do not hear from your partner for a set period, or he does not answer your calls, you might feel panic rising and demand to know what is going on immediately.

7. Fear of being alone. Spending every moment of the day in the same vicinity as your partner, in other words, being clingy, even having trouble sleeping without your partner being nearby.

In the long term, people with abandonment anxiety may develop other mental health issues, such as depression, mood swings, or even anger issues. These mental health problems may influence your future relationships, making potential partners feel alienated and force them to leave, thus restarting the cycle of abandonment.

Therapy

Therapy for abandonment anxiety can vary, and it mainly depends on the source of stress. For instance, we treat anxiety that has roots in abuse differently from those that stem from the death of a caregiver. However, most people who suffer from abandonment anxiety, manage to overcome their issues by combining more than one type of therapy. Here are some of the most common treatments used to combat abandonment anxiety:

1. Eye movement desensitization and reprocessing (EMDR) is used for treating trauma and can help people with abandonment anxiety if the root of it is in some past traumatic experience. It was first developed to treat PTSD but can also be used to treat any other type of trauma. EMDR is a type of therapy that will reprocess memories connected to the trauma and change your response to those memories.

2. Dialectical behavioral therapy (DBT) is one on one treatment with a professional, and it can teach you the skills needed to overcome abandonment anxiety. Mindfulness and emotional regulation are one of these skills. It helps you learn how to talk to your partner and how to control your emotions and reactions.

3. Cognitive-behavioral therapy (CBT) will bring awareness to your past experiences that are causing your abandonment anxiety. By being aware of them, it will be easier for you to overcome them. It will help you set an objective view of your experiences and teach you how to differentiate the present situation from your past. This will also help disconnect any anxiety resulting from your past experiences and teach you how to behave in triggering situations.

4. Psychodynamic therapy can bring awareness to your attachment styles, and it can teach you about how you relate to others. You may learn how to change your bad habits which are related to the bonding process. It will also make you understand which defensive mechanisms you developed to cope with abandonment, and it will attempt to improve them.

5. Couples therapy for abandonment anxiety. One or both partners may be dealing with abandonment anxiety. Couples therapy can help them deal with their issues, as well as relationship issues. It will also help them grow closer to each other and understand each other better.

6. Fear of abandonment couples therapy: This will help both partners understand each other better. If only one partner is suffering from fear of abandonment, the other one might not understand how past experiences can still influence his loved one. On the other hand, a partner that is suffering from anxiety will not understand how his loved one cannot put up with his behavior. His demand for attention and reassurance is not met. He does not see how that demand is negatively impacting his partner. Through couple's therapy, both partners will learn how to better interact with each other. They will learn how to express their needs in a healthy way and communicate properly.

7. Emotional abandonment couples therapy: If you, or your partner, are dealing with abandonment anxiety that stems from a present situation. It could be manifesting itself through an emotional barrier between the two of you. Couples therapy may help you reconnect and find the system of bonding which suits both of you. A counselor can help you realize where the barrier is coming from, and help you explore your feelings to prepare you to be open again.

In addition to all the options above, you can attempt self-care for abandonment anxiety. It is needed that you learn how to take proper care of yourself if you are the one suffering from abandonment anxiety. To overcome this fear, you must:

1. Learn to keep calm once the triggers overwhelm you. Find a safe space and attempt to objectify your fears.

2. Build your trust in others. Do not isolate yourself; instead, learn how to rely on others to better yourself.

3. Practice mindfulness. Pay attention to what you think and try to understand your fears, and ask yourself why do you feel this way, and where do your fears originate.

4. Learn how to communicate your needs. Instead of demanding attention and saying, "I need you to be there for me," say something like "I would feel safer if you would be there for me." Learn new communication skills; they will significantly reduce the number of misunderstandings you might have with your partner.

5. Acknowledge your past traumatic experiences. Do not ignore them, it will only affirm your fears, and it will not help your relationship.

Find the cause of your abandonment anxiety. Knowing the source will help you practice self-care with more ease. Your past abandonment experience happened, but you must realize it is not a pattern, and it will not necessarily happen again.

Helping your Partner

It is difficult to help someone who is suffering from abandonment issues, mostly because their reactions are unpredictable. If you bring up your concerns regarding their anxiety, they might lash out in anger and attack you, or they might completely withdraw within themselves and refuse to communicate. However, there are some things you can do to ease their anxiety and help them on their path to recovery:

1. Leave the conversation: If your partner becomes highly emotional, an interview will be unhelpful. Both you and your partner might say things you do not mean to satisfy your needs. Step away from discussions like these, and let your partner know you care but do not give in to emotions. Instead, hold your partner, and show him with body language that you mean well, and return to having a conversation once emotions are less intense.

2. Do not respond to behavior triggered by anxiety: Your partner will demand attention by saying things like "I do not want to talk about it" or "leave me alone." If you continue to insist on a conversation, you will be trapped and unconsciously affirm his fears. Instead, take him for his word and do not respond. Let his emotions pass before engaging in a conversation.

3. Say how you feel: Be honest and tell him how his abandonment anxiety is influencing you, and how it is making you feel. He will realize it is not all about him and reconsider his actions to avoid hurting you.

All the solutions listed above can help you understand how your abandonment anxiety came to be. You may learn its source and how to manage it, as such behaviors are influencing your relationship for the worst. Therapy can demonstrate you the skills you need to avoid or change those behaviors. With time and patience, this will lead to a happy and healthy relationship. Your insecurities and intrusive thoughts might return occasionally, and you might feel the need for more therapy, but do not get discouraged. Overcoming abandonment anxiety is a long process, and it requires devotion and self-care.

CHAPTER 3:

Jealousy

The green-eyed monster can destroy even the strongest of relationships. It breaks down trust and creates tension in the relationship. One partner takes on an offensive role while the other becomes defensive. In this kind of dynamic, both parties are miserable and the relationship begins to feel like a burden.

Jealousy is in most cases driven more by your insecurities than by your partner's actions or behavior. It can lead to people making rash decisions that end up causing more harm to the relationship. Lashing out, revenging and even aggression are just some of the ways in which jealousy manifests.

Eventually we all experience jealousy. Sometimes it is founded while in others it can be as a result of an overactive imagination and fear. Whatever the case may be, jealousy becomes a problem when you start giving in to it. Learning to manage your emotions is one of the most effective ways of overcoming jealousy and its effects on your relationship.

If jealousy has become a permanent undercurrent in your relationship, it is time you learned how to deal with the green-eyed monster. Here are some procedures to help you overcome jealousy in your relationship.

a) Identify your jealousy triggers

Are you afraid of being abandoned? Do you have low self-esteem? Is a lack of confidence making you feel insecure? In most cases, jealousy is triggered by the mental experiences that we have in our minds.

Maybe someone lied on you in the past and that led you to have trust issues. Or you developed negative attachment as a result of a difficult childhood. Delve behind your jealousy and find out what is really driving it.

Identifying what your triggers are may not eradicate your jealousy but you will be less likely to overreact when you understand where your feelings are coming from. This means that you must have a level of self-awareness that enables you to acknowledge that your insecurity has more to do with your fears than your partner does.

b) Learn to self-regulate

If you do not manage your emotions, they can wreak havoc in your life. Jealousy can cause you to do things that you normally would never consider. Aggression, lashing out, and seeking revenge are all signs that you are having a hard time controlling your emotions.

No matter how aggrieved you feel, destructive behavior is never acceptable and will not solve anything. Learn to keep your temper in check by not acting on your emotions. Mindfulness techniques such as deep breathing exercises and meditation can help you keep your emotions under control. Avoid giving in to obsessive thoughts that stir up your negative emotions.

Write down how you are feeling as a way to let out pent up emotions. This not only relieves some of the pressure you are feeling but helps to put things in perspective. Confide in a friend or someone you trust, talking through your feelings can also help you to overcome them and feel calmer.

Find ways to stay busy and mentally engaged so that you are not just ruminating on negative thoughts and emotions. Learning to self-regulate may just be one of the best things you can do for yourself and for your relationship.

c) Let go of your past

Most of our fears are fed by past experiences. We assume that just because one relationship ended severely that the next will follow the same path. Emotional baggage can stop you from having beautiful relationships by painting all your relationships with one broad brush.

Get closure for your past and leave it there, in the past. Nobody likes to be compared to your former lover or get judged based on someone else's mistakes. Just because you had an unfaithful partner does not mean that everyone cheats. When you bring your past hurts into your relationship, you have already affected the health of that relationship. You start to punish your partner for the mistakes of other people.

Depending on how deep-seated your emotional issues are, you can find ways to get closure yourself or even talk to a therapist. Get rid of any reminders of your failed relationships and give yourself a clean slate to work with.

b) Trust

In any relationship trust is an essential component. You need to trust your partner and you also need to trust yourself. When you trust yourself, you acknowledge that it is possible your relationship may not work out but you will be fine nonetheless. This liberates you from the burden of constantly worrying about losing your partner which is one of the fears that promote jealousy.

Not all relationships are built to last. This does not mean that you should live your life in fear or dreading that you will be abandoned. It simply means accepting that in every relationship you have to be willing to be vulnerable. Once you trust yourself enough you will be able to enjoy your relationship without continually feeling threatened.

Trusting yourself starts with loving yourself. Acknowledge that you are worthy of love and that your partner is with you because he chooses to be. Keep a positive mind frame by avoiding negative self-dialogue and self-defeating beliefs. Resist the urge to compare yourself with others in order to feel worthy of love or affection. Your partner will love and accept you the way you are if you allow yourself first.

The other aspect of trust is trusting your partner. Unless you have a valid reason to be suspicious, trust your partner to do right by you. Resist the urge to monitor and check up on your partner regularly. The world is full of other people and you cannot stop your partner from interacting with other people just to make yourself feel secure.

When you hold on to something too tight, you end up cutting off its circulation and killing it. Let your relationship have enough freedom that your partner does not feel like he is imprisoned or confined. Putting someone on a leash may work in the short term but eventually, without trust, your relationship will crumble like a house of cards.

RELATIONSHIP THERAPY

MICHELLE MILLER

CHAPTER 4:

Insecurity

Symptoms of Insecurity and How to Recognize Them

Blaming

If you are always reprimanding or blaming your partner for everything, you need a rude awakening. This happens when your ego is controlling your relationship and utilizing manipulative tactics to do it. Do you ever assume responsibility for the things that you do? Would you be able to move to one side and think from another perspective without accusing the other person? The ego will want you to find fault and scrutinize for others' mistakes. It will do everything and anything to transfer blame and criticize another person. Shockingly, that thing we evade is generally what we end up receiving in our relationships. If you fail to take responsibility for yourself, your ego will help you project all this onto your partner.

Playing the Victim

Is it safe to say that you are playing the unfortunate victim card in your relationship? Do you always compare yourself with your partner? Is it true that you are continually putting yourself down? An unhealthy ego will help you reinforce negative actions as opposed to positive ones. It will cause you to focus too much on your imperfections. If you are doing this, it is unquestionably time to venture back and conduct a recheck on your relationship. You are not a saint.

The time has come to be responsible for what you are bringing to the table and stop constantly blaming your partner for everything.

Being Jealous

Jealousy is the green-eyed monster, and it usually sets the stage for negative drama in a relationship. Ego tends to feed on self-esteem and the absence of acknowledgment. A cherishing relationship depends on regard and consciousness of each other. Love doesn't contribute to comparing, putting down, and criticizing as ego does. This is a show that turns into the most astounding type of negative drama in any relationship. If you are in an abusive relationship, your ego won't let you leave because of jealousy. What is making you consider these ideas? Does your partner make you question the validity of your relationship? This means you need to venture back and be straightforward about identifying the abuse in the relationship.

Fearing Rejection

This kind of dread prevents you from proceeding onward and accomplishing any of your goals. When you stop yourself as a result of this dread, you are unfair to your relationship. Changing the way you perceive things as opposed to being incapacitated by the anxiety and uneasiness caused by your ego will be a healthy way to increase self-esteem. Negative self-talk will only feed your ego. Don't compromise on who you indeed are to surrender to your partner's ego. This is anything but healthy. A loving relationship depends on mutual respect and acknowledgment. On the off chance that you are feeling rejected, maybe it's time to re-evaluate your relationship.

Always Having the Last Word

Your ego has a way of making every little thing about you and turning it into a one-person play. If you find that you talk a lot about yourself and don't ask about your partner, well, you are immensely ego-driven. The ego assumes a superb role in shielding us from accomplishing total harmony and joy. It is the mind's method for controlling. It will likewise create situations in your account that don't exist. If you find that you need to have the last say in all things, it's time that you venture back and discover the root of this need. Do you feel like you are better than others or second rate? Do you lack self-confidence and, in this manner, need to demonstrate that you are worthy despite all the trouble? The ego will make you conceal your sense of mediocrity by overhyping yourself. If you and your partner fight a lot, your ego probably fuels these fights. Is this how you feel necessary in your relationship?

It is essential to take a step back and observe your relationship at times. You need to identify when you are the one in the wrong and making mistakes. Take a look at your actions and acknowledge when they are driven by ego. You have to let go of your ego if you want a robust and healthy relationship with your partner.

So if you have a big ego or your love is egotistical, what should you do?

For the narcissist, being correct all the time is deeply connected with their sense of self-worth. In this way, the individuals who can't relinquish their ego do and say anything they want, and they always think they are correct. Tragically, this will be at the expense of a lot of other things. Their need to always be correct can cost them their relationship with colleagues, supervisors, kin, relatives, and more often than not, their partners. Sooner or later, you have to understand that the bogus self-esteem that you get from adhering to your ego and "being correct" doesn't exceed genuine happiness.

Being true to yourself and practicing mindfulness will enable you to understand that you can't be right in every circumstance. There will be certain situations where you make a mistake, you have a wrong mentality, or you're mostly on the wrong side.

It may be hard to admit this at times; however, having the ability to concede when you're wrong can be quite liberating. Assume responsibility for your actions and decisions, and you will soon see that the ball will be in your court!

You don't have to be better or higher than everyone around you. The need to be this way can be quite destructive for you. A great sense of ego leads you to believe that you are superior to every other person. It is similar to remembering that you don't need to be correct always. Understand that you don't have to be better than everybody else either. That is not a healthy level of competitiveness in anyone.

There will always be somebody better, prettier, more astute, quicker, wealthier than you. No matter how old you are, this will always be the way of things. The sooner you understand that you cannot—and ought not to feel committed to—be superior to other people, the sooner you can repair and improve your relationships.

Rather than contending with others along these lines, why not consider improving yourself? You are entirely unique. Focus on how you can improve yourself, and every one of your relationships will take a turn for the better.

Exercise – It is imperative to see how activity impacts the body as well as the mind too. Daily use is essential in the individual life. At the point when you practice regularly, your account discharges endorphins into your circulatory system, which improves your mind-set. Also, your psyche is occupied from your restless musings. Practicing has been deductively to help your general state of mind and decrease the indications of nervousness and sadness. As physical exercise increments, so makes the improvement of your anxiety. A few activities to take an interest in that have been explicitly connected to assisting with tension are yoga and judo. This is because these activities for an individual to be careful in their developments and center while clearing their brain. As you structure an everyday practice with your activity, your body will start to deliver serotonin and endorphins previously, during, and after exercise. These synthetic concoctions that are provided in mind are appeared to diminish melancholy and uneasiness fundamentally. Training supports confidence, improves certainty, enables you to start to feel engaged and reliable, and causes you to manufacture solid and new social connections and companionship.

Begin a healthy diet – The mind requires an enormous measure of vitality and sustenance to work effectively. Healthy nutrition can bring enormous changes in your physical health. A terrible eating regimen implies that you are not providing the supplements that are required for your mind's synapses to work effectively. In light of that, it might be worsening the manifestations of your nervousness. By eating a sound eating regimen and filling your plate with entire and new nourishment, drinking the perfect measure of water and guaranteeing that you are taking in the correct nutrients, minerals, and trans fats day by day, you are giving your cerebrum the proper nourishment to capacity and battle anxiety. A solid eating routine likewise implies dealing with your gut and stomach related tract. Recollect that a sound eating routine methods removing improved beverages like frosted teas, soft drinks, and prepared natural product juices. Studies have demonstrated that individuals who drink over the top measure of pop each day are over 30% bound to experience the ill effects of nervousness and melancholy than the individuals who don't. Unsweetened beverages like plain espresso, homegrown teas, and water that has the organic product in it are a far more beneficial alternative when keeping your body and cerebrum hydrated. Caffeine is likewise a supporter of tension side effects and ought to be curtailed to battle the symptoms of caffeine.

No more liquor – liquor is a focal sensory system depressant and is a known reason for tension as we all know that it is very harmful to our health. A few people do attempt to dull the impacts of their nervousness by drinking liquor; however, actually, alcohol is regularly the base of your tension. Liquor intrudes on rest, gets dried out the body, and occupies an individual from managing the current issues as opposed to going up against and recognizing the root and reason for their anxiety.

Catch up on your rest – Bad dozing propensities affect an individual's state of mind. This is because the mind's synapses need time to rest and recharge to keep the body's mind-set steady. Legitimate, eternal rest enables the cerebrum to adjust hormone levels and allows an individual to all the more likely to adapt to their anxiety. Unfortunate dozing propensities and sleep deprivation needn't bother with synthetic compounds to be amended. Awful resting propensities can be rectified utilizing standard techniques including melatonin, teas, homegrown mixes, exercise, and contemplation. At the point when you ensure that you are getting high, quality rest, your mind will start to address its hormone levels.

Begin to address your feelings– This covers dealing with your negative contemplations and frames of mind broadly, and being restless miracles the body's hormones and powers the brain to create more synthetic concoctions to attempt to feel upbeat. In the end, the cerebrum gets exhausted and can't deliver the hormones expected to battle sickness and tension. Via preparing your psyche to consider reflection emphatically and care thoroughly, you can change your recognition on what's going on and start to assume responsibility for your negative considerations. By battling and hushing your very own negative contemplations, you can work through your nervousness, ensuring that you are better ready to recuperate in your relationship. Make sure to rehearse all types of positive confirmation, which incorporates excusing yourself, appreciation for your life, and consideration to other people. At the point when you can get positive, uneasiness begins to slow, and you are better ready to speak with your accomplice without negative, foolish conduct subverting you. Continuously recollect that you are responsible for your own life. If there are circumstances that are making your tension erupt, you can transform them.

MICHELLE MILLER

CHAPTER 5:

Attachment

The relation is helpful and essential for human interaction, but how a person interacts or communicates with others can be related in positive and negative ways to various facets of his life. Attachment types were identified as one of the earliest elements in the creation of a human. This indicates that problems relating to relationships and mental health disorders can be attributed to the forms of attachment developed during childhood and modified through interactions.

Type of Relationships Formed

According to Martin (2017), relationships can be measured on the basis of three major attachment styles:

- Healthy attachment – that can build a stable, supportive relationship, where the person is confident to communicate his / her desires and emotionally intimate.
- Resisting attachment – a more solitary environment, while the person will spend a lot more time alone and resist contact, as the name implies before the interaction is too painful to drive others away.
- Nervous attachments — contradictions in relationships that may be demanded by the person, but which are ignored at a time. These individuals are generally called sticking, but because of this discrepancy, they do not have healthy relationships.

Martin (2017) adds that these types are created through interactions between parents and children and influence adult interactions. The type of attachments which we make affect not only the human being but also his self-confidence.

Description of events

An association is created because the caregivers are diligent and compliant with the wishes of the individual. In adulthood, a good friendship with a partnership or other intimate interaction may do this. These three imbalanced communication types are negative, concerned, and evasive. This happens whether the caregiver is withdrawn or irresponsive in childhood or prior relationships. This adds to an uncomfortable sensation anytime a friend attempts to be more vigilant. Finally, when the caregiver became unreliable, nervous, and distressed, attachment forms arise. The person is not aware of whether the affection is continuously there so that they are vulnerable and comfortable when being so far apart, they feel free from the expected dismissal. Application to therapy a specific interaction or interview may decide the form of commitment formed by the person with respect to their perceptions of a partnership. You will decide how your communication style impacts your present relationships as well as the challenges following the life objectives. The childhood experiences related to the development of forms of attachment are suggesting mental health conditions such as anxiety into adulthood, according to Schimmenti and Bifulco (2015). The knowledge of the style of the relationship of the client helps the therapist to tailor the treatment to the circumstances leading to the development of these disorders. The root of the attachment form is the critical source of effective counseling (Mikulincer, Shaver, Berant, 2013). If the heart of the attachment pattern can be established, the therapy cycle can ultimately be guided to the heart of the inability to form stable adult relationships. It is essential that the practitioner has a full understanding of the various attachment styles, the assignment context of these styles, and the associated events assigned to these styles to help determine a customer's best course of treatment. Attachment may mainly be rendered through childhood, but different partnerships may have modified the attachment type from one area to another by the provision or non-provision of a stable attachment matrix. Therapy should be customized to produce optimal results for the patient. It is essential that the client feels confident in thinking about their connections and other familiar things that have altered their communication patterns, as it is necessary for the therapist to be able to establish a successful partnership with the practitioner. Approaching the beginning of relationship issues without understanding these types of attachment will compromise the client's best result.

Do you understand the look of an established partnership between your customers?

Why Attachment Matters in Adult Relationships

The relationship between parent and child is defined in attachment theory by the willingness of parents to react physically and emotionally to their child. The bond is described as stable or vulnerable based on the ability of the parent to establish protection and how the child reacts. A child must have faith in his parent to think that the relationship is a safe haven and that the world is a safe and stable environment. Children need to trust innately that their parent is there for them when they are in need. I don't know a lot of people who argue that this is not the best way to raise all babies. This need for connectivity is innate in any human being. We don't seem to talk in adult relationships about attachment, but it is equally necessary. The affection in adult relationships is very different because it is mutual. A parent doesn't expect a sense of protection from their kids, but a partner certainly looks for that (even if they are unaware of it). Adults do need to believe that a connection provides stability and protection so that they can have a deeper, better expressed, better coherent, and optimistic sense of self and others. The fact that there is a sexual aspect is another distinction in adult relationships. Here too, we see how intimate the sexual relationship between partners is defined by the need for health and protection. "No defense, no sex" is a traditional refrain of adult intercourse. At the very heart of a marriage is the question, "Are you there for me?" If I need you I can count on you to be there physically, can I count on you to be there for me if I have an emotional need? Can I count on you to understand that my relationship demands protection and security, so that I can reveal my true self? Will this protection allows me to explore the planet and find my place there? The sensitivity and openness of each partner to the other's emotional signals in relationships determine whether there is a sense of a stable foundation on which to travel. This sense of stability and safe connection are missing in strained ties. Isolating or disconnecting a parent or partner from an attachment source is painful intrinsically. Emotional disconnection drives people into anxiety and uncertainty. The brain reads the actions of a partner as "dangerous," and because of our hard work to survive, we take a posture of challenge, flight, or freeze.

Each activity responds in a mutual feedback loop from a partner. It looks at a couple all over in a destructive loop that may lead to the collapse of the relationships between spouses. The more frustration and hopelessness the relationship, the more reactive, linear, and self-intensive the emotional and behavioral responses between spouses become. Couples are trapped in a destructive circle between repetitive attitudes and misunderstandings. Whenever a person struggles to respond in a moment of great need, a sense of fear and vulnerability develops until a few individuals get trapped in an assault loop and protect themselves over the moment. These loops are guided by rage, sadness, loneliness, shame, and terror.

Securely connected couples cannot go into a negative cycle as profoundly and can easily exit either cycle. Such couples will convey precisely what disturbed or caused them. Partners can control their emotional pain through separation and can give simple, consistent signs of needs when reunited. Surely attached partners will support each other and embrace warmth and reassurance. Moments known as vulnerable or dangerous can be recognized and addressed. Couples should draw on their experience and construct a coherent, clear account of their relationship.

In short, it is possible for securely attached pairs to address a potential deterioration without triggering a negative attack/retirement period. Couples tend to be more open and direct and also prefer to connect more to their friends. There is a stronger emphasis on individual needs and a broader sense of concern for the spouse. Communication is polite, as well as constructive. In reality, this is "successful dependency," the ability to feel connected to others and trust that they are autonomous.

Why Do Relationships Fail? - Basic Problems

Your companion has finished your link, and your mind is spinning. This is the end you can't believe, and you want to know how to get together with your ex. The first step in this cycle is to figure out what was wrong first and foremost in your relationship. There are all kinds of little issues that might have gone wrong and put the friendship to an end. In the end, though, all six basic questions can be traced back to the causes of a broken partnership.

Envy is not brought on by someone else's thinking or doing. Really, it's a feeling from inside you. There may be envy for many reasons, such as lack of confidence, a weak self-image, anxiety, or insecurity. Jealousy not only makes you cynical and depressed, but it also ruins a relationship.

Attachment you want to spend time with the person you enjoy while in a relationship. However, that can be pushed too far. You have been too emotionally dependent because you want your partner to share every single minute with you, or you are just waiting for undivided attention. From time to time, everybody wants some personal space. In a partnership, it is necessary to recognize and agree that. Domination it is only normal for someone you care for to want the best. It is also natural to make recommendations and interventions in this way. But you cannot impose your will on others regardless of how good your motives are. You will value the thoughts and ideas of doing things of your partner so that you have a stable relationship.

Egotism Itself is an essential explanation of why marriages collapse. It is human nature to put yourself first often. However, you alienate your mate even when you talk about your interests and wishes. Your desires and preferences must be matched with those of your spouse. Give and take is a real friendship. No time. It's important to make room for the things we care about. Relationships don't just arise and don't just end. It needs time to hold them and money. Seeking fault we are individuals, and all have flaws. You will never find someone who satisfies any of your standards. However, to sustain a relationship, you have to recognize the flaws considered by your mate. It is cruel and impractical to expect others to adapt to suit your best partner's needs. Relationships are tough. Overnight, they don't break apart. It takes time to fail in a relationship, and the failure is usually attributed to a combination of the above issues. There's always hope if you're not ready to give up your friendship. You must first recognize and fix the issues that caused the split. Only then can you spend all your energies on getting your wife back together.

MICHELLE MILLER

CHAPTER 6:

Negative Thinking

Are you a person more of a glass half empty? You know, more than ever, one who gets up on the right side of the bed? On the way to work, it will probably stop at the red lights rather than it would be via orange, it will be more comfortable than the one that is traveling on the traffic lane, somewhat likely that you will be on the left, while you will be in the right path?

So, when you're busy, grumbling so grumbling, do you feel like you're the only one walking under the rain cloud through your day? Would you feel an increasing sense of loneliness and rejection when those sunnier colleagues avoid you like any afflictions that you are infectious? So, as you walk back home as you think about your day as you crawl in more snarled traffic, do you wonder that you would have no luck if you had no bad luck?

Whether you know something about this that you can relate to, you should know that your self-limiting thoughts and actions don't have to be permanently crippling. The mental and emotional self-defeating states in which you have become compulsively and physiologically dependent do not have to control, even describe your life.

Perhaps you've seen DVD's like "The Key," or "What the Bleep We Know?" Maybe you've absorbed a self-help library. You may have been performing regular affirmations and meditation. But you're still looking. Within a few days or weeks, nothing will change your thought and behavior.

So, what's wrong with you in the world? How is it so difficult to reconcile your thoughts and emotions with the information and knowledge you gain so that you can build the interactions we all want in our lives by simply adjusting your expectations? However, if you thoroughly understand what experience you have acquired, even if you firmly accept that this information is accurate and right, somehow it seems to be beyond your capacity to incorporate it and use it in order to enact positive and consistent change.

This information and experience that you have often tried to apply in your life is right. We can do more, be more and enjoy it only by shifting our thoughts. That is evident in so many biographies and in countless stories of ordinary citizens who seem to have accomplished the impossible. It is because all the proof provided to you and all the suggested approaches are insufficient and, thus, faulty that the experience has not been available to you.

Let me first share with you some of the exciting research and development carried out in this field before I disclose more about this topic. NeuroVector Neuroscience Laboratories is a private research facility in Melbourne, Australia. The research facility - they are situated in an area adjacent to Western Sydney University and within minutes from the top three of Australia's major neurotechnology research universities. They are also always in contact with universities and research organizations in the USA and around the world, to keep up to date with the latest findings and technology.

Their research has contributed to the creation of a groundbreaking neurovector brainwave synchronization audio technology that, when used as directed, creates significant and long-lasting improvements in nervous system structure and function. In reality, their advanced neuroVector technology has been extensively tested and is working for all. They guarantee totally that your life will change dramatically in ways that would always amaze you.

Throughout their research work, laboratory staff discovered the neurologically occurring deficiency that prevents one from successfully applying all the simple sound ideas and methods which their various authors were trying to communicate. It is when a person remembers an incident with a positive disposition that they are likely to remember only positive aspects and the most important milestones. Our current thoughts and perceptions are wrongly filled with memories of real events from the past which produces an impression of ease and simplicity that is not the actual experience.

People find it difficult even to do things they felt they had mastered easily before. This is because they want the job to feel as simple as it is now. The brain holds all the memories, including their joys and losses, but when we remind ourselves of these memories, we only have access to the parts of them that relate to our present mood and motives.

With the NeuroVector TREA technology, researchers and developers have created a realistic and efficient way of shortening the complicated and complex journey of the winner's mindset. When using neuroVector TRAE's audio technology, the electrical activity in the brain aligns with those of people who spent decades shaping their minds to a higher degree of consciousness.

Researchers found that unpleasant memories and emotions are nourished in a loop. Any positive aspect of a memory or feeling loses its meaning in this negative emotional state, becoming more difficult to view or ponder.

In most cases, the brain functions are limited to some areas of the brain that are indicative of the self-defeating mental and emotional disorders on which the person is compulsively and physiologically dependent. The electrical activity of your mind (brainwave) throughout the brain, using neuroVector technology, creates new neural pathways that stimulate new thoughts and feelings.

New neural pathways have been documented in brain imaging studies and have been shown to allow faster communication between neurons in the brain. This increased activity in the brain equates to more' processing capacity' in the mind, i.e. higher IQ.

NeuroVector Neuroscience Laborators ' patented audio technology is today the safest and most successful way to alter one's thought habits—more efficient than the conventional binaural beat recordings that motivated the research and creation of this modern and groundbreaking technology.

My advice for the control of the negative ways of thought:

Negative thinking brings you stimulation, just like the monkey in my case. If you think about the fatness in the mirror, the brain makes neuronal connections to support this assumption.

Nerve branches and networks continue to create a system of thoughts to communicate with each other, so that in future you can consider these thoughts again as your mind believes. Neurologists have a saying that echoes this: the nerves that fire wire together.

Your thoughts, like a film, have a theme for them. Which would you say is regular the focus of your dreams? Think of the past, present, or future? Is your fitness, your job, your relationships, your sex or your money or otherwise? How much time do you waste to the point of fatigue worrying about these things? Often it seems like you are trapped in a pit you can't come out of–you go deeper and deeper and deeper. Break the cycle early, as mentioned above, by not allowing the thoughts to stand. Don't fuel your mind further with the same feelings.

There's an explanation why you have pessimistic feelings. What's the reason for this? What (negative thoughts) are they trying to tell you? One of the troubling concepts that make me scared is "what if you fail and never fulfill your mission and dream?" Thoughts alone shake my heart, because it means a lot for me to live my life. The pessimistic thoughts remind me that I have to change regularly and survive NOW, not in the future. The premise is an appeal for action to break and never give up. Which is your negative thinking pattern which requires or needs you to do?

Negative thoughts appear in waves at the door of your mind, just like a virus. You have a quest to penetrate your soul. You have a' whatever' strategy. So, what is the best option when a force moves in your direction? Function with energy, go with flow. Being a thinker needs at first some intellectual discipline. I propose that the best course of action initially is to become conscious of your feelings. Notice the duration (if it helps, then hold a diary). Problem of thoughts-does the thinking have any truth? What's the opposite of that idea? If a bank robber appeared at the counter asking for money, would the counterman take the weapon out of his hand? Perhaps not. The best move for the dealer is to turn over the cash (give in to his demand). When the needs of the thief have been met, action will be taken, i.e. call the police (asking you to inquire and question your feelings by bringing them to the forefront of your mind).

This is a fascinating image that includes a certain Buddhist thinking. What is thinking? Who is thinking? Of course, you say "I" think. What do you know whatever you think? Prove it! Prove it! When I asked you to be a thinker, who is watching the observer? You question the thoughts without getting carried away with riddles, and you thus shorten the cycle.

The mind is a complex one. It likes models. It wants to learn the next thing, how, where and why. Trick it, like a little girl. Trick it. It would give up and leave because you didn't fan the fire by embracing its thought process because of enough practice and patience. By giving up, the mind will continue to flood you with negative thoughts, but they are not charged so strongly.

CHAPTER 7:

How to Solve All Problems in 7 Steps and Change Habits

StePl: Build A Day-To-Day "Stress" Cycle

It's hard to be successful in your day-to-day tasks when fear and stress overtake your mind and divert you from work, school, or home life. This is the place the strategy of delaying stress will help. As opposed to attempting to delay or dispose of an awkward inclination, authorize yourself to do as such, at that point put off worrying until some other time.

Construct a "think cycle." Pick a fixed time and place to think about it. In your time of concern, you're encouraged to think over something on your head. The rest of the day, though, is a space free of anxiety.

Write down some of your questions. If you have an unpleasant thought or concern in your mind throughout the day, make a short note of it and then resume the day. Note that you'll have time to talk about it later, and there's no reason to stress about it right now.

Move down your "anxiety list" at the duration of your anxiety. If the emotions you feel are disturbing you, urge yourself to consider them, yet just for the measure of time you've accommodated your season of concern. When you discuss your issues in this manner, you will also find it easier to gain a more rational viewpoint. So, if your concerns don't seem to matter anymore, just cut your time of concern

Step 2: Challenge Nervous Thoughts

When you have persistent fear and stress, odds are you're looking at the universe in terms that make it feel more daunting than it actually is. For starters, you can overestimate the likelihood that things could turn out poorly, leap to worst-case scenarios automatically, or interpret any nervous thought as though it were a matter of fact. You can even disprove your own ability to deal with life's challenges, believing you break apart at the first hint of difficulty. "If something isn't fine, I'm a complete loser." Overgeneralization from a single bad event is believing it to stay true indefinitely. "I haven't been recruited for the role. "Focusing on the negatives when ignoring the good ones.

Make misleading assumptions without any clear facts. You're behaving like a mind reader: "I can tell you she really hates me." Or a fortune teller: "I just think something bad is going to happen." Accepting that the manner in which you act is a result of the real world. "I have an inclination that I'm such a moron. Somebody will snicker at me. "Keep a clear list of what you can and should not do and punish yourself if you break any of the rules. "I was never going to want to initiate a conversation with her. I'm such a dumb guy."

Marking yourself dependent on failures and seeing inadequacies. "I'm a failure; I'm boring; I want to be alone." Taking blame for events outside your influence. "It's my fault that my son was in an accident. I was meant to advise him to drive cautiously in the mud. "How to question these thoughts In your moment of concern, address your pessimistic thinking by reminding yourself: Where is the proof that the hypothesis is true? Isn't that true?

Is there a more optimistic, rational way to look at the situation?

What's the likelihood that what I'm fearful of would really happen? If the likelihood is small, what are some of the more likely outcomes?

Was the thinking helpful? How's it going to help me, and how's it going to hurt me?

What should I say to a friend who was concerned about this?

Step 3: Recogne Solvable And Unsolvable Issues

Evidence recommends that when you are stressed, you are marginally less apprehensive. Playing over the issue in your cerebrum possesses you from your feelings and causes you to have an inclination that you're finishing something. Anyway, there are two very surprising issues to consider to fix issues.

Problem management involves determining the problem, taking practical measures to deal with it, and then bringing the solution into effect. Worrying, on the other hand, never contributes to a solution. Regardless of how much time you waste focusing on worst-case situations, you're able to deal with them should they eventually happen.

Is worry resolvable? Unproductive, unsolvable problems are those on which there is no subsequent intervention. When the fear can be overcome, continue brainstorming. Create a list of all the options you might think of. Try not to be too caught up to find the right answer. Focus on issues that you have the ability to alter, rather than situations or facts beyond your

reach. Once you've assessed your choices, make an action plan.

If the fear is not resolvable, embrace the confusion. Unless you're a persistent fighter, the vast majority of your nervous feelings are likely to fall into this camp. Worrying is also the way we try to foresee what the future brings – the way to stop unexpected shocks and monitor the results. The question is that it doesn't work. Focusing in worst-case situations would only deter you from loving the positive stuff you have at present. To stop stressing, discuss the need for clarity and urgent answers.

- Will you like to expect that negative stuff will happen only because they're uncertain?
- Provided that the risk is very remote, it is easy to survive with a slight probability that something bad may happen.
- Tell your friends and family how to cope with confusion in different circumstances.
- Stay in line with the feelings. Worrying over confusion is also a means of suppressing negative feelings.

Step 4: Stop The Loop Of Worry

If you stress constantly, unpleasant thoughts can appear to run through your mind constantly. You may feel like you're spiraling out of control, going insane, or about to blackout under the weight of all this fear. In any case, there are steps that you should take currently to stop every one of those apprehensive sentiments and give yourself a break from relentless nervousness.

Get up there and get moving. Exercise is a sheltered and fruitful enemy of nervousness treatment that actuates endorphins that mitigate torment and stress, improve essentialness, and fortify your feeling of prosperity. Most explicitly, by simply pondering how your body reacts when you walk, you can stop the steady surge of stresses that experience your brain. Focus on the sound of your feet contacting the ground as you walk, run, or move, for instance, or the pace of your breath, or the impression of sun or wind against your skin.

Taking a yoga exercise or a kendo exercise class. By keeping your thoughts on your movements and breathing, performing yoga or kendo holds your fixation on the occasion, assisting with clearing your musings and add to a quiet perspective.

Ponder that. Contemplation works by changing the consideration from pondering the future or living in the past to what's happening at the present time. You will break the relentless cycle of pessimistic feelings and fears by remaining completely involved in the current moment. Just find a calm, relaxing spot and select one of the many free or affordable mobile applications that can direct you through the meditation process.

Gradual relaxing of muscles. This will assist you with getting away from the steady pattern of tension by focusing your consideration on your body rather than your feelings. By tensioning and afterward loosening up different muscle groups in your body, you soothe muscle aches in your body. So as your body unwinds, your intuitive will comply.

Try to breathe slowly. When you think, you feel nervous and breathe harder, sometimes leading to more fear. Be that as it may, by doing profound breathing activities, you can quiet down your psyche and calm unpleasant musings.

Step 5: Talking About Your Issues

It can seem like a simple methodology, however talking up close and personal with a dependable companion or relative — somebody who tunes in to you without being addressed, offended or continually sidetracked — is one of the most impressive approaches to loosen up your sensory system and diminish dread. As the issues heighten, pondering them will cause them to appear to be even less risky.

Having you worrying just helps them to pile up until they become intimidating. When the concerns are unjustified, verbalizing them will show what they are — needless worries. So, if your worries are valid, sharing them with someone else will create ideas that you would not have thought about on your own.

Develop a strong support network. We're not supposed to be raised in solitude. But a good support group doesn't automatically mean a large network of friends. Try not to think little of the rewards of a couple of individuals who you can depend and rely on to be there for you. So if you don't believe like you have someone to trust, it's never too late to develop new connections.

Know how to stop when you feel nervous. Your stressful personality can be something you've experienced since you've grown up. If your mother is a persistent addict, she's not the right one to call when you feel anxious — no matter how close you are.

Step 6: Exercise Mindfulness

Young woman sitting back in a chair that cradles her back, hands crossed in a lap, chin up, eyes closed. Thinking is typically based on the future — what could happen and what you're going to do about it — or on the past, rehashing stuff you've said or done. This technique is focused on noticing your thoughts and then letting them go, allowing you to recognize where your behavior is causing issues and getting in contact with your emotions.

Recognize and consider your questions. Don't want to dismiss, fight, or monitor them as normal. Alternatively, clearly consider them as if from an outsider's point of view, without responding or judging.

Let go of your fears. Note that while you're not struggling to control the nervous feelings that crop up, they'll quickly disappear, like clouds rolling through the sky. It's only because you're immersed in the problems that you get trapped.

Keep concentrated on the present. Pay attention to the way your body sounds, to the pattern of your heartbeat, to the ever-changing feelings, and to the thoughts that float through your head. If you find yourself caught in a single thought, bring your mind back to the present moment.

Rehash each day. Utilizing care to stay concentrated on the moment is a fundamental thought, however, it requires time and practice to appreciate the advantages. You'll likely notice from the start that your psyche props up back to your concerns. If you don't mind, endeavor not to get resentful. Each time you turn your psyche back to the occasion, you build up another psychological schedule that will assist you with breaking free from the terrible circle of concern. Step 6 - Talking:

If stressful situations occur, conversation can be the most productive way to get through the question. Many issues are best kept unsaid; it is not advisable to dig up old disputes when they aren't completely necessary. When we chat, we will continue to think about constructive issues; look for stuff that we reflect about and should work on together.

Step 7: Adapting techniques

If your tension is moderate and all around controlled, you can have the option to take a few to get back some composure on it effectively by pondering the examples and considering elective social methodologies. For most individuals, though, the fear of abandonment is embedded in deep-seated problems that are impossible to resolve on their own.

Professional help is also required to move past this anxiety to develop the self-confidence needed actually to alter your emotions to behaviors.

CHAPTER 8:

Some Exercise to Control Anxiety (Muscle Relaxation and Breathing)

This is one of the best ways in which you can relieve stress and overcome anxiety by relaxing your muscles.

This technique involves tightening your core muscles and then relaxing them progressively. This is often done in a bottom-to-top manner.

The good thing with this exercise is the fact that it helps the whole body release any tension along with the stress levels so that you lower anxiety feelings and relax. In most instances, this has been shown to lower such problems as headaches and stomach problems, and improve the quality of sleep.

Based on the fact that people with anxiety and depression often feel tense throughout the day, it can be hard even to recognize how relaxation feels. However, when you start practicing progressive muscle relaxation, you will know the difference between tensed muscles and relaxed muscles.

Start by setting aside at least 15 minutes every day for exercising relaxation. Find a place with minimal destruction. When you are just starting, you can try out this exercise at least twice per day for the first two to three weeks. As your body gets used to the exercise, you will realize that you achieve relaxation faster. It does not mean that once you feel calm, you stop exercising. You can keep doing it as part of your daily workout routine.

Step 1 Tension

Start by applying tension to a particular part of the body. It does not matter what muscle you are trying to target because the tension you apply is the same. Once you tense the target muscle group, the next thing is for you to take in a deep breath slowly as you squeeze the muscles tight as possible. Hold that position for about 15 seconds and then release it.

As you keep practicing, you will realize how easy isolating muscle groups can get. You must be careful while exercising to avoid hurting yourself when tensing the muscles. If you feel intense pain, stop the exercise. It is advisable that as you tense the muscles, you make it deliberate but very gentle. If you have pulled muscles or broken bones, ensure that you seek medical advice before engaging in this exercise.

Step 2 Relaxing tense muscles

This involves a quick relaxation of the tensed muscles. Once 15 seconds elapse, let the tightness flow out of your tensed muscles. As you let go of the tension, exhale, and feel the muscles loosen up. Take note of how different it feels when you relax the muscles as compared to when they were tended up.

Maintain this relaxed state at least for 30 seconds before you move to the next muscle group. Repeat this tension-relaxation step one muscle after the other until you have completed all the muscle groups in the body. Try not to beat yourself up if you have not yet mastered the difference between tensed and relaxed states. It takes practice and often uncomfortable to focus on your body. However, with time, you will start enjoying it.

Diaphragmatic breathing

This is also referred to as deep breathing. The good thing with this technique is that it boosts the supply of oxygen to the lungs and slows the rate of respiration – countering the fight and flight response.

This is a perfect technique when you are feeling stressed and anxious. Naturally, newborn babies, yoga practitioners, wind instrument players, and singers breathe using this technique.

So, why is this technique important?

First, what you need to bear in mind is that breathing often changes whenever we feel anxious. You start to take in short, shallow, quick, and hyperventilate breathes. With this technique, your body can manage over-breathing.

While this technique is very beneficial in calming you down from your anxiety, the truth is that it takes a lot of practice. The major aim of this calm breathing is to try as much as possible to avoid anxiety.

How do you achieve that?

This technique involves taking in slow, smooth, and regular breaths. You must do this when you are seated upright rather than when you are lying down. This ensures that the capacity of the lungs increases to fill it with air. To take the weight off your shoulders, place your arms on your laps or the side-arms of your chair for support.

Now, start taking in deep and slow breathes using your nose and into your belly. Then hold your breath for at least 5 seconds before you breathe out slowly for another 5 seconds. Then pause for a couple of seconds before you can resume breathing.

To decrease anxiety and depression, it is advisable to go for 8-10 rounds of these breathing cycles within a minute. However, you must try to establish your comfortable breathing rhythm. When you do, you will be able to regulate the amount of oxygen you take in so that you get enough and avoid tingling, fainting, or getting giddy sensations.

The trick is to ensure that you are not hyperventilating. The best way to do this is to pause in between each breath. Try as much as you can to breath from your diaphragm. As you do that, you must keep your shoulders and chest relaxed. This may be challenging at first, but with time, you will get the hang of it. Try lying down on the floor and place one hand on your heart and the other on the abdomen. As you breathe in and out, watch your hands rise as the chest expands.

Some of the rules that govern this practice are to do calm breathing for at least five minutes every day. It is not necessary that you feel anxious before you can do this exercise. The trick is to practice it even when you are feeling calm and collected. It is important that when using this technique while calm, you are comfortable with it. With time, you will begin to master the feel and skill, and your anxiety will go away before you know it.

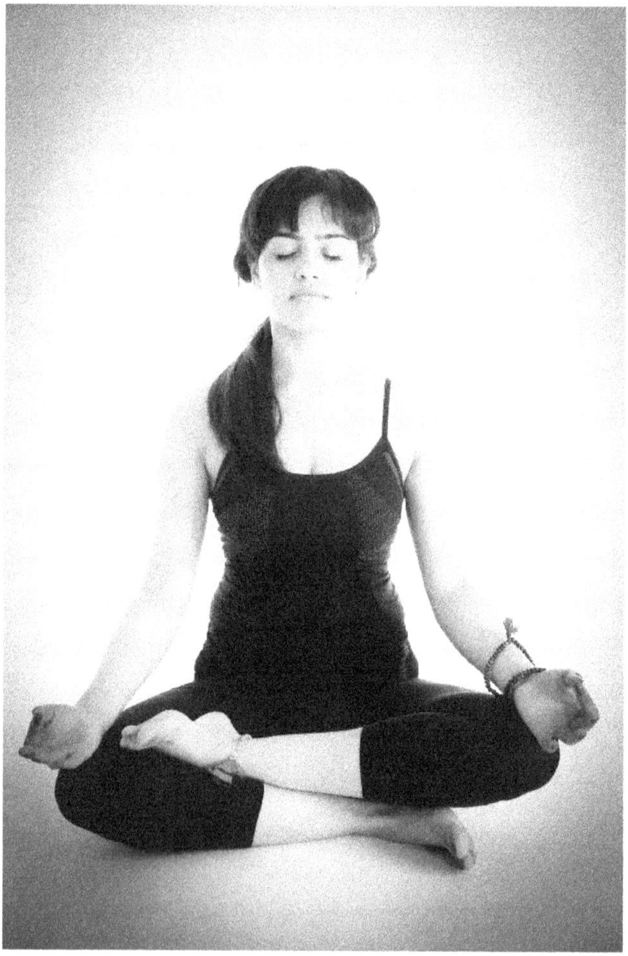

CHAPTER 9:

Advice for Couples

All of us desire a long and happy relationship. However, we do not get lessons at school on how to be in and maintain a lasting relationship. There are so many distractions in the world that keep us from achieving perfect and happiest relationships. You have the power to design your relationship and how you feel about it. First, you must be open to a constructive relationship. Secondly, you must commit daily to avoid all distractions that do not serve any purpose in your relationship. Thirdly, do not give up too first.

Every relationship is different and the person you love might not be the choice of another. A happy relationship will feel positive, additive, deep, equal, and acceptable and has room for vulnerability. From the beginning, you have to make choices and have the clear intention of heading somewhere. How can one cultivate a long and happy relationship?

a. Be clear from the beginning

While some people take time to get into a relationship, others hit it off on the first date. Regardless of whether you decide to be in a relationship on the first date or after years of friendship, you have to be open to each other about what you want. Talk about your true self as soon as the relationship starts. What do you want from the relationship? What can you do to ensure that you meet the desired goals?

Staging your needs clearly from the beginning ensures that you understand whether you and your partner are compatible.

It also helps you to know if there are things you will have to compromise on. Do you want to get married and have kids in the next two years? Say it as it is. Do you want to be in a long term relationship or a contract kind of relationship? Tell your partner.

b. Share your most deep secrets and dreams

Sharing creates room for intimacy. It also invites the other person to open up. In fact, it is okay to talk about your childish desires like building a tiny house on the edge of a cliff and spending the rest of your life there. Again, this sharing helps you to determine if you are compatible. If you realize early enough that the relationship will not work because of incompatibility, then you will spare yourselves a lot of heartaches.

c. Have a wide-open communication channel.

Communication determines if you will be happy or sad in your relationship. Every rule of a happy relationship is linked to proper communication. If you want a happy relationship, make sure that you communicate openly, even when the topic is uncomfortable. Pay compliments when deserved and ask questions if need be.

None of you should be afraid of what will happen if they bring a particular subject up. Address issues calmly and use compassion and empathy in your communications.

d. Embrace your self

There is nothing wrong with loving yourself. Your life has different facets and you must embrace them all. Embracing yourself is the first step to understanding yourself and knowing what needs to be changed or otherwise.

e. Support each other

Everyone has dreams and goals they would like to achieve. A good relationship should allow both parties to offer to each other. If you offer support to your partner and he/she reciprocates, that relationship will last.

f. Explore growth together.

Life is about change and there are things every couple wants to change in each other. Everybody wants to live their best life. It is important to expose every opportunity of growth together, Support one another through the changes.

g. Work towards being better partners.

We are work in progress and learners. Remember that no one teaches us how to be in a relationship, therefore, we have to learn on the go. Probably, there are things you wish you had done differently in your previous relationships. Maybe you need to use more love language or how to open up to your partner. Everyone should strive to be a better partner.

h. Dream together

A relationship is about two people. The future belongs to both of you. Therefore, it is important that you sit and talk about tomorrow, a month from now, a year and even forever. What would you like to achieve together? Talk about everything, for instance, kids, a home, finances, vacations, etcetera. Realize that the more you talk with a person, the easier it is to determine if they are a good fit.

i. Be present

Sometimes we are overwhelmed by other things that we forget how to connect with our loved ones. For instance, you might have gotten home after a long day at work and all you want to do is shut people out and rest. On the other hand, your partner might have hard a tougher day and is looking forward to sharing with you. Relationships require sacrifice and that means putting the needs of your partner at heart. So, be present for your partner.

RELATIONSHIP THERAPY

CHAPTER 10:

How to End Anxiety

No matter what kind of person you play in life, the skill to properly control and express your emotions is sure to play a vital role. You also need to be able to know, interpret, and respond appropriately to emotions that others around you have as well. Contemplate about how it would be if you weren't able to tell when one of your close friends was feeling sad or when one of your coworkers was mad at you. When you are not only able to express and control your own emotions but also interpret and understand the emotions of others, you are said to have emotional intelligence.

To keep things simple, emotional intelligence refers to your ability to perceive, control, and evaluate feelings whether they are your personal emotions or emotions that someone else is feeling. Some people have a great emotional intelligence and are able to control the emotions that they have in many situations while also responding to the emotions of those around them. In contrast, some people have poor emotional intelligence; these are the individuals who will burst at almost anything and barely take the emotional state of others into consideration.

Let's take a look at the distinction between someone who has emotional intelligence and someone who doesn't. Our first person is someone who takes life as it comes. They understand that most of the time when things go wrong, it is out of their control rather than seeing it as the world attacking them directly. They hardly get upset, especially over the little things and recognize the proper times to show their emotions.

In addition, this person reacts well to how others are feeling. When a colleague comes and starts yelling at them, they don't respond in kind. They recognize that something must really be bothering that person and they step up to try and help or correct the issue at the heart of the problem. When one of their friends is having a bad day, they talk through it and help that friend feel better.

Now, let's look at our second person. This person has a difficult time controlling their emotions. When they are upset about something, they will explode at others (whether it is that other person's fault or not), they cry easily, and they may have anxiety. These individuals will often have the idea that the world is against them and little things, the things that don't matter that much, will set them off.

When it comes to responding to others, this is barely a thought. They will ignore the feelings of their friends and only process events based on how they are personally affected by them. When someone else is mad at them they think that they are being unfairly treated. The world is against them and everyone just doesn't understand them.

The first person we met is someone who has a high level of emotional intelligence. This person knows how to recognize and control their emotions and can even hone in on some of the emotions of others around them. The second person has a low level of emotional intelligence. They get upset over everything, probably have no idea why they feel the way they do, and they don't even pay attention to the feelings of others. Of course, there are variations that happen between these two extremes and figuring out your own level of emotional intelligence can be important for helping you to improve.

Some people believe that you are able to improve your own emotional intelligence with some hard work. But there are others who believe that this is an inborn characteristic, something that you are born with which makes it extremely difficult, if not impossible to change. There is probably a grain of truth to both schools of thought. We are all born with a natural level of emotional intelligence which we can then either nurture and improve or let it grow fallow through disuse.

The four parts of emotional intelligence

There are four main factors that are going to determine your emotional intelligence. These include:

- Perceiving emotions: the first thing that you need to do in order to understand emotions is to learn how to perceive them properly. This can include learning how to recognize nonverbal signals like facial expressions and body language.
- Reasoning with emotions: the next thing that you need to do is use your emotions as a way to promote cognitive activity. This can be hard at first, but emotions can help prioritize what we are paying attention to and reacting to, and we can pay attention to this to learn something about ourselves.
- Understanding emotions: there are many meanings that can come with the emotions that we perceive. For example, if you observe that someone is angry, you may have to take a step back and see why they feel the way they do. A boss may be mad at you for your work because they got in trouble with their boss, they fought with their wife, and they got a speeding ticket, or for a whole host of other reasons and

someone with a high level of emotional intelligence will be able to recognize this.
- Managing emotions: next is the ability to manage your emotions effectively. You need to be able to regulate your emotions, find an appropriate response, and then respond as an important part of your emotional management.

There are several ways that you are able to measure your emotional intelligence. There are some tests that can be done to check on this, but it is also possible to figure out your own emotional intelligence and change it through hard work and perseverance. By learning how to recognize your emotions, what is causing them, and the appropriate response to the situation at hand, you can easily improve your own emotional intelligence in less time than you might think.

So why would you want to spend your time working on emotional intelligence? There are actually quite a few situations in your life where a high level of emotional intelligence can make a big difference. For example, in the workplace. Employees who have a higher level of emotional intelligence are the ones who perform better because they pick out jobs that they are passionate about, do better with other employees, persuade other people to their ideas, and also avoid conflicts. Think about how some of these skills could help you in your own career, whether you are trying to advance or just stay on top. Everyone could use a brush up on these skills to help them do better in the workplace.

Another crucial area where you will really see the benefit of working with emotional intelligence is in your relationships, whether these are with a partner, with your family, or even your co-workers. Each person that you encounter is going to have their own feelings and being able to recognize these and respond in the proper way will make it so much easier for you to get along with them. When conflict does arise, you will be able to keep your emotions in check, preventing a bigger blowout than is necessary no matter what kind of relationship you are trying to work on.

Emotional intelligence is something that everyone is able to improve upon and there are so many benefits to so. However, it is important to realize that it is also a skill that takes some time to master. You will not be able to wake up after practicing for a day or two and have total control over your emotions. In fact, this is probably something that you will have to work on for quite some time before it becomes a habit. But when you understand this from the start and work hard to observe, understand, and manage your emotions you will be able to reach your goals in no time.

MICHELLE MILLER

CHAPTER 11:

The Areas that Most Impact Anxiety

Anxiety Triggers

Certain areas of your life may trigger anxiety. The following are some common reasons why you may start to feel anxious. Keep these triggers in mind to discover what parts of your life might be causing you the most stress and as a result, causing you to be snappy or uncommunicative with your partner. Anxiety stemming from any of these areas can and will impact your relationship if you are unaware of your feelings because people commonly project what they are feeling in other parts of their life onto their relationship, hurting that relationship in the process.

One of the main areas that people feel anxiety is work or school. People need to make money and create a path for their future. Accordingly, there is a lot of pressure to succeed in professional environments. Plus, making money is often a necessity for survival, which only heaps the pressure on. With all this in mind, it's no wonder that work causes people to get stuck in their heads and feel unable to cope with their workplace duties. Your job probably gets overwhelming, and that's normal, but you don't want to bring these negative feelings home with you and inflict them on your relationship, getting angry or upset at your partner when those work stresses have nothing to do with your relationship.

Relationships beyond the one you have romantically can be huge trigger points for many people. Whether it is your relationship with a friend or a family member, sometimes things can get tense, causing you to have anxiety related to those outside relationships. Those feelings in outside relationships can also start to creep up on you when you're with your partner because those insecurities and doubts you have with other people are fresh in your mind.

Another area that causes distress is the way your body looks. People are often super critical of how they look, and society encourages this fixation on external appearance. Thus, with so much focus on looks, even in a secure relationship, you may begin to have doubts about not looking good enough. You may worry that people think less of you because of what you wear or how you do your hair. People do judge others based on these things, but anxiety pathologizes this fear until you are so obsessed with how you look that you can't focus on anything else.

Believe it or not, diet can actually impact your anxiety levels. Research has suggested that your mood impacts the foods you crave, but it has also shown that what you eat can influence your anxiety levels. For one, major dietary changes can cause increased levels of anxiety, so don't make drastic dietary changes overnight. Further, while the impact of diet on individuals varies greatly because of different eating patterns and feelings associated with certain childhood foods, high-fat diets tend to reduce anxiety while high sugar diets can increase it. Of course, that's not to suggest that you should start only eating fat and eliminating sugar altogether because the best results are found in balanced diets. Most importantly, if your body has the nutrients it needs, you will feel clearer, brighter, and be able to resist anxiety. Physical health translates to better mental health.

Drug use, including caffeine and alcohol, can also cause anxiety. Again, like with diet, that doesn't mean that you should cut coffee and alcohol completely and you very much shouldn't stop taking any prescribed medications, but it is still something to be aware of. Both prescribed and illicit drugs could shift the chemical balance in your brain and make you more prone to anxiety. When starting new drugs, monitor how you are feeling. If you start feeling more spikes of anxiety as you begin a new drug, you may want to ask your doctor about potential alternatives or turn to a psychiatrist to help you with your anxiety.

Illness can be another factor in anxiety. Mental or physical illnesses can leave you worrying more than is healthy. A person with cancer, for instance, is likely going to have some anxiety about their condition. Around forty-five percent of people with cancer show symptoms of clinical anxiety, which is a staggering number. Chronic conditions like IBS also may show increased anxiety levels in people, proving how triggering illnesses can be in anxiety. Further, mental illnesses can often be comorbid, so someone with depression or other mental conditions could have increased odds of anxiety. Accordingly, don't neglect your feelings when it comes to medical diagnoses because an illness can make forging a relationship even harder with all the complications it provides.

Negativity, in general, will naturally cause anxiety. If you're a glass-half-empty kind of person, you're probably more jaded and more anxious. You'll tend to look at your partner with this same kind of cynicism, making it hard to establish trust. Those who are persistently negative struggle to look at the world and not be afraid. Negativity is a perfect spot for anxiety to crawl into. Luckily, just recognizing when you are in a negative head space is a great step forward, and positive thinking is pretty easy to curate with time and practice.

Arguments are another one of the main causes of anxiety. They don't have to be full out yelling matches to be harmful either. Even just a disagreement with a coworker can lead to you coming home irritated and feeling worried about your situation. Unresolved arguments are especially anxiety-inducing because they fester. If the arguments happen with your partner, for obvious reasons, double the strain is put on your relationship, but having arguments with someone else could still result in you picking fights with your partner. This could because you're just feeling irritated or it could be because you feel disempowered with the other person you're fighting with but know that you can safely argue with your partner without immediate consequences. A yelling match with your boss could never happen, while a yelling match with your partner won't singlehandedly destroy the relationship. Although, arguments can be harmful if you don't learn from your mistakes.

Solving Anxiety Triggers

While you inevitably will have things in your life that trigger anxiety in you, you don't have to let those triggers ruin your ability to handle anxiety and cope with your issues. There are ways to manage your anxiety and prevent some flare-ups even if you cannot prevent anxiety altogether.

A good first step is to determine what triggers you and address the root cause of your triggers. There's a whole list above outlining some of the common ones, but anything that causes an unsettled feeling in the pit of your stomach can be a trigger. These triggers will often relate to your past traumas. Think of the times you've felt the most helpless and afraid. Those events should give you a better idea of what your triggers are. Triggers could be little things that you barely consciously consider. For example, maybe a smell of a perfume that someone you'd rather forget always wore causes a visceral reaction or maybe confrontations with your boss make you feel like a small child being yelled at by your father. It can help to go to your trusty journal during this step. Write down times when you feel peaks of anxiety and see if you can find overlap of causes for that anxiety and connect these causes to past hurt.

When anxiety takes hold of you suddenly, don't forget to breathe. This is one of the simplest suggestions, but even if you have a deadline and are anxiously rushing to get done with your work, sometimes you need to stop for five minutes and recollect yourself. Stop and let yourself breathe and give your brain a bit of a rest too. It seems like a waste of time to stop to breathe when you could charge through your work, but if you take that time for yourself, you will ultimately be more productive and better able to handle the work you have in front of you. If you can get your anxiety under control, you will be more productive and feel less burnt-out when you come home. As a result, you'll be able to spend after work time with your partner and be more present instead of feeling like an overworked zombie.

Another easy change is to limit your alcohol and coffee intake. Both substances change the way your brain works like illicit drugs would as well. Coffee, for example, is a stimulant. Accordingly, the impact it has on your body can feel like a fight or flight response and make you feel even more anxious. So, maybe instead of drinking three cups you can try just to have one. Alcohol, meanwhile, is a depressant, but it can also be detrimental to your anxiety levels. Alcohol can help you calm down and relieve some of the stress you are feeling, but with long term use, the impacts become lessened and you end up less able to handle the anxiety on your own. Further, excessive drinking has a myriad of mental and physical symptoms that can cause you additional stress rather than less stress. Thus, while substances can make you feel good temporarily, they may make you more anxious.

Exercise is a great option for people who feel like they have a lot of pent up energy as a result of anxiety. If you feel like a shaken soda bottle ready to explode at any interaction, physical activity can improve your mood by sending a surge of feel-good chemicals through your body and letting you use some of that anxious energy for a better purpose. Some studies have found that exercise reduces people's chances of having depression or anxiety by twenty-five percent. For those who already have anxiety disorders, symptoms of anxiety were reduced an average of twenty percent just with the addition of routine physical activity. Accordingly, even for those with less severe anxiety, exercise can still ease the worry. Plus, working out makes your body healthy, which gives you less to worry about when it comes to your health. You don't have to try extreme activities or even intense ones. Anything you can do to get your body moving will suffice. Find something that challenges you, but it also enjoyable.

Give meditation a try. Many people think that meditation sounds silly, but it doesn't have to necessarily be the stereotypical image that comes into your mind of a yogi humming and sitting with their legs crossed on the floor. Yoga can be a great way to meditate and be mindful, but it isn't the only way. Meditation is simply the method of becoming aware of yourself and your body and reconnecting with your emotions and allowing them to exist without worrying constantly about them. It allows you to be mindful, which means that you are present and fully in the moment rather than bogged down by outside concerns. Sixty percent of people who try meditation and stick with it over an extended time reduced their anxiety levels within a year. Meditation can also be good for your heart, blood pressure, insomnia, depression, and even PMS symptoms, which means that it can help improve areas of your life that might otherwise cause you even more stress.

CHAPTER 12:

Self-Evaluation of Anxiety in a Relationship

How do you know you are anxious in a relationship? What are the signs that show that you are having a negative emotion concerning your relationship? What are the effects of anxiety on your relationship? All of these questions will be answered when you carry out what is called a self-evaluation of relationship anxiety. This focuses on the self-evaluation of tension in a relationship. The essence of this is to evaluate the issue to put an end to it.

Anxiety can spring out at any time in a relationship. The fact is that everyone is vulnerable to this problem; the tendency to become anxious in a relationship increases as the bond becomes stronger. So, there is a need for everyone to carry out a self-evaluation.

Do you spend most of your time worrying about things that could go wrong in your relationship? Do you doubt if your partner really loves you? A sure sign of relationship anxiety is when you become worried all the time as a result of those question running through your mind.

For proper self-evaluation of this problem, you need to know the signs that show that you are already becoming anxious. Also, you need to weigh the causes and effect of this problem on your relationship. As I have said earlier, the purpose of evaluating is to address the problem before it develops. This is structured to give you maximum benefit, and I will try to be as explicit as possible.

How to Know if You Are Getting Anxious in a Relationship

You might be neck deep in relationship anxiety without really knowing, so this will point out the symptoms of this problem to you. If you notice any the signs that will be mentioned below, you will benefit greatly from the self-evaluation process.

1.   When you feel jealous of your partner

Take a cursory look at your behavior. Do you feel like breaking somebody's head when your partner is close to the opposite sex? Are you threatened by any friends of theirs who you fear may "steal" your partner away from you? This is jealousy, and it is one of the signs that you are feeling anxious in your relationship. Sometimes, you might even have the urge to test your spouse's commitment and love; this is an indication of anxiety triggered by jealousy.

2.   When your self-esteem is low

When you are always cautious of how you behave because you don't know what your partner's reaction will be, or you can't express yourself freely in front of your partner due to fear of rejection, this is an indication of low self-esteem - a sign that you are anxious in your relationship.

3.   Lack of trust

Your partner is one of the people you should trust the most. If you always have to confirm whatever your wife, husband, boyfriend, or girlfriend says before you believe them, it shows that there's a lack of trust in the relationship. Many times, the lack of trust is caused by past betrayal. However, you should not allow past betrayals to impact negatively on your relationship, provided they were one time occurrences. Realize that your partner is not perfect, and once they have assured you that such incidences will never happen again, believe them.

4.   Emotional imbalance

Today you are frustrated, tomorrow you are angry, the next day you are happy – this is emotional instability. You might not be aware of this, but constant mood swings are also a sign of emotional imbalance, and they do not help the matter. They only worsen it. Whatever problems or issues you are facing, discuss them with your partner. When the two of you deliberate on a problem, you will get it solved quickly. When you discover that your mood is not stable, it is a symptom of anxiety in a relationship.

5.   Lack of sleep and reduced sex drive

The aftermath of constant worry is insomnia, which is the inability to sleep, and when you are unable to sleep, your body is stressed, leading to decreased libido.

If you are experiencing one or more of these symptoms, what you need to do is to figure out the possible causes and deal with it. I am going to give you examples of likely causes of these problems.

Possible Causes of a Relationship Anxiety

Most times, relationship anxiety could be a manifestation of a deep-rooted problem. Here are the common causes of relationship anxiety:

1. Complicated Relationship

When you are uncertain about your relationship, or it is not clearly defined, it can be classified as complicated. This applies to those that are dating. For instance, a woman may not know the intentions of the man - whether he wants to marry her or is just in it for fun. Also, a long distance relationship could result in anxiety. In such cases, partners must learn to trust each other.

2. Comparison

Comparing your current relationship with past ones should be avoided as much possible. You might begin to entertain feelings of regret if you discover that your previous relationship was better in the areas of finance, communication, sex, and other aspects. To avoid this feeling, you should never compare your marriage or relationship to that of others or the ones you have had in the past.

3. Constant fighting

When you are always quarreling with your partner, you might never stop worrying because you don't know when the next altercation will crop up. This is one of the causes of severe anxiety in a relationship, because your bid to avoid quarreling will not allow you to have a pleasant time with your partner.

4. Lack of understanding

Partners that do not take the time to understand each other will always face difficulties. As mentioned earlier, the constant quarreling will result in an anxious relationship. Are you noticing the symptoms of anxiety coupled with miscommunications? Lack of understanding might be the reason for your relationship anxiety. Get to know your partner better, and encourage them to know you.

5. Other issues

Difficult experiences in past unhealthy relationships might result in many other issues. Not only that, neglect during childhood, abuse in the past, and lack of affection are some of the reason why someone can feel anxious in a relationship.

Once you have identified the root cause of your relationship issue, getting rid of it will be the next step. Do not forget, the primary reason for the self-evaluation of any problem is to get rid of it. We are going to examine the effect of anxiety on a relationship with logical steps towards putting an end to it.

Effects of Anxiety on Relationships and How to stop it

This is a relevant that you need to read carefully, as it opens your eyes to how anxiety manifests in a relationship and the effective ways to stop it no matter the way it appears.

1. Anxiety makes you continuously worry about your relationship

Persistent worry is one of the manifestations of relationship anxiety. If you are continually having thoughts such as, "Is my partner mad at me, or are they pretending to happy with me? Will this relationship last?" These kinds of views indicate one thing – WORRY. If you discover that you regularly entertain these kinds of thought, do the following:

- Clear your mind and live in the moment
- If negatives thoughts are continually running through your mind, then stop, clear your mind, and think about the beautiful moments you have shared with your partner. Think about the promises your partner has made, and reassure yourself that your relationship is going to stand the test of time.

- Do not react impulsively - think before you take any step. Share your feelings with your partner rather than withdrawing from them - make an effort to connect.

2. Anxiety breeds mistrust

Anxiety makes you think negatively about your partner. You will find it difficult to believe anything they say. In some cases, you may suspect that your partner is going out with another person. These kinds of feelings inevitably come between you and your partner. It makes it hard for you to relate to them well. To put an end to this, follow these practical steps:

- Ask yourself, "Do I have any proof of my suspicion?"

- Go to your partner and talk things over with them

- Start again if you notice that your relationship is suffering from a lack of trust

- Reestablish the trust, date each other as if it is your first time, and gradually build the trust

- Do the things you did when you first met each other

3. Anxiety leads to self-centeredness

What anxiety does is take all your attention, making you focus solely on the problem while every other thing suffers. You don't have time for your partner; you are withdrawn to yourself. You focus mainly on yourself and neglect the physical and emotional needs of your partner. Here are the things to do to get rid of this attitude:

- Rather than magnifying and focusing on your fear, pay attention to your needs

- You can seek the support of your partner when you discover that you cannot handle the fear alone

4. Anxiety inhibits expression with your partner

Anything that stops you from expressing your sincere feeling to your partner is an enemy of your relationship. Anxiety is the culprit here; it hinders you from opening your mind to your partner. You think that they might rebuff you, or that telling them how you feel may cause an adverse reaction from them. This makes you keep procrastinating, instead of discussing the critical issues right away with them. How do you overcome the fear of rejection? Consider the following quick steps:

- Focus on the love your partner has for you

- Voice out what you feel to get rid of anxiety

- Approach your partner cheerfully

- Discuss heartily with them

5. Anxiety makes you sad

Anxiety breeds these two problems – limitation and fear. A soul battling with these two evils cannot be happy. Anxiety is that culprit that steals your joy by preoccupying you with unnecessary agitation and worry. Happiness is the bedrock of any relationship, so stop being sad and start enjoying happy moments with your partner by taking the following steps:

- Dismiss any thoughts that make you sad

- Play your favorite music to occupy your mind

- Become playful with your partner

- Relive the sweet moments you have had with your partner

- Be humorous, laugh with your partner

6. Anxiety can either makes you distant or clingy

One way by which you can recognize anxious people is that they tend to be extreme in their actions. If they are not aloof, they will become too attached. Both of these behaviors are extreme and unhealthy. Have you evaluated yourself and discovered that you are guilty of these extremities? Take the action steps below to restore your healthy relationship with your partner:

- Figure out your feelings
- Work on yourself
- Get yourself engaged with things you enjoy doing

7. Anxiety makes you reject things that will benefit you.

It makes you see everything from one point of view - fear. Anxiety results in indecision in a relationship, because you won't know which way is right. Here is how you can stop this problem:

- Acknowledge your confusing thoughts and deal with them
- Weigh your decisions carefully without being biased
- Seek your partner's help if you discover you need support

CHAPTER 13:

How to Improve your Mood

Some people, when they start dating, think that having differences in opinions about politics, religion, values, or morality means they will always be fighting over things from day one. This is far from reality and only becomes a problem when both parties refuse to take into account each other's viewpoints. Instead of accepting them or viewing them as a new perspective, they perceive it as something negative and thus, are always trying to change them. Opinions can be changed, but they don't always have to. If we take things back to the day you two met, was it not your differences that attracted you to each other in the first place? There is a strong backing behind opposites attract – proven both by science and psychological experts.

Having a different opinion does indeed complicate things slightly in a relationship but there are many ways to deal with it.

I Have Something to Tell You

The moment couples start living together, they are bound to come across diverse opinions – most of which may not match yours. This can lead to misunderstandings as well as arguments over even the smallest of issues such as what to dress your kid as on Christmas. If you come from a Jewish family and your partner is a hardcore Christian, this argument may seem quite valid as Christmas isn't a celebrated holiday according to the Jewish tradition. They celebrate Hanukkah instead. The same differences can also be seen in how the money is spent in the house, which gets to make the final call, which gets to discipline the kids, who is responsible for housekeeping and raising the kids, etc.

But where do these differences come from?

For starters, we all come from different households, neighborhoods or different sides of the country. Partners may have been raised in a certain way that conflicts with the other's way of living. In some houses, it is considered bad to talk back to your husband; whereas, in some homes, nearly all the major decisions are taken mutually after thorough discussions. This diversification of environments and early childhood experiences play a crucial role in personality development. Your partner may come from a family that spent every summer vacation out in the woods, but you may have never experienced anything as outdoorsy. Therefore, when it comes to taking the kids to someplace, your partner may insist on renting an RV and heading for the woods while you might be more interested in visiting the entertainment hub of the country for some family time together.

Then, we also have different educations, different exposures, different jobs, and different perspectives about life. All of these can easily become problematic when going unheard or unresolved.

However, these differences don't mean that your partner is right and you aren't or in any way demean you. Accepting others' opinions is a crucial aspect of every marriage. A relationship can be fostered with unity and understanding where every different idea gets discussed with an open mind.

Why You Should Listen to What Your Partner Has to Say

We believe everyone should see the world as we do. We think of it as the right way and are rarely keen on changing our minds about it. When we are paired in a relationship with a partner who has a completely different point of view than yours, it is so easy to blame them for being misinformed or living with a distorted opinion about reality.

But they think the same about your views too. So how to go on living with them when you constantly feel that they are wrong and vice versa?

First off, each individual is entitled to their opinions. Opinions are formed based on real events and make the individual who they are.

They aren't wrong, just different.

When you two are journeying together, keep in mind that it is never going to be easy or simple as a straight line. You both chose to be together and thus must provide each other with some space and understanding about the things they solely believe in. Having a partner with a different opinion is also a healthy thing for many reasons. For starters, it will enrich and broaden your vision about reality. It allows you to question your own beliefs and opinions and see if you are wrong. A different opinion can also give you the chance to ask them what made them think that way or why do they believe what they believe in. The newfound information can help you two understand each other better and strengthen your relationship, as then you will be more considerate when discussing important issues with them.

Thirdly, when you acknowledge and accept your partner's opinions, they will feel more valued and understood. When they feel that, they will be more open with you and feel safe sharing their deepest thoughts and ideas with you without feeling judged. The level of trust between you two will blossom, and your partner won't need to amplify their views just to be heard.

It also helps to bridge the gap between you two as you learn to respect each other's viewpoints. Moreover, there may be times when one of your decisions may require more thinking on your part and your partner may help you see it. For instance, you are thinking of getting a new job. You are thinking of a good pay raise and fewer working hours. However, you might overlook aspects like long commute hours and heavy traffic. If your partner knows how frustrated you get when you drive for long hours, they may ask you to reconsider. You might feel a little taken aback by their idea and believe that they don't want to see you succeed. But when you two sit down to discuss why you think it's a great idea and why they think otherwise, a different point of view may change your mind. You may come to realize that their worry wasn't about you earning more but rather about your mood and health. So a different point of view can help you see past all the glittery stuff.

You can also visualize the long-term impacts of your decisions. For instance, if we follow-up with the same example as above, your primary objective was short-term goals. You just wanted to work a few hours less and get paid more. However, your partner's concern was more about your health. Who knows, ten days into the new job and you are back to hating your life again and regretting ever leaving your previous job.

A difference of opinion can also help you overcome your weaknesses. As humans, we have the habit of underestimating our skills and talents. We always think that we aren't good enough. That is your opinion of yourself. Chances are, you may have backed down on some good potential opportunities in the past due to the same fear. Now enter a partner into this situation who thinks no one can beat you at the skill you are good at. This positive and refreshing boost of an entirely different opinion of yourself will improve your self-confidence.

How to Resolve Contradictory Opinions without Fighting?

Differing opinions will arise between partners – that's a given! How you are going to resolve them is the more important question. Sometimes, these differences in views can become the reason for fights and arguments between couples. So how can they move past that and accept and respect each other's opinions without breaking into a fight?

We have some great advice to offer. Take a look!

Negotiation

Negotiation or compromise is a suitable way to come out of a difference in opinions during complex situations. When you two want to do something you're way and the partner intervenes with their methodologies, opt to compromise. Find a way in which neither one of you feels left out or disrespected. If you two can't reach a consensus and aren't; willing to give up on your stance, it is best to avoid attempting it at all. After all, nothing can be more important than your relationship, right? Don't be hell-bent on proving yourself right all the time.

Don't Argue

Sometimes, it can be very hard to change someone's perspective about things because they are very personal to them. In that case, it is unfair on your part to expect them to give it up. You must understand where they are coming from and why they think a certain way. If no mutual ground can be found, you must retreat.

Be Sensible

What your partner is saying might be rational, and you know it, but if you continue to argue, then that is just egoistic on your part. Try putting yourself in your partner's shoes and look at the world from their eyes for once. If you know that they are right and you keep fighting for the sake of being right, then you need to back up and accept it as a mature individual.

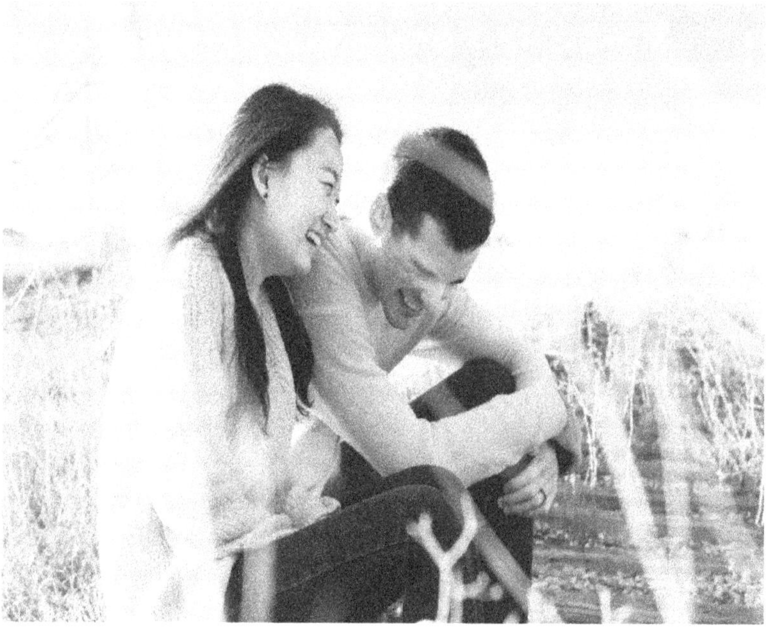

CHAPTER 14:

The Diamond inside Anxiety

They consider me right in the throes of fear, and the fear most often focuses on their intimate relationship. A series of questions lead them to fear that they are in the "right" relationship or whether they make a "mistake." I have said it many times, but it is worth repeating it: all of those who find me are in good and good relationships, and the fear of playing them is simply nervous. There is a small number- maybe 5 percent of people who know that their concern comes from a specific location. They are an indication of significant red flag issues in the relationship, but these are evident from my initial interaction with them and are not correlated with the positive feelings that follow the anxiety in a relationship.

To the vast majority, fear strikes like power from the depths and literally draws them into an infernal world in a blast of panic from their highly functioning everyday lives. Where they were once excited to move into a healthy married life, now they are so concerned about it that it hampers their ability to feed, sleep and work properly, let alone to plan a wedding. You would like the anxiety to disappear, thinking incorrectly that it is an indication that you are in the wrong relationship and that the only solution is to leave. That's when they find their way to Google's "engagement anxiety" or "marriage terror."

The first and most important step in working through the fear is to reverse the yearning that it will vanish and to understand that within the coat of suffering is great wisdom. It is clearly a challenge to make; nobody would want to live with the demon of fear, so you should understand why you want the demon to vanish. Yet there can be no real healing without the ability to discover its origins and heights.

It is a strange and counterintuitive assertion, but what all my clients realize eventually is that the fear-based thoughts and repetitive questions contain great information. This will help you reach this knowledge by dressing like a hero or heroine embarking into what Joseph Campbell calls the "Hero's Journey." Then you can have the ability to dive into your psyche's darkest areas and keep a light of reality about what you are seeking in them. And here's a nugget of confidence to combat the fear of looking inside: you can find nothing to do with your partner and everything to do with you. There is an unharmed warehouse of sadness, a soft space of vulnerability, a shy person, a river of terror, a warehouse of myths about love, marriage, romanticism, and intimacy. And when you learn to take care of your difficult feelings and to substitute false assumptions with the truth, you will find a degree of harmony, confidence, and healing, which you had never learned. The uncertainty you feel about your relationship is not new, and you have not felt insecure in your life for the first time. If you like most people who find me, you have frequently or continuously suffered from anxiety throughout your life. Now is your chance to repair it.

The magic of this deep soul research shows what the soul is trying to express. The soul wants wholeness, peace, and serenity, but it does not always know how to fulfill these wants. Instead of specifically requesting more life, for instance, we prefer to project the will into our partner in the form: "He's not interesting enough." If we stick to that concept and assume it's real, we lose the chance to mine for the diamond within anxiety.

I've always told you that the purpose of concentrating on the negative attributes of our partners is to shield or protect yourself from the hard feelings caused by transitions: the remorse of letting go and the dream of the ideal mate, the uncertainty of jumping into the unknown, and the insecurity accompanying the danger of love. But I realized recently that, while the thoughts defend against painful feelings, they are also gates to expand our consciousness and to deepen our emotional and spiritual development.

To break through the nervous barrier and hit the inside gem, it is important to understand which questions lead to what diamonds. I have grouped the most common issues according to their positive role to promote this process.

Finding Your Way through the 'Mirror Maze' Of Emotions and Relationships

It may also feel like a day-to-day life for those with shyness and anxiety. If you are an insecure or shy guy (or woman), you probably have smart, talented, funny, affectionate, and interesting friends, but you are still so unsure about yourself that you are lost in trying to find out who you should be rather than who you really are. You think your true self is "too isolated" from those around you. And when you care about others, lead and take responsibility, you doubt your own worth and how you make a difference for others. You certainly have worked hard to be a member of the community or, more frequently, to avoid being insulted by a lack of attributes that will make you attractive or appealing to others.

You may be married or have relationships and are involved in caring for others, but you feel you've never been able to express your thoughts, emotions, dreams, and interests directly. You could doubt whether anyone would hear or care, even if you spoke out. Your days and hours are full of tasks and events, but despite what you are doing, you find very little satisfaction.

Relations and social interactions can be a labyrinth of reflections and dead ends to us, shy men, like this hall of mirrors. When you obey one rule, you will never know how to find your way out, keep your eyes on your feet, and know where you are. You will concentrate on placing every foot carefully before you if you are not disturbed by flashing lights, changing colors, and tenting views of the exit. You can check your way and move forward with each stage.

Fear and anxiety work best when disturbed and unsure. The confounding wind of interactions, talk, and movement around you may become daunting if you feel that you are responsible for following these sometimes conflicting currents and reacting to them. When you concentrate on knowing yourself and being attentive to yourself, your own values, perceptions, emotions, and awareness, you have the ability to start the journey out of the stormy labyrinth.

CHAPTER 15:

How to Master Your Emotions

One of the most important things that you can do to help you gain more emotional intelligence is to master your own emotions. This can be a strenuous process but the results are well worth it if you persevere. When you encounter many negative emotions, like anger, sadness, fear, and so on, they can be extremely difficult to get a handle on, especially if they take you by surprise. When this happens, we have let go of our mastery over our emotions, and only negative outcomes will follow.

Mastering your emotions can be one of the hardest things that you work on in this whole process. It is much easier just to let the emotions come and take over your life, without considering how they will affect you and others along the way. Here we are going to discuss some of the things that you can do to master your emotions better so they don't just take control over your life.

Know yourself

The first step that we will look at is how to know yourself. Are you familiar with how different emotions affect you physically? Do you know where tension or anger is held inside of your body? When you feel anxious or sad, do you know the physical responses related to each?

There are so many times that we will react to a situation without really knowing why. You feel the emotion come on suddenly, before springing into action, already in a defensive stance and ready to fight. However, with enough practice, it is possible to tune into these emotions before they start to take over. You can learn where they are inside of your body and, over time, you will even be able to spot some budding emotions early on, taking control of them before they take control of you.

A good thing to try out if you would like a chance to get to know yourself better is to spend a bit of time each day, even if it is just five minutes, in quiet contemplation. You can take this time to use meditation, sitting down and journaling, going on a walk or doing another activity that lets you be alone with your thoughts. The point here is to think about your life, no matter where you are in it, and how this makes you feel.

It doesn't take much time each day to see the results of this practice. By looking at your life and understanding your prevalent emotions, you will be able to gain a sense of your own self that most people don't have. Our modern world does not encourage this quiet contemplation. We are too busy running from one place to another to get things done and then never have enough time to finish it all. This then makes it impossible to recognize the things that may be bothering you with so much external stress and anxiety flying about, it is no wonder that so many people are ready to explode.

Protect yourself

After you have had a chance to begin your quiet time, you can also use it to think about ways that you can protect yourself. First, you may be asking what this all means? It basically means that you should take some time to look at the external influences that are in your life and how they make you feel. Some of them are going to pop out right away as things that make you feel anxious, upset, or angry while others will take a bit more work to classify.

One place that you should look is to the media that you consume. Things like magazines, newspapers, radio, news, and television can all place you into an emotional storm first thing in the morning, but only if you let them. If you seem anxious and stressed, especially after reading or watching the news, it may be time to reconsider how you spend your mornings. This can save you time, which you can use for meditation, while also protecting yourself emotionally.

The company that you keep, or the people you spend your time with, can also influence your emotions. Are these people uplifting and ready to make you feel great, or are they the kind of people who like to complain and bring you down all of the time? If you are uncertain about how they are making you feel, take note of your emotions and thoughts when you leave their company. Do you feel uplifted and like you just spent your time in a positive fashion or do you feel like you were just stomped on and are now more anxious than when you arrived? If you don't like your answer then it might be time to mix up your social circle. There are so many things out there in the world can negatively affect your emotional intelligence, what's worse is that some of them are out of your control. It is hard to change your coworkers and it is hard to tell the news to stop broadcasting the bad stuff, but you can make some decisions in your life that will eliminate, or at least reduce, the effect these negative influences produce.

Controlled expression

You may find that when you are anxious or upset, for example, that spending a few minutes on a brisk walk can help to calm the anger down, or writing out your emotions in a journal can help you to see that things really aren't as bad as they may first appear.

Learning how to move that anger into something that is much more positive is so much healthier for the body. The issue is that most people don't have these outlets for their emotions. Instead, these emotions are allowed to drag on for days, making you fall into a negative emotional pattern. This loop will make it difficult to perceive anything in a positive light while also reinforcing itself at every turn which can make it especially difficult to break free of.

Luckily, there are many different ways to control your emotions successfully. You can stick with choosing an outlet for the emotion so that you can get it all out and then move on or you can think about the emotion and whether your response was actually warranted. Regardless, the important thing is that you learn how to turn off the negative emotion, to not constantly think about the situation that dragged you into the state in the first place. If you can let go of that, you are going will certainly feel better in no time flat.

Time travel

Another exercise you might find effective is known as time travel. Time is one of the best ways to change your personal perspective to the feelings you have. If you find that you are getting caught up in a type of negative state that feels insurmountable, then maybe it is time to stop what you are doing and take a break. Close your eyes and take in a few deep breaths before you ask yourself a question: "Will this (issue, circumstance, or whatever), matter a month from now?"

Make sure that you are honest with yourself when answering. Yes, you feel the emotion pretty strongly now, but it is unlikely that you are going to care or even remember it by the time next month comes around. If this is the case, then you need to ask yourself is it really worth getting bent out of shape about now? If it is possible for you to feel a bit better in the future about this situation, it is definitely possible for you to feel better now.

Now, you may be really upset about the situation at hand or it could be something really big that is bothering you. You may go back to that question from before and decide that yes, I will still be upset about this in a month. If this does happen, it is time to go to the next step.

Tools

When it comes to dealing with negative emotions, they are going to occur because there is a little blip that happens in your circuitry now or then, similar to when a fuse happens to blow in your home. Until that circuit gets back to work, everything connected to it simply won't work as intended.

Your negative emotions work in the same way. They make you blow a fuse and you will respond by going offline with a lot of negative emotions. Learning how to properly deal with these negative emotions and gaining the tools that you need. I will make it a bit easier for you to stop the negative emotion and also to fix up the circuitry. You will still feel the emotions when this happens, but it helps you to stay in control even when the negative emotions come calling.

Mastering your emotions can be hard. These steps will definitely help you to get going on the right path, but it will take time to go from letting your emotions control you to being the one in control of your emotions. However, once you get the right tools in place, make sure that you recognize those emotions, and find a good outlet for them when they do come, you will gain mastery over your emotions in no time.

CHAPTER 16:

Toxic Relationship

Anxiety isn't always the element which affects a relationship. Sometimes it's the other way around, and the reason you have anxiety is because of a toxic relationship. But what exactly does toxic mean? We refer to a relationship as toxic when it isn't beneficial to you and it's harmful in some way. The building blocks for a healthy relationship are made from mutual respect and admiration, but sometimes it just isn't enough.

However, there is a difference between a problematic relationship and a toxic one, and that is mainly the noxious atmosphere that surrounds you. This kind of relationship can suffocate you with time and prevent you from living a happy, productive life. Many factors lead to toxicity. It is most often caused by friction that can occur between two people that are opposites of each other. In others, nothing specific is to blame, and the toxic relationship grows from the lack of communication, the establishment of boundaries and the ability to agree on something, or at the very least compromise.

Take not that not all toxic relationships develop because of the couple. Sometimes there is an outlier seeking to influence conflict because they will benefit from it in some way. This type of individual preys on other people's insecurities, weaknesses, or manipulates his way inside a relationship from which he has something to gain. In some cases, a toxic person seeks to destroy a relationship in order to get closer to one of them. He or she may not even be aware of their damaging behavior because of a self-obsessed focus that does not extend to anyone else. Personal needs, emotions, and goals take priority over anyone else's wellbeing.

With that in mind, let's briefly explore the characteristics of a toxic relationship:

1. Poisonous: A relationship that is extremely unpleasant to be around as it poisons the atmosphere around it. It makes anyone around the couple anxious, and it can even lead to psychological and emotional problems such as anxiety and depression.

2. Deadly: Toxic relationships are bad for your health. In many cases, it involved risky, destructive, and abusive behaviors. Some people end up harming themselves with alcohol, drugs, or worse. Injuries and even death can become the final result.

3. Negative: In this kind of relationship, negativity is the norm. There is no positive reinforcement, even when children are involved. The overwhelming lack of approval and emotional support is standard.

4. Harmful: Toxic relationships lack balance and awareness. Those involved are never truly aware of each other and lack the most positive principles that a healthy relationship needs. Toxicity also promotes immoral and malicious acts that harm a romantic relationship.

What we have discussed so far may lead you to think that toxic people are psychopaths and nothing more. While it is true that some of them are, that's not always the case. However, psychopaths are expert manipulators due to their ability to mask their true feelings and intentions. These people have a psychological disorder that makes their personality imposing, pretentious, and even impulsive. Many aren't aware of their behavior and the effects it has on others. They tend to be self-absorbed and expect a great deal from others while being narcissistic and deceitful. In other words, they lack insight as well as empathy. Psychopaths are people who seek attention, admiration, and acceptance, but they will need to accept their responsibilities and the needs of others.

Why and how would anyone end up in a relationship with someone who displays psychopathic traits? The answer lies in their ability to maintain appearances and manipulate others. If they realize you see through their charade, they will do anything to convince you that they are a good person. They may start doing good deeds, not out of empathy and love, but out of the need to redeem themselves. In many cases, these people can recover if their psychopathic disorder isn't too severe. With help, they can gain control over themselves and their toxic behavior, so they can live a productive life without hurting others in the process.

As mentioned earlier, toxic relationships don't always involve psychopaths or those who display similar traits. In many situations, these relationships are the way they are due to decent people that are terrible decision-makers, or that lack social skills. Taking a wrong turn in life happens to everyone, and many people change but not always for the better.

Warning Signs

Now that you can better identify toxic relationships and the kind of people that are involved let's see if you're in one or not. Humans are complex creatures, and the traits we don't necessarily make someone toxic. Some underlying issues and disorders can make people behave negatively. However, they can still be excellent partners. With that said, here's a list of questions you can ask yourself to learn more about your relationship:

1. How do you feel in the company of your partner?

2. Do you feel happy, safe, and nurtured in the presence of your significant other?

3. Are all the other people involved in your relationship safe and happy? For instance your children (if you have any), parents, and friends and so on. As mentioned earlier, people tend to avoid toxic relationships instead of being in contact with them.

4. Do you experience anxiety or panic attacks when you are about to discuss something with your partner?

5. Can you think of any scenarios in which you were manipulated to do something that wasn't for your best interest?

6. Is your partner pushing the limits of what you would consider ethical? Is he or she even crossing the line of what is legal?

7. Does your partner to push you to perform challenging tasks that you consider entirely unnecessary? These challenges may seem pointless, and that you need to resolve just because it's what your partner wants.

8. Do you feel emotionally strained and exhausted after interacting with your partner?

If you can answer a few of these questions, you are likely in a toxic relationship that may be making you anxious and damaging your health. You then need to decide for yourself whether you wish to stay in this kind of relationship to repair it or leave. If you do decide to stay, there's a series of decisions you need to make. For instance, you need to feel in control with the idea of resisting all the negativity that comes with a toxic partner, because you will need to endure feelings of anxiety and stress. You need to ask yourself whether you are gaining enough from that relationship and whether it's worth sacrificing yourself for it.

Handling a Toxic Relationship

As mentioned, a toxic relationship can be a powerful source of anxiety. It doesn't have to be a romantic relationship either. Some of them you can avoid by cutting contact with some people to feel relief. However, there are certain people you simply cannot break away from, whether they are romantic partners or your mother in law. This is why in this we are going to discuss how to deal with such a relationship.

The first step is to accept the inescapable situation. When your options are limited, you cannot achieve relief by avoidance, and acceptance leads to a decrease in anxiety. You may be tempted to be hostile towards that person, but it won't help. Instead, it will just add to your worries and stress. At this point, your only alternative is managing your anxiety by admitting to yourself that you may never be able to get along with that person. In addition, you can attempt to ignore him or her completely by never going spending time together and ignoring any contact. However, none of these tactics usually work.

Resistance can help short-term, but it will continue generating anxiety and stress because the toxic person knows how to get under your skin and take advantage of you. Accept that this relationship is difficult and challenges you but you are doing your best to make it better. That doesn't mean you should completely surrender. By accepting your situation, you will allow yourself new possibilities and new options instead of repeatedly punishing yourself.

Take note that for the process of acceptance to take hold, you need to be consciously aware that you are not responsible for anyone else's emotions and reactions. Toxic behavior often makes people blame you for their situation and feelings. Do not accept any of that, as you are not the reason for their suffering. They need to take responsibility for their thoughts and actions instead of blaming others.

The second step is telling the truth. If a toxic relationship is creating stress, likely, you often lie to avoid conflict, which causes even more anxiety. The problem is that when you lie to such a person, you enable them and become partially responsible for the reality they create — leading to the toxic environment surrounding them.

For instance, let's say you intentionally didn't invite the problematic person to your birthday. When confronted about it, you may be tempted to say that you sent an invitation but used the wrong address, or it went into the spam folder. Lying isn't easy, especially if you are an anxious person. People can tell, especially if you tend to make excuses for yourself often enough. Instead of lying you should tell the truth, and the real truth. This means that you shouldn't use an excuse. Just say they make you uncomfortable and extremely anxious, that is why you didn't invite them. Telling the truth can be difficult and even painful because it affects others. It takes a great deal of courage and once you get through the experience, you will feel a powerful sense of relief. In the end, it's better to get something off your chest instead of carrying it.

RELATIONSHIP THERAPY

CHAPTER 17:

Know Your Partner

Who are we as partners in the relationship? How do we step (literally as well as figuratively) towards and away from those on whom we depend? I am also amazed that people can be together for fifteen, twenty, and even thirty years. They don't know in too many ways what ticks each other. Like we have seen before, getting to know our ordinary people and ambassadors allows us in some way to address these questions. But in a relationship, not everyone is able to respond in the same way. Power balance varies from person to person inside and between primitive and ambassador camps. In reality, you and your partner can encounter various interactions between your primitive men and ambassadors due to the variance of your brain.

And we are all at the table with a specific sort of partnership. We may know the style of our partner, but it is sometimes unaware of that. Unhappy couples also assert ignorance, and maintain claims of ignorance ("I just don't know what planet you're on") during relationships, "If I knew you were this way I would never have met you." We will go through why and what you can do to solve this mystification in your relationship. I have found, as a couple of therapists, that these statements of ignorance are inherently false while the people who say them may be real. They are incorrect because we all have a relationship style that is consistent over time. As we grow up, relationship types with our parents or caregivers are the norm we have learned to conform to. In other words, our social cabling is at a young age. This wiring remains mostly unchanged as we age, given our intellect and access to new ideas. For example, I frequently hear new parents say, "I'm never going to do what my parents have done to me," so they don't repeat the mistakes their parents have made in times of distress. It's just a matter of human nature and genetics, and I don't say it with judgment.

Many partners are unaware of their relationships and how they connect in a married couple environment. They try to show themselves in the best light, as in any audition. In the first day it wouldn't make sense for anyone to say, "I have been alone as a child a lot of time, and I still am. I don't like being intruded in my time alone. Once I'm ready, I'll come to you. And don't get bothered to come to me because then I know you're asking me and I don't like that. "An equally quick way to give a hill date would be to say," I just cling and get mad when I'm abandoned. I dislike and neglect silences. I do not seem to receive enough from people. Still, I don't get compliments well, because I don't think people are genuine, I tend to reject something positive. "Partners may provide insights during the initial stage in a relationship about their necessary preferences for physical closeness, emotional privacy, and health and security concerns. Yet this preference comes to life only when the relationship is irreversible in one or both partners' minds.

We do much of what we do almost automatically and without thinking. Mostly, it is the work of our primitive people. One of the aspects that partners usually don't think about in relationships is how they step emotionally with each other. Early in childhood, our intelligence reacts to physical closeness and duration, influenced things like where you choose to sit or stand in connection with each other, how you can change the distance between yourselves, how we embrace, how we make love. Everything we do involves physical movement and static space. Since we are primarily working on the autopilot, we are unaware of the whole aspect of our interactions. Also, physical contact during courtship is treated differently than in more involved phases. For instance, many people are continually touching while dating, but when they commit, the amount they touch drops dramatically.

Who Are You?

No one likes to be categorized, but it is mostly because we have minds that organize, sort, compare knowledge and experience by their very nature that we classify people and things around us. In reality, for centuries, people have described the human condition and still develop new ways of doing so—Scorpios or Capricorns, from Mars or Venus. We are liberals or libertarians, geeks, or Goths, atheists or religious fanatics. Before we deplete or dehumanize anyone, those definitions will help us comprehend each other.

A significant aspect of this manual is that you identify your partner's interests and relationship types, explain and eventually mark them. It's much easier to work together and address problems when you know and appreciate each other's styles. It makes it easier to forgive and genuinely help because of the belief that "I know who you are." I'm not showing new or completely my designs. They are based on research findings first popularized almost half a century ago by John Bowlby (1969) and Mary Ainsworth and their fellow workers, who describe how babies develop an attachment. Over the years, I have found that most spouses have been part of one of three critical styles of partnership with a range of tips that I will present to you.

First, don't try to push yourself if you don't figure out which style suits your partner best. The "mileage you get" from this information may vary. I presented these styles in their purest form. One of the three types are known by the vast majority of people. In reality, people can be a mixture of different types, often making it hard to choose the most prominent. No worries, if that's the case to you. You should recall and use the one that best suits in a particular situation. Second, my goal is to encourage reverence and empathy in discussing these types of what I believe are natural characteristics for human beings. Do not find them as flaws of character. Don't turn them into your partner's weapons. Alternatively, accept these types as the reasonable and necessary changes made by each of us in adulthood.

How We Develop Our Style of Relating

As I said, we have a young age in our social wiring. It is how our parents or caregivers respond to us and to the world that decides whether we grow up to feel fundamentally safe or insecure. Parents who value relationship are more likely to defend their loved ones than parents who value other things. We prefer to spend more time with their children face-to-face and from skin to skin; be more curious and interested in the spirit of their child, concentrate more closely, be more sensitive and respond to their children's requirements. They build a healthy place for the child in this way.

The dynamics of this early relationship are physiologically distinctive. Neuroscientists have found that adult-post based children appear to develop more neural networks rather than adult brain-detached children. In general, these children can control their emotions and desires by well integrating with the primitives and ambassadors of secure children. Its amygdalae are not overwhelmed, and its hypothalamus carries out regular operations and feedback contact with the pituitary and surgeon glands, the other hazard cogs and the tension wheel, and when appropriate turn this device on and off. We have a well-developed dumb vagus and intelligent vagus. Thanks to good connections early on, healthy children tend to have the right brain and insula well-formed, so they can read their expressions, thoughts, feelings and sensations of the body and get the whole thing. Their orbito-frontal cortex is particularly well-formed, with neural connections that provide input to their other ambassadors and primitives. We seem to display more empathy, more reliable moral judgment, more substantial impulse control and more intense aggression than anxious children. In general, healthy children are more resilient to social tension slings and arrows and perform much better within social circumstances.

Playfulness, engagement, versatility and aesthetics define a healthy partnership. Pleasant sensations prevail because bad feelings are rapidly alleviated. It's a beautiful place! It's a place where fun and excitement and innovation are to be expected as well as relaxation and comfort. We are taking it to adulthood when we encounter this kind of healthy foundation as a child. Even in early childhood, we didn't all have stable relationships. Perhaps without one who was always available or trusted, we had many revolving caregivers. Or maybe there were one or more caregivers who appreciated more than the relationship, like self-preservation, beauty, young people, success, intellect, skills, money or reputation. Maybe one or more caregivers emphasized integrity, anonymity, freedom and autonomy in commitment to relationships. Nearly everything can change the meaning of the partnership, and sometimes it is not by design that this happens. Unresolved traumas or injuries, immaturity and the like can interfere with the sense of safety of a child. When we do so, then we, as adults, are connected to a pure vulnerability. Instead of seeing ourselves as an island in humankind's ocean, we should maintain our communication and prevent too much communication. And it can lead to ambivalence as we interact with others and become more like a wave in that situation.

CHAPTER 18:

Therapy and Treatment for Anxiety

Seeking out a Therapist

Sometimes, the best thing you can do for persistent anxiety is seeking out a therapist. This is far easier said than done, but even if you feel like you do not need one, it may be worthwhile to consider. Therapists are not evil or a waste of money they are actually quite useful. They can help you navigate through all sorts of negative thoughts and ensure that you are able to handle yourself better no matter what the situation at hand. Through these processes, you will get customized content that cannot provide for you. You will get real-time feedback, telling you how you are doing and whether you are making a mistake in the execution of something that you are doing.

If you think that actively seeking out a therapist may be useful to you, you should make an appointment with your primary care provider to get advice or a referral. Sometimes, insurance will not cover any therapy without a referral, so this is one way to skip that step. As a bonus, your doctor will also be able to ensure that there are no physical causes to the symptoms you are having, particularly surrounding your heart. You only have one of those, after all.

When you have gotten a referral for therapy, you can then begin to consider what kind of therapy would work best for you. Would you want a cognitive behavioral therapist? Traditional talk therapy? Some other kind? There are several different forms of therapy for anxiety, and ultimately, the one you pursue will be your own choice. When you have made your decision, you should then check out any in your area that accepts your insurance, or if they do not, that is affordable to you.

When you do eventually meet your therapist, keep an open mind, but also keep in mind that you need to click with the individual. You want to make sure you feel comfortable with the person that you are talking to. However, it is hard to judge that after a single session in many instances. Try to meet with a therapist at least twice before deciding that he or she is not right for you. Finding the right match for you is essential if you want to make sure that your therapeutic process is actually effective.

Worst Case Scenario Role-play

Another technique some people find useful in managing anxiety is to engage in what is known as a worst-case scenario role-play. In this case, you are challenged to imagine the worst possible ending to whatever you are anxious about. For example, if you are anxious over getting a divorce, you may then stop and consider what the worst-case scenario would look like you plan out exactly what would happen. Perhaps you fear that your soon-to-be-ex will get full custody of the kids and get to keep possession of the house, leaving you with a massive child support bill for children you never see, and your children are quickly alienated against you so they no longer want to interact with you at all. Maybe this goes a step further and you lose all contact with your children, and all you become is a wallet for all of the activities, medical insurance, and everything else the children need while your ex marries someone else who gets to be the parent to your child that you wish you could be.

Stop and play out that situation. Then, you need to consider how realistic that is. How often do parents lose all contact with their children unless they are doing something that is bad for the children? How often do you hear about people who do drugs retaining custody of their children, or people who abuse their children retaining custody? How likely is your ex to stop, take the kids, and run? Why would your ex want to do something that is so bad for your children, who would benefit from having both parents present, barring any abuse or neglect?

As you dismantle the situation, you start to realize that the chances of your worst-case scenario actually happening are exceedingly slim, and that gives you some of the comforts you need to move on without further anxiety over the subject.

Play out a Situation to the End

The last of the methods to cope with anxiety that you will learn is to play out a situation until the end. In this case, you will be thinking about considering your fear and allowing yourself to think through what will really happen in that particular situation. For example, perhaps your fear is that you will lose your job when you go to work tomorrow because you were sick for a week and missed a lot of work. Your anxiety is keeping you up and you know you need to sleep, but you just cannot manage to do so.

In this case, what you should do is stop, think about that fear, and then play out how you think the situation will go. If you are afraid that you will be fired when you show up, imagine what you think will realistically happen. Perhaps you imagine that you will arrive, and your boss will come over. Rather than telling you that you need to talk in private, however, your boss asks you if you are doing better and says that you were missed. He does not say a word about you being sick because he is a good boss and he understands that people get sick sometimes.

Because you play out the realistic ending, you are able to contrast it with the worst-case scenario that you may have also developed for that particular situation. You are able to look at the two and realize that you will be okay. You know that being fired is a possibility, but it is always a possibility. There is always a chance of being fired at any job for any reason. You are then able to relax a bit and tell yourself that things will be fine, which enables you to fall asleep and get the rest that you need finally.

Strategies for Improving Quality of Life

Now, you are going to be walked through several steps to improve the quality of life you have. These are other ways that can benefit you that are not necessarily directly designed for anxiety in particular but can help you find more enjoyment and value in the life that you have. As you go through this process and read through these four different activities, imagine how you could apply any of these possibilities to your own life to develop the life you want to lead. You may realize that there are several different ways you could implement more positivity into your life that may have a pleasant side-effect of lessening your anxiety.

Understanding Body Language

In learning to read other people's body language better, you do two things you teach yourself how to read others, so you know what they are thinking at any given moment in time. You also ensure that you are able to develop the skills to get yourself acting in ways that are directly related to the mood that you would like to be in. Remember fake it until you make it when you engage in learning to read other people's body language, you are able to better engage in the body language that you, yourself would need to get your mind thinking in certain mindsets. Further, you also develop the idea to recognize your own body language, learning what your own body language means, and in doing so, you are able to understand your own moods better when you are struggling to read them.

Studying Emotional Intelligence

In doing so, you are making yourself more capable in social settings. You are ensuring that you know how to control yourself and your own behaviors. You are ensuring that you can always behave properly because you know how best to regulate yourself. You also are developing the self-confidence that you need to get the skills desired to keep your own anxiety at bay. By learning to be emotionally intelligent, you are saying that you want to better yourself, recognizing that you can always improve and that you can always find a light in a dark situation, no matter how small that light may be. That light can guide you to a learning experience that you may find is incredibly beneficial to you.

CHAPTER 19:

Conflicts in Relationship

Conflicts arise in relationships from time to time. It could be due to financial problems, your families who interfere in your decisions, your professional career, the education of your children, or your new life with the addition of a baby. All of these elements and more are the source of arguments between you and your partner and can lead to conflicts in the relationship. When this happens from time to time, do not worry too much, because arguments can sometimes be for the good for the relationship.

Nevertheless, you must learn not to let negative situations last too long, otherwise your relationship may be greatly weakened. Indeed, conflicts in your relationship are synonymous with the first step that destabilizes a relationship. You therefore need to be able to manage these situations well to find serenity, complicity, and thus revive the flame. To make sure your relationship can continue or even get off to a good start, you should never let things get worse by standing idly by or thinking it will be better tomorrow.

Love is not a given - you have to work on yourself and your relationship constantly. If you do not act in time and allow a conflict to persist in your relationship, you risk getting dangerously close to separation.

What Are The Reasons For Conflict Between Couples?

In order to face the monster in your relationship and face your fears, the first step is to understand the origin of the conflict between yourself and your partner and to fix it properly.

Indeed, you will not be able to completely adjust the tensions in your relationship if you do not put your finger on the exact origin of the issue. In order to solve a problem effectively, you must know its roots. Otherwise, all you can do is put a band-aid on the problem. Small tensions can trigger big fights when issues remain unsolved.

The first thing to do to overcome conflicts in your relationship is to identify and acknowledge them.

As I mentioned in my introduction, there are many reasons for the situation your relationship is going through today. I will go over some of these reasons.

Conflicts caused by professional life

Tensions can arise because you care more about your career than your partner - or at least, one of you may think so. This situation can make your partner or yourself react strongly. There is nothing worse than feeling abandoned by someone you love.

Focusing more on your professional life than your personal life is not only unhealthy when you're single, it is detrimental when you're in a relationship.

It is sometimes really difficult to reconcile work and family, especially when you want to start a business or have a very stressful job. But, to have a balanced life and to avoid conflicts in your relationship, it is imperative to learn to disconnect from work and to enjoy life with your loved ones.

Infidelity and Inappropriate Behavior

There are attitudes to ban when you are in a relationship. If you stick to a behavior that your partner considers to be unforgivable, you will have trouble picking up the pieces and inevitably your relationship will experience periods of turbulence.

There may also be conflicts between couples in the case of infidelity. If you are in this situation, you'll be dealing with struggles beyond the scope. Seek out therapy, whether for yourself or for you both.

When Your Partner No Longer Meets Your Expectation

Life evolves, grows, and changes. Relationships do, as well. Sometimes, two people in a relationship grow separately and reach a point where they are no longer the people they were when they began the relationship.

When this happens, sit down and have a conversation about it. What expectations do either of you have that aren't being met? Are these expectations reasonable? The only way to gauge where the relationship is to talk about it.

To overcome the conflicts in your love life, whatever the source of the tensions are, the first thing that you must seek to understand is why the conflicts are there to begin with. To do this, talk to your partner. The discussion may be uncomfortable, but it is necessary. Your anxiety might be heightened, but don't let if force you into rash behaviors. Calm discussions do more for conflicts than anxiety-fuelled arguments.

Many couples try to avoid fighting as much as possible. Others will blame the other person for being the cause of arguments. These reactions don't resolve struggles and may even exacerbate issues.

Struggle are an ordinary part of life and relationships. When ignored, they cause more harm. When faced head on, they become the tools to help couples grow closer by solving conflicts together.

Struggles can emerge from mistaken assumptions about:

- The nature of the relationship
- Varying assumptions regarding how things ought to be done around the house
- Work
- The various obligations of each partner
- Contrasts in morals, values, needs, or wants
- Poor communication

What Conflicts do to Anxiety?

When problems crop up in a relationship, you might feel like all of your anxieties are warranted and finally proving to be true. Don't give in to this way of thinking! Anxiety stems from the unknown, and conflicts arise when expectations are not met or differences in opinion to light. They are healthy when handled properly, while anxiety is nothing but detrimental. Some of the ways conflict might affect anxiety include:

Increased Heart Rate

Conflict can cause a release of adrenaline, which anxiety only makes worse. This can lead to rapid heartbeat which in turn causes shortness of breath and increased anxiety thanks to these physiological symptoms. It's a vicious cycle. The best way to combat this is to approach conflict with calmness. If you avoid raising your voice, becoming upset, or reacting in anger, you won't trigger an adrenaline release and thus will quell the feelings of anxiety.

Nervous Energy or Movement

Again, thanks to adrenaline, your entire body will react by suddenly filling with energy that has to be used in some way. Since during an argument you most likely won't be running or fighting, that energy translates into pacing, toe tapping, hand wringing, and general nervous movement and energetic tics. These can be uncomfortable for you and distracting to your partner when you're in the middle of a conflict. Of course, it's not your fault, but that knowledge doesn't make it go away. As above, approach the situation with calm rather than anxiety to prevent the release of adrenaline.

Panic and Anxiety Attacks

Anxiety can lead to anxiety attacks? How shocking.

This might not be new information, but it's beneficial to your health to remember that in conflicts, it's in your best interest to keep calm if you have difficulties with anxiety and panic. The situation can trigger an attack, which can make everything worse. Panic and anxiety attacks are typically characterized by:

- shortness of breath
- difficulty focusing
- sweating
- racing thoughts
- feeling of impending doom

Needless to say, these are not fun symptoms, and it pays to be mindful before entering into an argument that if you don't remain level headed, you could stir up an attack.

Defensive Behavior

Nothing is more detrimental to constructive conflict resolution than defensiveness. Anxiety can block the more rational part of your mind that can think through a situation logically. Without this logic, you may have a hard time concentrating on what your partner is saying an, instead of listening, cause you to lash out and go on the defense, even if your partner is not attacking you. While you should absolutely defend yourself when unjustly treated, if your partner is seeking a peaceful resolution the best course of action is to match their intentions and drop the defensiveness. Of course, when you have anxiety, that's not so easy.

Shut Down

Instead of becoming defensive, you might just shut down entirely. The anxious mind may be unable to process what is happening and lack the energy to work through the situation, leading to a total shut down.

When this happens, you are unable to focus or concentrate, you can't call on logic or rationality to work through a conflict, and you may even be unable to comprehend what your partner is saying. On the inside, you will feel heavy and empty, like you are a battery that was suddenly drained. The best thing to do when this happens is to rest and recuperate. Conflicts will keep until you're able to take back your mind and put your rationality in charge.

The Key to Overcoming a Bad Dispute in a Relationship

When faced with a conflict in your relationship that is growing, think about the way you express your feelings or talk about this conflict with your partner. Good communication is where everyone can take stock and try to understand the attitude of the other. The conflict will be easier to manage when it's not exacerbated by angry tones and unnecessary insults.

For effective conflict communication, there are 3 rules to follow:

- Avoid raising your voice and keep calm whenever a conflict happens.
- Allow your partner to talk and develop their argument, because communication not only involves talking, but also listening.
- Find a middle ground, but do not make compromises that can have negative consequences in the future.

A couple who argues but who respects these three rules will find it easier to come to a resolution.

Actions needed to overcome conflict between couples

Relationships are not always easy, and you are constantly learning. Is it possible not to repeat the same mistakes and stabilize one's romantic relationship? How can you manage conflicts in your relationships without becoming a doormat?

Follow these recommendations to rebuild the love in a struggling relationship:

- Once you understand the reasons for the tensions that are shaking your relationship, you can move on to the more "direct" phase of reconciliation. It is true that the

first step can be very psychological, because you have to communicate with your partner.
- It is necessary to put in place more technical and thoughtful actions to find the heart of your partner and to overcome the crisis of your relationship.
- The actions you have decided to put in place must correspond to the different issues, otherwise the latter will not have any particular effects and may perhaps even aggravate the situation. Don't seek
- Don't assign blame on either side. Relationships are a team effort, and both of you need to be in it fully, or not at all.
- If your partner or yourself are not feeling fulfilled in your relationship, you need to spend time together to understand better your issues and what both of you need from the relationship.

Every relationship experiences conflict at one point or the other. It is important to know that disagreement is not necessarily a bad thing - it is a way by which people express their diverse views on a situation or topic.

CHAPTER 20:

Anxiety and Miscommunication

Communication with others is difficult, even in the best of situations. It requires you to come up with a way in which you can communicate a message that matters to you, something that you do care about and that you do want to be translated, to someone else in hopes of being able to better relate to them or in order to convey a message that matters. The most basic of transmitted communication could be as simple as a quick glance at each other—a knowing look in which you are positive that you know what is going on inside the mind of the other person. It can also be lengthy, expertly-sculpted emails in which you spend two hours on one paragraph, trying to find the right way that you can communicate with them.

Communication is a fundamental pillar, a backbone of any relationship, along with trust and faithfulness. However, communication is also something that is incredibly difficult to get right 100% of the time. Sometimes, miscommunications happen. Sometimes, you say the wrong word, or you try to pass off the wrong meaning. Sometimes, you completely misunderstand what the other person is talking about entirely, while others, you may feel like you simply do not know how to convey what is really the matter with you. No matter what happens with you, however, one thing is for sure—you must be able to spend the time learning to communicate with the other party if you hope to truly be able to recognize what matters in life and if you hope to be able to manage your relationship truly. Without some mode of communication, you and the other person cannot come up with what matters. You cannot come up with solutions that benefit both people equally. You cannot figure out the best way in which you can better deal with those around you.

The Problem with Miscommunication

Miscommunications are a major problem. They are something that should be avoided and mitigated whenever possible, but it is not always something that can be done. You cannot possibly always ensure that you will be able to communicate perfectly clearly. You can try—but sometimes, someone will get the wrong idea. Sometimes, it may be you that is misunderstanding, but sometimes, you could be unclear enough that the other person is the one that is struggling to understand what is going on. No matter which end you are on, however, it can hurt a relationship.

When you miscommunicate with your partner, you and your partner are not on the same page—and that is inherently a problem. The partnership between the two of you ought to be one in which you can both rely on each other, but if you cannot communicate properly, you may as well be speaking different languages entirely; you will be that far apart. Think about the last time that you miscommunicated with your partner. What was the last time that you argued really about? Was it what you thought it was or was it something underlying it all? Did you both have expectations that went unmet due to a lack of a common understanding? No matter the cause, struggling to communicate properly will kill the relationship that you are in. it will lead to you failing to thrive. It will lead to you failing to get everything figured out in time.

Happiness and health in a relationship require both parties to recognize how to communicate. It requires both parties to be able to very calmly and very thoroughly, discuss what matters the most. It requires both sides of the relationship to know how they can better improve upon their own communication skills and how they are able to ensure that, next time, they can avoid the problem entirely. Communication is hard, but when you have anxiety clouding your mind and guiding you to speak from a place of emotion far too often, you can have other problems as well that will need to be solved in some way.

Miscommunication and Relationships

The causes for miscommunication can vary greatly from person to person and from relationship to relationship. However, there are very common communication problems that occur in many different people. These can greatly influence the way in which you are able to communicate when you do have to talk to someone else. When in a relationship, you are aiming for as open and honest of communication as possible. You are looking at a point in which you and those around you are able to communicate better what is going on with you and how you can better understand each other. Now, let's go over some of the most common miscommunication causes in relationships to understand better where the problems are likely to arise in the first place. When you know what to expect and when to expect the problems in your relationship, you can also then begin to fix the problem in its entirety as well and that is highly powerful. The sooner that you can fix the problem, the sooner that you can avoid the problem and that matters greatly.

You Use the Wrong Tone

Sometimes, when you are speaking to someone else, the tone that you use it comes out the wrong way. You may ask a question with the wrong tone underlying it. Perhaps, for example, you woke up in the morning and realized that your partner did not get up and do the dishes like you expected. They would do. You go over, wake them up, and ask them, "Why didn't you do the dishes?"

When you say that, the tone matters immensely. It could be that you calmly ask your partner why the dishes are not done. You use a calmer tone of voice that is meant to convey curiosity. You genuinely want to know what happened—you come from a place in which you would be able to help the other person. However, if you were not careful, you could also wind up saying it in a way that is harmful instead. You could have it come out just a bit too harsh actually to be productive, for example. Instead of caring and wanting to be able to help your partner, you instead demand an explanation from a point of anger or frustration, and when that happens, you run into further problems—you run into the problem of saying the wrong thing and therefore not being able to solve the problem better.

You Are Not Listening Actively

Another common cause of the miscommunications that you likely suffer from is a lack of active listening. You may pay attention to some degree, but as soon as something is said that you disagree with or as soon as you feel threatened, those good listening habits are out the window. You want to be heard and listened to—and your partner does, too. But if neither of you are being listened to, you have a huge problem here—you run into the problem of neither of you being able to trust and rely on each other truly. If you do not actively listen because you are too quick to go on the offensive or get offended by something, then you are not doing either of you a favor. You must be willing and able to entertain the fact that your emotions matter, but that you must also be willing to listen as well.

Active listening is difficult—especially if you are in a fight. When you are doing this, you have to be really focusing on listening. This means that you are not focusing on coming up with your next rebuttal for why your partner's twenty excuses about not cleaning the kitchen are all entirely wrong and nothing but made-up lies meant to distract you from the truth—you are focusing entirely on what your partner is saying. You must be willing and able to listen to your partner if you hope to really be able to get anywhere with your own communication, and any attempts that you make to avoid or skirt around that fact are not going to be met with a good relationship at all. You must be willing to see how the way that you change your own behaviors matters. You must make sure that you are listening.

Avoiding Conversations

Sometimes, we can fall into the trap of trying to avoid having a difficult conversation desperately. It could be that you know that the conversation is going to be a problem. It could be that you recognize the ways in which what you are trying to do or trying not to talk about are going to be difficult, and so rather than attempting to get it over with to keep you and your partner on the same page, you chose to attempt to ignore it. You attempt to bury your head and avoid the conversation altogether.

While ultimately, avoiding the conversation about the toilet seat may not have any ill effects, especially if you are willing and able to put up with the changes and the interactions that would come with it and you are willing to simply accept that your partner will never put it down if you never say anything, other conversations that are more serious need to happen. It is not right to string someone along simply because you are not really willing to have that conversation with them or because you are afraid of what will happen if you do attempt to have it in the first place. That is not right—at all—and that is a huge problem. You may find that ultimately when you do this, you will see that there is a problem with how you are interacting and how you choose to communicate.

You Apologize Too Much

Perhaps one of the most quintessential problems that you can have when you are anxious when it comes to communication is constant apologies. When you are anxious, it is easy to feel like you are constantly stepping on the other person's toes—it is easy for you to feel like ultimately, what you are doing is irrelevant or what you are doing is going to be a problem, and so you default to apologizing. You may start to constantly tell them that you are sorry for what you do or why you do it. You may say that you are sorry even when you have done nothing wrong, or even when the other person is actually the one at fault.

This is a major miscommunication=-- it is essentially teaching your partner that you will take the blame for just about anything. You are ensuring that you are not afraid to be the one at fault, and rather, you are usually the one that is at fault because you believe that you are the one that is the problem. Your anxiety is able to essentially convince you that you are the problem so you believe that you are the one that has had those problems in the first place. When this happens, your anxiety is typically telling you that there is something wrong with you or that you are too flawed.

CHAPTER 21:

Build a Healthy, Long-Lasting and Loving Relationship

All relationships need nurturing. You and your partner need to be able to walk together through life. This can be achieved only if you trust each other and you know how to communicate effectively. Even when your relationship is at its worst, to be able to survive, you both need to invest in it. But relationships also need you to understand that you and your partner are separate individuals that have their own differences. Never try to change your partner. Relationship means compromise.

Change Naturally

We all do change through our lives due to new experiences, and we can't be the same person we were before this relationship. But that kind of change is natural, and people don't even notice it. But don't force the change, don't insist on it and don't expect it in your partner. Observe the ones that happen to you, they are important lessons and they need to make us better person. For example, before you met your partner you never really gave a thought about exercising. Your partner loves to hike and to spend more time with him you decide to join him. This new activity you share with your partner made you realize how your body is changing for the better, you come to conclusion that your health improved due to hiking, and you decide to give even more to it. You start going to the gym every now and then and you take care of yourself more. This is influencing you; you changed something about yourself in a positive way, and it is making both you and your partner happy. This is an example of good change that happened naturally and it came from an experience. The forced change would be your partner making you go hike with him even if you don't want to. He forces you to go to the gym by conditioning you with various things. You don't like it, but you feel obligated to do it for your partner. Given enough time, your insecurities will trigger and you will start arguing about it. After all, you are doing something you don't want to. It will build anxiety between you and the relationship will suffer.

Keep the Connection Alive

Partners drift away from each other sometimes due to everyday stresses. It can be related to work, family, or friends. Our attachment styles, the same ones that cause insecurities, may give us an early warning and we have the advantage of having the time to react and work on reconnecting with our partner. Keeping the connection you and your partner built requires work. There are things you can do so you don't allow your relationship to suffer from loss of connection:

Set a daily ritual. At the end of the day, spend some time with your partner talking about the experiences you had that day. Listen how your partner spent his day and get involved by asking questions. Be an active listener and ask how he felt. If they were bad, show compassion and affection. Tell him about your day, what you did or who you met. Talk about your family and shared friends. If you don't feel like doing this, consider making plans with your partners for the future. Spend time just the two of you and share ideas about the future. It can be individual things you want to do or something you want to share with your partner. Conversations at the end of the day often provide support and a feeling of coming back to something secure, your relationship. It will help you to share through difficult times or share your happy times. There is no need to spend specific time talking, do it as long as you feel comfortable but do it every day. The routine of these conversations will leave you with the feeling that there is something to be happy about at the end of the day, and there is security at home.

Spend quality time together. This is about experiencing the same thing together. Without this part, the relationship might not exist. Couples do get caught up in their personal lives and they do forget that they need to spend more quality time with their partner to be happy. We live in an age when we have to work most of our time, and we work when we are home. Instead of spending our free time for ourselves and our partner, we often use it to catch up with work or school. It is important to spend quality time with your partner. It can be going to a concert, dinner date, enjoying a sport together, or having a movie night. It is not enough if your partner is next to you and your attention is on your work. That is not quality time. It's just being in the same room. Remember how exciting it was at the beginning of your relationship to spend each moment of the day together? You can relive those times if you give yourself a bit of time to share activities with your partner.

Share a project. Many couples say that the best spent quality time with their partner is when they shared a task. From repainting the house and playing together with your children, volunteering together for the same cause, couples find it helpful to reconnect if they have a common goal. Working together on a project will reveal the true meaning of the word "partners" and it will shed light on how to plan your life together, how to communicate better and how to focus on each other. It is a great way of combining obligations and quality time.

Show Love through Actions

In a relationship, both you and your partner do nice things for each other. But couples often take each other for granted, especially later in the relationship when it matures. When this happens, they feel disconnected, lonely and even rejected.

When there is a lack of affectionate actions in the beginning of the relationship, you might need to ask yourself if he or she is really the one for you. Is the attraction going both ways or are you the only one who is interested? Maybe it's just your insecurities of rejection or failure that make you want to continue seeing this person or maybe he is triggering your insecurities and your attachment style keeps you feeling affection for your partner.

Some people expect from their partners to know what will make them happy and believe that if there is a need to say out loud what you want. It invalidates the action their partner took to please them. But is it really fair to expect your partner to read your mind? Nobody can know you that well to be able to predict things about you. You have to ask yourself is the action really more important than your partners intention to make you happy? After all, if you are obsessing about the action itself, or the gift itself, you are completely missing the point of relationship. Show off your newly learned communication skills in situations like these. Be mindful and tell your partner openly what would make you happy. You can even ask for it, just be smart about it.

Be Honest

Trust and honesty are very important key ingredients for successful relationship. They are also probably the most difficult to maintain. It takes hard work from both you and your partner to be able to maintain them and keep your relationship from falling apart. There are guides on how to keep the honesty in relationship to a satisfying level, and both you and your partner need to follow so you can make each other happy.

Promote honesty. It is essential in building a healthy relationship. Attraction and love were just the components that made the relationship happen, what will keep it going and make it last is honesty. Forget about little white lies you've been practicing with your previous partners or friends and family. If you want this relationship to really work, be completely honest. We use white lies mainly to make our partner feel better or happy, but if he or she finds out the truth, it may crush them, trigger their own insecurities and make them not believe you in future.

Be emotionally honest. You need to stop with closing your emotions away. Learn how to express them and most of all, be honest about them to yourself. There is no benefit of avoiding emotions, lying yourself about them. If you are unable to acknowledge them, how do you expect your partner to do so? How do you expect him to behave in your relationship if he is unsure of how you feel? Take time to think about your emotions, acknowledge them for what they are and then talk about them with your partner. To practice "the emotion talk" start with simple stuff. Don't just tell your partner what you did today, also tell him how you felt about things you did.

Don't keep secrets. Unless they are birthday surprises, Christmas presents, or just surprise affection acts. Those are safe to keep. Anything else can lead to your partner not trusting you anymore. It is same as with white lies; keeping secret might hurt your partner and start the downfall of your relationship. Most people find out if the partner kept a secret so what's the point? Avoid any uncomfortable situations and see that it's only beneficial for your relationship if you don't keep secrets from your partner.

Once the trust is broken, it takes building up the relationship from the beginning to gain it back. It is a very difficult and long process, but it can be done. Communicate with your partner what went wrong and why was the trust broken. Only through understanding can you move on. Don't just shrug it off because it will return and bite you. Broken trust is the number one reason for a breakup. The key to rebuilding trust is to live in the present. If you made peace with the fact that your partner lied to you, don't think he will always lie. Don't evaluate all of his actions to see if he is being truthful. That means you are not able to let go. Observe his actions in present and don't associate them with past lies. Trust yourself to be able to detect if he is being untruthful, don't go above and beyond searching for lies. If you are the one who committed the lie, there is no action that will prove your honesty to your partner. There is nothing you can do to convince him or her that you will never do it again. Such a promise is a heavy one, and what if you can't fulfill it? Let your partner regain your trust in time in his own way. The only thing you can do is practice honesty at all times. Don't give in to old habits, be truthful and considerate. Your partner will see your good intentions and will accept your honesty again.

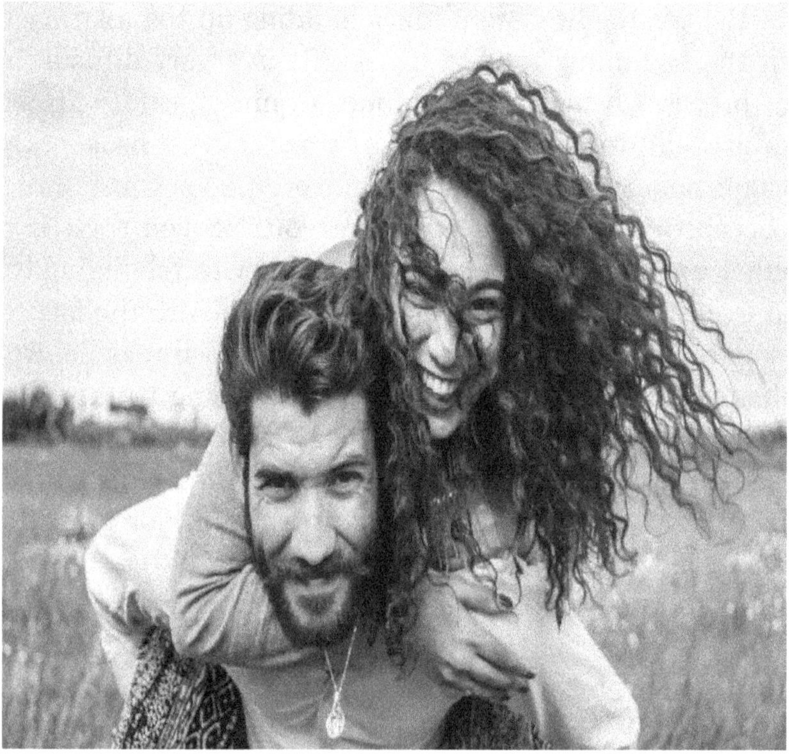

MICHELLE MILLER

CHAPTER 22:

Wrong Mental Habits

Since I do not think about my partner the whole day long do I really love him?

This is a question that lingers in the mind of the people with the fear of love or in one word, the people who have Philophobia. Thinking about someone all day long when you are in love is normal, but if it is the only thing you do and if you cannot come up with any other reasons as to why you love that person, then you are infatuated. Do not be confused between true love and infatuation. Some people think having butterflies in your stomach and thinking about the person all day long is the only signal that they love the person, this is completely wrong. It is fun but not love. If you are not thinking about him the whole day wrong, stop worrying it is normal.

You should be asking yourself if you feel calm when you are with him. Are you able to communicate with him easily? If yes, this means you are into him, it does not necessarily mean you think about him all day for you to know if you love him. If at the end of the day you look forward to being with him, being near him, whether you thought about him all day or not, this means you love him. Think about this, you have this new dress and every time you are thinking of wearing it while going out, yes you wear it every time because it is the only thing coming to your mind; eventually, this dress will bore you. The patterns will start pissing you off; you will feel like you should change into something else. This is the same in the relationship. If he is the only thing on your mind every single second of your time, will you not get bored? Of course, you will be bored, and if you get bored, you will start looking for other alternatives which will ruin your relationship.

If you are still thinking that maybe all day thoughts about him are a testament of your love, ask yourself, how much do you know your partner? You might be beating yourself up to that you do not think about him a lot, whereas there is nothing to think about. For example, you have this new movie, you have kept it in your movie drawer, without a bother of watching it, and how can you talk about that movie even if you know the title of the movie? It is impossible to understand what the movie entails. You cannot possibly think about it. Same to the relationship. While you are busy beating yourself up for not thinking about him a lot, in actual sense, there is absolutely nothing to think about because you do not even know the guy.

Do you have any clue about his life? If not, what then do you want to think about? You do not know what he likes, what color he loves, what meal he loves, his hobbies, which work he does, the people he hangs out with and so many other details. How can you think about someone you do not know? Getting to know your partner well might reduce these thoughts but again it is not a must that he is on your mind all day.

Think about it this way, you waiting for him to call you after some time and not all day. If that call finally comes in and puts that wide no reason smile on your face just because you have heard his voice, then yes you love him, it is not a must that he is the only thing on your mind.

Is he the one you think about when you are upset and believe that he is the only person that can make things better? Then yes, you love him. Imagine your worst pain, a pain that you think you cannot pull through, and then there is that one person who comes, and just by him telling you it is going to be fine and him being there with you, your pain starts melting away. Isn't that wonderful? Yes, it is and whether he is on your mind once a day or twice a day or name the times you think about him, you love him. He does not have to compete with the cells in your mind like he is there now and then for you to convince yourself that you love him.

If this habit of you thinking that he must be on your mind all day long is in your mind, you should look deep inside you. Make sure that you are not thinking about your ex-partner. That might be the guilt tying you around to the thoughts that you are not thinking about him enough, and therefore, you think you do not love him.

If you are just getting through a break-up, it is also possible to drive this habit home that is into your mind. Within no time that is the only thing, you are thinking of. You are the problem. This habit is manifesting because you only entered this relationship to try and get over your ex, getting over someone you once loved is not easy at all. It is among the hardest things that a heart can master, but letting it get under your skin and you start thinking you are not thinking about your current him each time and thus you think you do not love him is very wrong. It is a habit you need to squash down the drain.

The person who loves you does not like or care or want the perfect you, so you do not have to be perfect for him. For example, that bad mark you got from a surgery that you have never wanted to share being embraced, being touched, and being soothed as beautiful, that is love.

If you have this habit, try and spend more time with your partner. Get to know him better. Know his family though do not be pushy for some people love their privacy and like taking it slow, get to know the people he is hanging out with, know his job, the difficulties he is experiencing in his life and so many other details as long as you do not overstep. These things will equip you with something that will make you feel less guilty of ooh am not thinking about him every second of my life; this means I do not love him. You must understand that love is beyond seconds, minutes, hours, days, or even months of thinking about someone. There is a connection that one cannot understand and it cannot be defined by the frequency of how you think about someone.

You should be able also to ask yourself if you are seeing him regularly. If indeed you are seeing him regularly, why would he be on your mind every second? It will seem odd, more of infatuation. No, it is not wrong to think about him every time, especially when the love is new, but this when it has worn off, it should be ok. Normal. You will see him regularly, and this means anytime you are with him whenever you want to and you do not have to build yourself a habit of time-frequency trying to define your love for him.

You should stop making decisions when you are not sure, or you do not have the right information. When you are trying to think of not loving him because of him not being on your mind every second of the day, you should be getting some things straight in your mind and heart. Stop rushing to decisions when you are not sure if that is the case. Then the worry kicks in now, I do not think about him the whole day, could it be that I do not love him? No, you love him. The rate at which you think about him should not dictate to you how you feel about him. Get your facts right before jumping to a decision. So it is not necessary that you think about him all day to know that you love him.

I have noticed another attractive boy/girl, so does that mean I am in the wrong relationship?

You should understand that there is a difference between being attracted to someone and liking someone. This is a hard time for one to comprehend his feelings. Most people find it difficult to differentiate between the two. They mostly get confused; they do not know if they like the person or are simply attracted to the person. Attractiveness deals mostly with the looks. The good biceps he has, his mustache, his blue eyes, his fine ass, his lips movement, his dressing code, his hairstyles, and so many others. But liking someone, this is different, and it encompasses everything. It won't matter if he changed into what you did not expect him to change into, it does not matter if he has that ugly scar, does not matter if he is the most hated by people and so forth, you will still like the person, you will feel comfortable around the person, you will not judge him, you will be patient with him, you will feel complete and you will understand him.

When you are torn in being attracted to someone else, and you are dating the other, ask yourself why you are wondering about your feelings.

You should be able to ask yourself where the feelings are coming from, what is driving you; there must be something that is pushing you. You must be getting some motivation from deep down within you that is holding together the pieces and bring out the feelings. Maybe you are chasing an old love. You were expecting him to be like your ex, but this is not turning up that is why, but it still does not necessarily mean that you do not love him. Chasing an old flame is fine but thinks of what if it is not the old one but something new and worth to be with, then you will have to be with the new good him, or better him but you still will be attracted to the old flames out there.

However, it is a good thing to know if the chase of the old love, the expectation of your partner to be like your ex, is driving to your mind these ideas of not loving him and root it them out, because these ideas will develop into mental habits and might end up ruining your relationship.

Ask yourself, what your past experiences are, and if they are affecting you. Maybe you were hurt by someone else, and you are afraid that he will hurt you, that is why you are being attracted to someone else, someone you think might be better. Maybe you are afraid that it will turn out the opposite of your expectations, maybe you are expecting it to go wrong when it is going right. What if all this time you have been together you have never understood him and this is deeply making you attracted to some other boy? Get to know him better; it will ease your differentiation of liking and loving.

CHAPTER 23:

Repair Your Relationships When Dealing With Anxiety and Depression

Determining the link between emotion and relationships. Taking deeper into your relationship. To take positive action to strengthen your relationship. The results of your actions. Even if we say, we're not at all social. People tend to have friends and family with whom they talk, even if they just talk about a trip to buy food. We work better with support. Our moods improve, and our ability to cope with stress also increases. It should, therefore, be obvious that all the relationships we encounter somehow affect us, from relative strangers to close friends and families. Taking the time to improve every partnership will definitely improve your mood and make you feel very relaxed.

You will learn how to strengthen relationships and how to use these strategies more and more. More importantly, we shall examine intimate relationships as they have the greatest consequences for our mental health and learn to cope with the loss of a relationship, which often causes anxiety or despair.

How does a relationship with your emotions connect?

If you're anxious or depressed, all that worries you is concerned. Each relationship is put on the back burner. You spend all your energy on your own issues and concerns. All this attention and anxiety are drained out mentally and emotionally and are supplemented by the people who care about you. They become frustrated and helpless when they are not successful and cause them to pull away from you, and the relationship suffers more.

Take a few moments to answer the following questions concerning an important relationship in your life and see whether depression or anxieties are harmful.

1. Did I pull the relationship away? What are the ways?

2. Did I get less affectionate? What are the ways?

3. Did I get more critical or irritable? What are the ways?

4. Am I less empathetic or less complimentary? What are the ways?

As always, it's not black and white. There may always be other reasons why a relationship doesn't work. Consult with specialists in mental health who are trained in couple therapy.

Have you ever heard of a child claiming that you've got a pet for the first time? I explain how well the animal is being handled. How well they can feed and walk and clean it up afterward. Parents then embrace the newly found obligation of their child and go out and get a cat. The first week is fantastic. The child does all the same, as they said. Nonetheless, at the end of the third or fourth week, the parents find themselves mostly cleaning up or feeding their pets and have to ask their pets to walk or take care of them otherwise. The beauty of the animal and its excitement is disrupted by life and complacency. This boy has not gone out of his way to becoming reckless, but it is that life has taken precedence.

Relationships begin in a similar way. We are excited to spend time with and enjoy with another human. We laugh and complement each other, and when we interfere with life one day and begin to forget our responsibility for the relationship.

We forget about calling or organizing. Failure to pay attention causes the relationship to fail. We build our relationships with constructive actions and words, and the techniques you learn help you to strengthen almost every relationship.

Communication is the basis on which relationships are built. In all of our relationships, positive communication is necessary because it's healthy and keeps us free of stress. We are introducing a few exercises to maintain such a positive environment. The first is the Daily Bulletin. That's when you take the time to talk to your partner and listen. The aim is to improve intimacy and should be done often.

1. Meet with your friend to decide for 20 minutes when you are going to sit and discuss daily activities.

2. The goal is daily, but 3-4 times are also beneficial.

3. Engage yourself in meeting times and keep them written where you can both see them.

4. Let your partner start and talk for 10 minutes.

5. Ask questions, nod your head, and make brief comments so that you can tell them how they feel.

6. After they are finished speaking, try to summarize positively what they said.

7. Ask your partner if you understand correctly and ask for clarification if you don't.

8. Take your time and ask your partner to follow the same rules about your day.

9. Take the time to think about how before and after you felt and what better understanding you felt.

The second exercise reminds you of the power of congratulations. It is hard to think of others if you're anxious or depressed, and how much you love them, but not voicing them can lead them to feel unappreciated and to a breakup. Take a moment to compose the top 10 things about my partner that I admire.

1. Write down first everything you love and admire your partner. Include items that you sincerely believe to be applicable, such as talents, intelligence, care, help, etc.

2. Congratulations to your spouse from the list you created or created a new one at least once daily.

3. Develop a plan every day to accomplish this mission. Make a habit of congratulating everyone.

After a few weeks of congratulations, think about any changes in the relationship.

If these two previous activities are not successful, we suggest that you see a couple's therapy therapist. When you can't think about anything, your relationship is in serious trouble.

Attending a broken relationship can be devastating if a friendship is lost. Life is imperfect; people are imperfect. Sometimes the loss we experience is due to death, but other times it is due to other factors, such as divorce, divorce, or relationships that break. In any event, the treatment of a loss causes stress and sometimes depression.

It is essential that you still look after yourself when you lose a loved one. Make sure that you eat and sleep and are safe, for grief is mental and physical, and all your resources are needed to get through. Make sure you ask for assistance. You should look for help from friends and family, religious outlets, support groups, and practitioners in the area of mental health.

When you are dealing with the loss of the loved one, the best solution is not to curl up in the bed or resort to drugs that only make things worse. Study the relationship and the significance of the individual to you. This process leads you on.

Take time to look at the following questionnaire to help you explore your complaint. Take as much time to reply and don't rush. Expect to feel sad or even cried, but please seek professional help if you feel that you can't do this workout at all.

1. What was this person's life like?

2. What have you loved about that person?

3. What's been hard about this person?

4. What lessons did I learn from this positive and negative relationship?

5. Now, what has changed in my life?

6. What thanks do I have from this relationship?

7. What am I really upset about?

8. What's this relationship I enjoyed?

9. Write a letter to the person you missed for closing. Express whatever is on your mind.

It is irreplaceable to be warnings and the connections we share. This being said, it is important to pick up the pieces and move on and fill your lives with meaningful relationships and activities after your loss and time to sorrow and have recovered. Take the time to help others out. Again, it will make you feel better and completely normal. Speak a little more, just a little more. Again, it becomes social. You don't have to be the life of the party, but simply talking with those around you will help you heal more and more. Go out and do something that is happy for you even if you don't feel ready to try something that will make you happy. Allow yourself to rejuvenate.

CHAPTER 24:

Helping Your Partner Deal with Anxiety

Watching your partner deal with anxiety can be very difficult. But if you don't know how to help them, you will feel helpless, too. If you don't really understand what your partner is going through and you only see them struggling, you might do things that can make the situation worse. Over time, your relationship will start deteriorating until you are left with a broken bond and a person whom you don't know anymore.

Not knowing how to help your partner can leave you feeling sad, frustrated, or even angry. Meanwhile, when your partner doesn't see any effort from you, they may feel isolated, lonely, and other negative feelings that can worsen their condition. You obviously want to learn how to help your partner and save your relationship.

To have the capacity to help your partner deal with their condition, you must first educate yourself. This is what you are doing now. You have already learned what anxiety is, the common signs that may indicate that your partner is struggling with anxiety, and how you can communicate more effectively with them. But we aren't done yet! There's still a lot to identify before you can apply your knowledge to your real-life situations. Finding out everything you can about anxiety will help you learn more about the condition. This, in turn, allows you to understand your partner better as they face their anxiety. When your partner sees that you want to help them, this can make them feel inspired to help themselves. Then this will awaken your desire to work together as you share the common goal of learning how to manage your partner's anxiety effectively.

Recognizing Panic Attacks and Other Irrational Behaviors

These days, it seems like anxiety disorders have become very common. Among the different stages of anxiety, a lot of people seem to reach panic-level anxiety, and when this happens, they experience an anxiety attack. An anxiety attack happens when a person gets an overwhelming feeling of fear, distress, apprehension, or worry and they don't know how to overcome it. For some people, this attack comes gradually but for others, it comes on suddenly and with incredible intensity. While the symptoms of this attack may vary, the most common ones are:

- Feeling dizzy, worried, restless, apprehensive or fearful
- Dry mouth
- Shortness of breath
- Excessive sweating
- Hot flashes or cold chills
- Tingling or numbness

Another kind of "attack" that someone with anxiety may experience is a panic attack. A panic attack is similar to an anxiety attack, but it has different causes, including stress, chemical imbalances, using drugs or caffeine, and even heredity. Panic attacks also occur when someone has a mental disorder such as anxiety. If this is something that occurs to your partner, you must learn how to help them get through the attack. Here are some tips:

- Help your partner realize that the symptoms they feel aren't harmful or dangerous. To your partner, these symptoms are exaggerated, which makes them feel frightened. Therefore, you should try to explain things to them in the gentlest and calmest way possible.
- Help your partner identify their feelings. This lessens the intensity of those feelings.
- Try not to add to the panic your partner feels by asking them questions like, "what are you so worried about?"
- Help your partner focus on the present. Talk your partner through the current situation so they don't worry about what might happen in the future.
- Distract your partner with a simple activity, like asking them to count backward, clap your hands with a specific rhythm and ask them to follow it, and other things that can help take their mind off their anxious thoughts.

Some of these strategies may work well for your partner, while others won't. Try out different techniques until you find those that are most effective. Some of these may even work to help your partner deal with anxiety attacks, too. The key here is to help your partner overcome the attack without succumbing to it.

Generally, feelings of anxiety can emerge when something triggers them. There are so many possible triggers and these triggers may vary from one person to another. Some people may have a single trigger, while others have several.

Also, some people may react severely to certain triggers while others need a higher level of exposure before they are affected.

Either way, some of the most common triggers of people who suffer from anxiety disorders are:

- Caffeine
- Conflict
- Financial problems
- Health problems
- Medications or drugs
- Negative thoughts
- Public performances or events
- Personal triggers
- Skipping meals
- Social events or parties
- Stress

Also, in some cases, you might be your partner's trigger. If this is the case, aim not to take it personally. Continue being supportive and loving, even if you find out that your partner's anxiety gets triggered when you're around. In such a case, though, try to find out why you have become your partner's trigger. Communicate with your partner and ask them questions to get to the bottom of things. After all, you can't help your partner if your mere presence sets off their anxiety.

Then, there are nervous breakdowns. People with anxiety are more susceptible to having nervous breakdowns, but the good news is, you can help prevent this from happening if you can catch it early. As you observe your partner for anxiety attacks, panic attacks, and general anxious feelings, try to recognize the signs of an impending nervous breakdown, too. The most common of these signs are:

- Unexplained changes in their appetite
- Changes in their grooming and sleeping habits
- Changes in their mood or energy levels

- Frequently feeling weak or fatigued
- Frequent muscle aches and headaches
- Breathing difficulties
- Having inappropriate reactions to interactions and events
- Not wanting to socialize with other people
- Issues with their memory, organization, and attention
- Gastrointestinal and sexual function problems
- Substance or drug use
- Sudden weight loss or weight gain

If you realize more than one of these signs in a partner who suffers from anxiety, then a nervous breakdown might not be far behind. When this happens, your partner will lose their ability to function altogether. Therefore, you must take the necessary steps to snap your partner out of it. Do this by helping them deal with their problems or lightening their load.

What Can You Do About It?

Whether it's dealing with panic attacks or the anxiety disorder itself, there are several things you can do to help your partner out. After learning about their condition and knowing how to identify the "danger signs," the next thing to do is to learn to help them deal with it. Here are some ways you can do to make things easier for your partner and yourself:

1. Learn to accept your partner's condition

Acceptance is key when you find out that your partner has a mental condition such as an anxiety disorder. If you cannot accept this, you won't be willing to help them out. Whether your partner told you about their condition or you found out yourself (and your partner confirmed it), learn how to accept this diagnosis. It may be difficult, especially if your partner developed the condition recently, but acceptance must come to you. Once you can accept that your partner is suffering from an anxiety disorder, then you can take the next steps.

2. Set boundaries in your relationship

Since your goal is to empower your partner, it's important to set clear boundaries. Before doing this, take some time to learn more about your partner's condition and how they are coping with it. For instance, if you see that your partner is trying hard to manage their condition, then you won't have to set boundaries that are particularly strict. However, if your partner is becoming too dependent on you, this is when setting boundaries becomes essential. Just make sure to communicate these boundaries in the gentlest, most positive way so your partner won't take things the wrong way.

3. Focus on your own self-care

Helping your partner is a noble thing, but in the process, you shouldn't forget to care for yourself, too. Don't offer so much of yourself that you have nothing left. Remember, if you end up developing anxiety because you have invested so much in helping your partner, you might be the one who gets a nervous breakdown. Practice physical, emotional, and mental self-care so you can remain strong enough to support your partner through their difficult times.

4. Take time to relax together

As you are dealing with an issue or a challenge in your relationship, try to find enjoyable things to do, too. Take the time to relax together as you did before this condition came into your relationship and made it more complicated. Try taking a spa day together, practice couples' meditation, or just take turns massaging each other. Doing relaxing things together makes your bond stronger and it can help alleviate your partner's anxiety.

5.   Come up with a backup plan for dealing with situations

Helping your partner deal with anxiety involves coming up with a plan that includes effective strategies to get through difficult situations. However, even if you plan everything well, unexpected things might still happen. For instance, when you attend a party with your partner, you can prepare for it by doing a relaxing activity first. But once you get there, your partner's anxiety might kick in which, in turn, might lead to an anxiety or panic attack. In such cases, you should always have a backup plan. You can either involve your partner in creating these backup plans or establish them yourself. As long as you have an alternative solution to dealing with difficult situations, you can help your partner get through the most unexpected events.

6.   Only bring up your partner's condition when they give you permission

Suffering from an anxiety disorder isn't easy. If you think having a partner with this condition is difficult, imagine how your partner feels. Furthermore, mental illnesses like anxiety are often stigmatized in our society. This is why people don't want to open up and communicate with others when they find out that they are suffering from such a condition.

If you learn that your partner has anxiety, it's okay to tell them that you already know. If your partner expresses relief and opens up about their condition, go ahead and start a conversation with them. But if your partner seems worried or shocked to discover that you already know, don't push it. Give them time to accept that you know and when they are ready, they will talk to you about it. As much as possible, don't push the topic, as this might make your partner feel more apprehensive about their condition. Just as you need time to accept that your partner has this mental condition, give them time to accept that you are aware of their condition already. This will make it a more positive experience for both of you.

These strategies are real and practical, but you might still feel some stress along the way. After all, this is something new that you both have to deal with. Just keep applying these strategies and hopefully, you will see improvements in your partner over time.

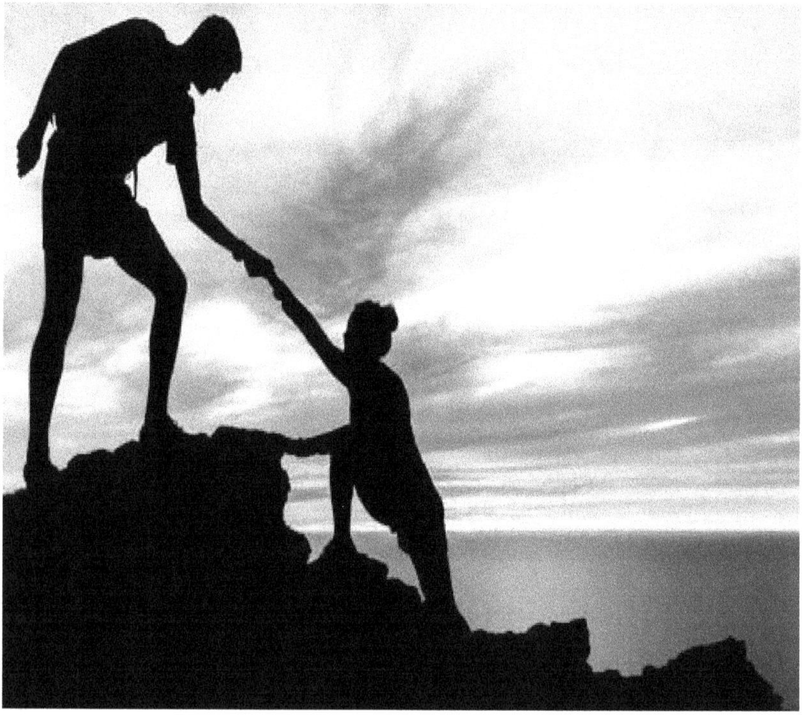

CHAPTER 25:

Put Anxiety in the Past

Even though you may have experienced extreme trauma in childhood that dictates how you react to situations as an adult, you have the power to overcome the anxiety that threatens to cripple you and put it in the past where it belongs. There are specific steps that you must go through in order to rid yourself of the demons that are writing the script for your adult life, but when you do, you will know true freedom for the first time. Even if you do not totally rid yourself of your anxiety and only learn to accept it and work with it, you will then have the ability to enjoy your relationships the way they were meant to be enjoyed.

Acknowledging and Accepting

Many people will say that a certain event gives them anxiety when what they really mean is that it makes them nervous. You will feel nervous when something is uncomfortable or unfamiliar, and this is perfectly normal. Feeling anxiety and feeling nervous are two completely different things. Anxiety is characterized by excessive fear or worry, and it has the power to affect your ability to go to school, hold down a job, or maintain a good relationship with that special person.

Your first step will be to recognize that you have a problem with anxiety. People will often only seek help for the physical symptoms of anxiety, weight loss or gain, the inability to sleep well, and the headaches and stomach aches. They and their doctor don't connect their physical symptoms with the possibility of an emotional issue. And some people will deny that they have a problem with anxiety, or they may feel sensitive if the possibility is suggested to them. But the first step you will need to take is to admit that you struggle with the issues that anxiety brings to your life.

You will not be able to solve your issues until you are able to admit that you have them. It is easy to ignore a problem and hope it will go away on its own. You can ignore your anxiety, and you can pretend that it is not affecting your life. But your anxiety is affecting your life, and the sooner that you can admit that, the closer you will be to overcome it. Making excuses and denying the problem will not fix the problem. It is true that the initial step in fixing a problem is to admit that one exists because you can't fix something you don't know is there. As soon as you are able to admit that you have a problem with anxiety, you can begin to figure out what causes your issues.

You might tell yourself that there is no way that you have a problem. But you do. You have a problem maintaining a solid relationship with your partner because you are letting your anxieties from the past infringe on your current way of life. You desire a good relationship with your partner, but your anxieties build walls that you can't quite get past. You need to be able to get past yourself in order to get better because, in the case of anxiety, you are your own worst enemy. The defenses that you built in response to the traumas you suffered are now controlling the way you arrange your adult life. The relief that these defenses give you will make you feel safe and good, if only for a little while. Even if you are not self-medicating with substances like alcohol, drugs, or food, hiding behind the walls, you have built that is your way to protect your feelings from getting hurt again. You will continue to do anything in your power to feel that good feeling, even if it means destroying the very relationship you are trying to cultivate. All that matters is protecting you.

Now is the right time that you need to do the exact opposite of what you really feel like doing. You might feel like admitting that you have a problem with anxiety means that you are weak, but it actually means the exact opposite. Admitting that you have a problem with anxiety proves that you have the courage to improve your life and your relationships by learning to deal with your issues. Denying that you have a problem will cause you more harm in the long run. The longer you wait to address your anxieties, to harder they will be to overcome. People who are weak will hide their problems and deny their existence. People who are strong will be able to admit that they have anxieties and will want to do whatever is necessary to overcome those anxieties.

Do not avoid your anxieties because that will just make them worse. Admit to the things that make you feel anxious and realize that your anxiety will not be so bad the next time, now that you have accepted the fact that it exists. Prove your anxiety wrong because right now, it is running your life and ruining your life. Accept your anxiety for what it really is and take the steps you need to take to overcome it.

Recognizing the Symptoms and Accepting Your Reaction

Your anxiety is usually driven by your anticipation of what might happen. It doesn't need to happen, and it may never happen, but it might happen. Try not to give power to those thoughts. Focus your mind on where you are right now and what you are doing right now. There is no past, and there is no future. Your anxiety level will begin to decrease if you simply remain in the present. Your anxiety level will increase if you allow yourself to recall past failures, fear feeling hurt or upset, or begin planning your escape from the situation. Stay in the present.

When those first feelings of anxiety begin to creep up, accept their presence. Do not attempt to ignore them, control them, or fight them, because right now they are still in control of you and the situation. Trying to get rid of them at this point will only make them stronger in their attempt to overwhelm you. See how your anxiety fluctuates down and up, and try to give it a rating for how strong it is. Slow down if you feel that you are trying to do too much too quickly. Tell yourself that it is okay to feel this way. Realize that you can still handle this situation even if you are feeling anxious. Continue doing what you need to do, even if you are feeling anxious about it. There is completely nothing wrong with not being in control of the situation, as long as you are not feeling totally out of control.

Do not add to your anxiety with a secondary fear. A secondary fear is the one that comes along with your anxiety. You might feel that you are going to be suddenly ill, faint, lose control, or do something that is embarrassing. These secondary fears often start with sudden thoughts that are tied to your anxiety. It might look something like the following conversation that you are having with yourself in your head:

"I need to tell my partner how I really feel, but I am afraid."

"I feel lightheaded. What if I faint?"

"I feel like I'm going to faint. I need to leave now."

So you leave without ever facing the anxiety that is related to your fear of being open with your partner. Your anxiety about opening your heart up to possible rejection has won again. The anxiety is normal, but adding to it is not normal. Feeling the secondary fear is normal, but you do not need to act on it. The conversation should look more like this:

"I need to tell my partner how I really feel, but I am afraid."

"I feel lightheaded. What if I faint?"

"I am not going to faint. I am just feeling anxiety."

The same theory holds true if you suffer from panic attacks when anxiety hits. Do not add secondary fear to the panic attack. Accept your anxiety and your panic attacks for what they really are and realize that they will pass on their own if you just wait patiently. Also, don't try to make the panic attack go away or try to fight it in any other way. It will pass.

Do not try to avoid or escape your anxiety. If you try to, then you are just telling yourself that there really is something wrong with you. Try not to make resolutions based on what you are feeling, but take a moment to consider all of your options. The thing that is really causing you to fear is not the cause of your anxiety, but rather your imaginations of the horrible consequences that might happen. You will make a step forward every time that you accept your feelings and face your fears. Any time that you try to avoid your feelings or to escape your fears, you are giving up an opportunity to prove that you are stronger than your anxiety. Maybe the situation that you are trying to avoid, the situation that fills you with anxiety is too big for you to handle all at once. There is absolutely nothing wrong with taking it in small doses. If you have trouble telling your partner how you feel, don't start with a long soliloquy about your love. Start with something small, such as the fact that you don't care for steak as much as your partner does and that you would like to eat chicken more often. It's a small step, but you will be stating your opinion and telling your partner how you really feel about something that is important to you. While you are doing it, try to remain calm. Tell yourself that you are perfectly capable of doing this and not feeling overwhelming anxiety. You will need to be willing to have the anxiety, and then you must be willing to fight your anxiety. The goal here is not to make your anxiety go away forever but to change the relationship that you have with anxiety. You will need to be completely willing to feel your anxiety before you will be able to make it go away. Try to make your reaction to anxiety worse. Tell your palms to sweat more, your heart to pound harder, and your legs to shake more. You probably can't do it, but in trying to do it, you will see that your symptoms are beginning to subside. This is because you have owned the feeling and shown it that you have the power to control it, and not the other way around. You need to be committed to your recovery but not so rigid that you cause yourself even more anxiety. You do not need to be perfect. Anytime you are successful, no matter how small, give yourself some credit for your accomplishment. Never remind yourself of what you used to be like before anxiety took over because that person is gone forever. Sometimes you will not feel like you are accomplishing anything, and you will not feel any better than you did before. Be patient with yourself, and bear in mind that these things take time. You did not become an anxious person overnight, and you will not be better overnight.

Never try to assume responsibility for those things that are outside of your control. Right now, you can't control the fact that you suffer from anxiety, but you can control your reaction to those anxious feelings. So you are not responsible for having anxiety, but you are responsible for the way that you react to it. Write your own mantra, or use one of these, and use it to tell yourself that everything is going to be just fine.

CHAPTER 26:

Working It Out

Some truly intimate relationships involve some miscommunication, discord, or dispute. Though you tend to dwell on ways to avoid being neglected by your friend with tunnel vision to gain appreciation or love, you will certainly do everything you can to stop those issues. Chances are you will be sweeping your thoughts and desires under the rug. It is how you protect yourself. Over time, when you know exactly how alone you felt over your relationship, you will stumble over the ever-growing bump in the rug. You'll notice your wife's pain, and you'll even feel furious. It's a phenomenon that cannot keep you happy in the end. Luckily there is a more safe way out there.

By attentive self-awareness, you'll grow to support yourself, embrace the emotions, and be ready to confront insecurity.

You're likely to be more open to positive input from taking care of people in your life. As a result, you'll be able to interact more openly with your partner and listen to your partner's viewpoints without being sidetracked by how they affect you. The result of this approach coping with relationships is that you will be emotionally conscious and able to establish an emotional bond.

If you stay emotionally sensitive, caring, and articulate as conflict arises, you would be in a stronger position to maintain a healthy relationship. At the same time, you seek to resolve or cope with conflict.

This will take you through the dispute management process in just such a constructive manner.

Asking for support.

The method of clearly expressing what you want allows you and your partner to concentrate on strengthening your relationship together.

Focusing on two main activities could be helpful:

1. Share your thoughts, your expectations, and your wishes.

2. Tell what you want from your companion, clearly and concretely.

Types include:

As the husband Art goes out with his friends, Heather is angry. She generally stews in her thoughts but doesn't share them with Art — which makes her feel more isolated from him and more anxious about missing him. Finally, she wants to tell him, "I feel lost when you go out with your friends, and like I don't matter to you. I want you to have fun with the boys, but it's so hard for me." They're thinking about the issue, and he's saying he loves having time with his friends, so it's not a solution for her.

After some debate, they decide that he should also give her ample warning about his plans so that she can also make plans. He also promises that in the evenings when she winds up stuck at home, whether he's out or on his way home, he'll call or text her — just to let her know he's worried about her.

Sally often goes on work trips, leaving Max to feel depressed and doubt how much she truly cares about him. He has always helped her career, but he worries too much about her traveling, as he wants to spend time with her. He discusses this while making sure to stress that he encourages her to fulfill her desires.

While they do not come up with any answers to their differing needs, they believe they support each other. They reaffirm their engagement with the relationship and agree to talk and text daily when she is away, which helps.

Not all things do turn out that well, of course. When the discussions end poorly, make sure to go back to them when you're relaxed. Your objective is to find a way to feel cared about and relate to each other on an emotional level, even though you're struggling with a tough problem. The following method will help you overcome some of those thorny problems.

Exercise: Starting a Difficult Conversation

The way you put your friend up to a question sets the tone of the discussion. Indeed, the Gottman Institute, which performs work related to marriage and partnerships, found that they could not only predict the outcome of a fifteen-minute discussion in the first three minutes but could also predict which spouses would split and which would stay married (Gottman and Silver, 1999; Carrere and Gottman, 1999). But think about how to launch a dialogue and observe the following guidelines:

Take a socially relaxed moment to converse. Timing isn't all that, but it is a number. If both parties are in a strong enough emotional and behavioral state to deal with it rationally and peacefully, does a tough discussion go well?

State the issue in brief. The only question is how it affects you, no matter what the friend has done or the situation. So quickly state the question, and get to the real issue — how it affects you.

194

Allow no liability. Moving on for all the negative stuff the friend has done or referring specifically to the character's flaws would make him defensive. You're not going to get happier, and he's going to be more physically detached.

Concentrate on the experience. You just want him to understand and worry for you as much as you would want to lash out at or hide from your husband while he is bothering you. The only way he can do that is if you express your opinions and emotions freely.

One common way of doing so constructively is making assumptions about "I." If you initiate a statement with "I," you're saying something to your friend about what's going on with you — opening your life to him. In comparison, when you continue a sentence with "you," you're insulting your partner and stopping contact.

Imagine, for example, saying, "You rarely do something romantic anymore." This brings the point across, but you're far more likely to get the reaction you're hoping for by suggesting, "I wish you'd do anything sweet, like how you used to get me flowers for no reason." Or imagine that you and the husband spoke about his propensity to leave his dirty laundry on the floor, and he decided not to do something. You might say, "I feel frustrated with you for doing this. It makes me feel unloved, and like I am your sweetheart. I'm just getting so sad." Compare that with saying, "You're a slob and disrespectful. I don't know why I'm trying to talk about anything with you."

Need I say more?

Of course, you can often use "I" statements to be insulting, such as, "I think you're an asshole." And, "you" statements can be emotional, such as, "You've tried to be helpful, but often

I'm so angry that I can't take it in." So, when I'm dealing with people, I sometimes ask them to consider who they'd point out more when they're making the statement; this typically suits the person they're thinking about; the bottom line is that you want to open up about yourself and give your partner the chance to truly "see," support, encourage, and respect you.

Be explicit about your emotions. You may need to spend some time communicating your thoughts and identifying them. When you cannot do so, test the "Identify the Emotions."

Share this with your partner until you're sure about your thoughts. You may state, for example, "I feel depressed," or "I feel lonely." Say what your partner should do to meet your needs. He is strong. This also comes from expressing feelings. You might say, for example, "I feel unloved, and I need to know that you love me.

So if you squeezed my hand when we're out together or made arrangements for us to spend time together, that would be nice." And you might say, "I feel sad and want us to be together. And I'd appreciate it if we were able to spend more time just relaxing and laughing about dinner." When you're not sure what your friend should do to make you feel comfortable, speak to each other about having a happier location solution.

Talking Through Conflicts

In addition to sharing your feelings and desires, healthy communication requires you to listen to and "get" your partner — not just understand your partner intellectually, but see situations through the eyes of your partner, and empathize with her. You need to set your experience aside when doing so. Don't break your friend off; as you clarify, the goal is to agree with you—no minimizing or denying your partner's feelings to protect yourself from the hurt elicited by those feelings. Furthermore, you don't have to compromise with your partner when you do so or give up on what you want. It's just that listening will take turns, you and your friend. Both of you must be open to communicating, "reading" one another, and interacting positively and respectfully. Using that approach, even in the most intimate and sensitive interactions, you will foster a sense of confidence.

Much like you have to be careful whether to launch a tough debate, the strength of such a dialogue is not only in what you're talking about but in how you're doing it. This helps you be conscious, for example, that you do have prejudices and are fallible. Your willingness to see and accept this can encourage your openness to criticism, your sense of kindness, your willingness to apologize, and your capacity to forgive sincerely. Overall, to create a positive result, you must approach your partner to know him truly or her, express your thoughts, and emotionally become stronger. Instead, when you and your friend struggle to protect your viewpoints, you will find yourself trapped in different worlds, or at odds.

CHAPTER 27:

10 Habits That Can Make Your Partner's Anxiety Worse

As the partner of an anxious person, you can play a critical role in alleviating the symptoms of their condition and making life for them (and you) easier. As we have seen, there many different types of anxiousness that have historically been characterized as anxiety disorders, but if we think of worry as an emotion characterized by excessive worry or fear, then we can understand the common thread that often runs through anxiety disorders. We have also seen that some conditions characterized by worry or fear like post-traumatic stress disorder have recently been redefined by psychiatrists (at least in the United States) and may technically be seen today as "anxiety disorders." That being said, anxiety is a common thread in many dysfunctional ways of thinking or behavior patterns and keeping this in mind is an important step that can lead to change.

Regardless of the type of worry your partner faces, you can be of help to them by aiding them in avoiding habits that can make their symptoms worse. These are also habits that you can work into your own life to steer you away from developing anxiousness yourself and to help you interact better with the anxious person in your life. The purpose of this is to equip you with a useful skill. By recognizing these dysfunctional habits, you are able to minimize the impact of your partner's anxiousness and help place your relationship on the road toward being worry-free.

Habit 1: Setting Unattainable Goals

A habit that can certainly make your partner's anxious symptoms worse is setting unattainable goals. This is a habit that the partner too can develop and which can prove unhealthy in your anxiety-fraught relationship. By setting unattainable goals, the anxious person sets themselves up for a whirlwind of emotions that includes worries, fears, and anger. These emotions come from a subconscious realization that the goal may be unattainable resulting in time spent worrying about the outcome, but they also stem from the whole gamut of emotions that ensue when the goal inevitable fails.

As we have seen, anxious people can have intense reactions to things that may not disturb others. Having a plan or a goal fail (especially if it is an important one) can be devastating to even a person without a mental health issue so it is not hard to see why this would be a problem. By setting a reasonable, attainable goal, you and your partner can reduce the anxiousness that comes with reaching for something that cannot be achieved and then having to deal with the consequences that inevitably come along.

Habit 2: Unhealthy Dietary Habits (like excessive smoking or alcohol consumption)

This is an easy habit that an anxious person can drop (although it may be easier in some people than in others). It may actually come as a surprise to some that certain foods or substances can exacerbate worry. There are a number of these products that should be avoided, but the big ones are caffeinated products like coffee and energy drinks, alcoholic beverages, and tobacco-containing products. Do you really want to give your partner who stays up all night worrying about this or that an energy drink or a heaping pot of coffee a few hours before bedtime? Avoiding these substances will help you keep their anxiety from getting worse and maintain your own sanity.

Habit 3: Excessive Use of Social Media

We live in a period of social media addicts and many people do not have a full understanding of just how problematic this can be. Anxious people have a tendency to obsess over things or to blow things out of proportion. When you consider that much of the information that comes from news programs or is posted to social media is exaggerated or designed to inflame the reader or is outright untrue, it should become obvious why social media can be a problem.

It is a good idea to steer your partner away from using social media if you can. It is also a good idea for you to avoid using social platforms in front of them (or at all). Another part of this is using forms of communication other than face to face. By limiting your conversation to standard, old-fashioned face to face communication, you can prevent the worries and fears that come from unclear or misinterpreted messages.

Habit 4: Depriving Yourself of Sleep

Sleep deprivation can exacerbate the condition of someone dealing with mental health concerns. This is true of anxiety as well as other conditions like depression, bipolar disorder, and the like. The idea here is that the brain needs sleep in order to function normally and to maintain the body in homeostasis. Although scientists are actually engaged in an active debate as to why precisely sleep is so important, the value of sleep in individuals with mental health concerns is widely acknowledged. Do yourself and your partner a favor and try not to deprive them of sleep. Indeed, encourage them to get about eight hours a night.

Habit 5: Not Getting Enough Exercise

Exercise is not only important in keeping your body in tiptop shape, but it also releases endorphins that cause people to feel happy and energetic. Indeed, it has been argued that the sedentary lifestyle of modern people has impacted us in a number of negative and problematic ways, and the impact that being sedentary can have on the mind is often overlooked. You can help your significant other reduce their anxiety by encouraging them to exercise and by making sure that you are not the cause of why they are not getting enough exercise.

Habit 6: Not Being Honest About How You Are Feeling

A habit that anxious people share with depressed people is that sometimes they are not honest about how they are feeling. They may say that they are fine when in reality, they are feeling down in the dumps or are worried about something. You can help your partner avoid this habit and combat their anxiety by informing them that how they feel matters to them and that it is important to you that they are honest. You cannot help an anxious or depressed person feel better if you do not know how they feel.

Habit 7: Magnifying A Situation (Blowing Things Out of Proportion)

Anxious and depressed people tend to engage in something called catastrophizing. This is also called magnifying and it refers to blowing matters out of proportion in a dysfunctional way. Anxious men and women do not do this on purpose. Because they tend to over-worry or obsess about things, they can attach more importance to things that what really is there. Helping your partner drop the habit of magnifying or catastrophizing is an important step in the direction of salvaging or maintaining your relationship.

Habit 8: Not Listening

This is a habit that anxious individuals and their partners can be guilty of. Although an anxious person may hang onto your every word and hear you, are they really listening? Remember that anxiety-fraught individuals can misinterpret or misunderstand ambiguous words or communicated information (via text, email, et cetera). Listening, therefore, becomes a very critical skill to have in a relationship where anxiety is an issue. Drop the habit of not listening to one another and both of you will see all the ways that your relationship can be bettered.

Habit 9: Allowing Your Partner to Isolate Themselves

Depressed or anxious individuals can isolate themselves. In depressed individuals, this can be attributed to chemical signals that cause a host of symptoms that basically lead to them being more withdrawn, while in anxious persons it often may be due to avoiding situations that might trigger their worries, obsessions, or compulsions. Isolating yourself is a habit that anxious people will have to drop if they hope to get better, and as their partner, you will be making a big difference if you can help them here.

Habit 10: Managing Stress Poorly, both Inside and Outside a Relationship

It can be argued that anxious people, by definition, have difficulty managing stress, but managing stress will is important in any relationship whether there is anxiety or not. Think about a relationship where both partners work or have busy schedules. You want to make sure that you both have time for the things that relax you or that you enjoy and also that you have ways of diffusing anger-fraught or stressful situations. Managing stress poorly can, therefore, be a bad habit in any relationship, but in relationships where one partner is anxious, this habit can result in catastrophe. Do yourself a courtesy and talk to your partner about how the two of you will handle situations that stress you out.

CHAPTER 28:

Road to Healing

Healing is a unique experience for everyone who goes through it. For some, it is quick, for others lengthy, and still others fall somewhere in between. It has to do with the serious symptoms, willingness to change, and time spent working on reaching goals. Some people are able to achieve their happy ending on their own, by reading books like this one or doing their own research and finding techniques that help them manage their anxiety and continue living a normal life. Others might decide they need a little help to make it through a particularly difficult time, and that's okay too.

There are a number of tricks to manage anxiety and reduce the frequency of panic attacks, and everyone has their own tactic that works best for them. The key to these tips and tricks is to continue trying different ones until a person finds one that works. There are natural remedies such as essential oils, relaxation techniques such as deep breathing, and even cognitive behavioral therapy exercises that can be found online. Not each one of these will work for everyone, though, and people should not be discouraged if they try one method and it doesn't work for them.

Overcoming fears can be the most difficult part of taking charge of anxiety, but it is also the most important. Avoiding things a person is afraid of can only make those things seem scarier, but facing them head-on can often take away the mystery and fear. Sometimes to achieve this, a person will employ the help of a doctor or counselor to assist them with developing an action plan and staying on track. This can also help a person more accurately measure their progress and receive feedback from another informed person. This discusses ways a person can manage their anxiety, reduce the frequency of panic attacks, overcome their fears, and ensure their therapy is working for them.

Managing Symptoms

Learning to manage anxiety can be difficult and uncomfortable. It might mean going against all of the signals your brain is sending to face a fear that seems insurmountable. It is important to remember during this time that working with your doctor to learn new coping skills can be the best and fastest way to start effectively fighting off your anxiety.

Perhaps the best way to learn and practice these skills is by using mindfulness techniques. Being mindful of yourself and your thoughts can make it much easier to notice when they start erring toward anxiety and away from calm and rational. This way, you can take back control of your thoughts before they spiral too far down the wrong path. These techniques can also reduce worry and increase willpower. If a person is able to tap into their body's needs at any time, it can relax their sense of uncertainty and give them a feeling that they are back in control. These exercises can include setting intentions at the beginning of each day, meditating, going for a walk, or simply looking up at the sky to notice all the things that would normally pass by without a second glance. People can also make a point to put their phone down for an extended period of time to make time to take care of themselves and not have to worry about others. If they want to take this exercise to the next level, they can even leave their phone at home when they go out to experience a release from technology.

It is also important for people to remember that most therapies will not give results right away. They take hard work and dedication to start yielding benefits. Typically, cognitive behavioral therapy takes about 12 to 16 weeks before a person will start seeing marked improvement in their symptoms.

Along with managing their anxiety, a person can also work to reduce the frequency of their panic attacks. Learning to manage panic can be just as stressful as facing fears with anxiety, but once a person can learn to take control of their mind and not be intimidated by their symptoms, having a panic attack might not be the terrible thing it once was.

The first step a person can take to reduce their panic attacks is to make sure they are sticking with the treatment plan their doctor devised with them. It can be difficult to face things alone once you leave the doctor's office, but making sure you are practicing the techniques he or she teaches you is imperative to success. Sometimes joining a support group can help you to follow through with the action plan. People often find that having a group of others who truly understand and experience the same problems can help them see their issues from a different perspective or find the support they need to continue working toward their goal.

Just like people with anxiety, people who experience frequent panic attacks should limit or avoid exposure to stimulants and depressants such as caffeine, drugs, and alcohol. These substances can make it more difficult to deal with feelings and recognize what your triggers are, so it is best to keep them out of a routine.

Stress management tactics are another helpful way to get a grip on panic attacks. People can focus on turning their negative thoughts into positive actions; this might take a little more skill than if someone was dealing with anxiety alone because of the suddenness of panicked thoughts. They can also focus on being assertive instead of aggressive when they are feeling irritated by exercising regularly, and making a schedule to manage their time and tasks effectively.

Relaxation techniques also work equally well for managing panic attacks as with anxiety. Things such as yoga, deep breathing, and muscle relaxation can help the body to calm down even in the face of panicked thoughts or physical symptoms. Making sure you get enough sleep at night is another way to relax the body. Having a schedule for bedtime and wake up times can be incredibly helpful to calm the body because it has a predictable schedule.

If these milder approaches are not doing the trick, sometimes exposure therapy can be the best option for a person to face their fears and decrease the likelihood of a panic attack. This type of therapy involves a person subjecting themselves to the very thing that they are afraid will incite an attack. Typically, this process can be painful the first few times, but after a while, the person will realize the situation does not pose any threat and there is no reason to feel anxious or panicked.

Some people opt for home remedies to treat panic attacks, especially at their onset. Inhaling lavender essential oils, or putting some in a diffuser, is possibly the most common way people can ease their worry homeopathically. Lavender is known for its calming effects and ability to relax the nervous system.

Moving Forward

An important part of the healing process when someone is overcoming anxiety and panic attacks is to confront their fears. When a person continually avoids things that cause them anxiety, it can cement the fear in their brain and make it more and more intense as time goes on. To face their fears, however, a person needs to understand how their brain reacts in scary situations so they can start to identify their triggers and responses. Once they know these two things, staying ahead of the curve can become much easier and the odds of successfully controlling anxiety can increase.

The first step is to refuse to be afraid of feeling fear. Sometimes the suggestions of fear, such as a trailer for a horror movie, can be enough to get someone's anxiety moving. You can't necessarily avoid commercials for horror movies, though, so a person has to learn that the suggestion of fear and fear itself are two different things. Avoidance can keep a person from doing a number of things in their life, even things they used to enjoy. Fear can be a powerful motivator to stay away from something, but if a person can take a deep breath and acknowledge that it might not spark fear then they could have a better chance of confronting it without anxiety.

People can also overcome their fears by focusing on the positive things in life. You can take a piece of paper and write down all the things you are grateful for to shift your focus onto happiness. It can also be a great reminder of the different people and reasons that make fighting off anxiety, worth it. Using humor is also an effective way to lessen anxiety and forget your fears. If someone starts to feel worried, they can make up the most out-of-this-world worst-case scenario, such as aliens landing at the dinner party and there not being enough food to serve all of them, to help them realize how silly some of their worries really are. Learning to appreciate this sense of humor and not taking yourself too seriously can help reduce stress and anxiety simultaneously.

Even when a person is dedicated to facing their fears and reducing their anxiety, it can still be difficult to do alone. Deciding to start therapy can be a major decision for some people and once they start, they might not feel like they are making any progress in the beginning. Trusting a therapist can take time, but they are there to support and help you. A therapist can monitor someone's successes and progress and keep them motivated to continue with treatment. Having this consistent, unbiased support can help a person remember that therapy takes time and effort to work.

Most therapists who utilize cognitive behavioral therapy are frequently checking in with their patients and discussing their symptoms, goals, and behaviors. By assessing the person's emotional state and progress, they are able to keep them on track toward achieving their long and short-term goals. This is also how the therapist can make sure that the person is enacting their plan and working on changing their thoughts and behaviors.

If you ever feel concerned that you are not making enough progress while in therapy, you can always ask your doctor to give their opinion. They might discuss with you the steps you've taken in the right direction and things they think might still be holding you back. Most likely, however, they will tell you not to worry because everyone heals at different speeds and as long as you are putting in the work you will get the results.

Having a positive relationship with your doctor can also help you feel like you are making progress because it develops trust. It also helps you to open up and let them know all of your symptoms and feelings so together you can form a comprehensive, realistic action plan that targets them all. When a more detailed action plan can be created, faster results are more likely to occur because the doctor can target very specific things with realistic expectations. This can also help someone to trust their doctor more because they see the results they hoped for and are acknowledging that the hard work is paying off.

Finally, a person can also consider whether or not they are solving problems on their own. If they are, this can also indicate that they are working on achieving both their short- and long-term goals.

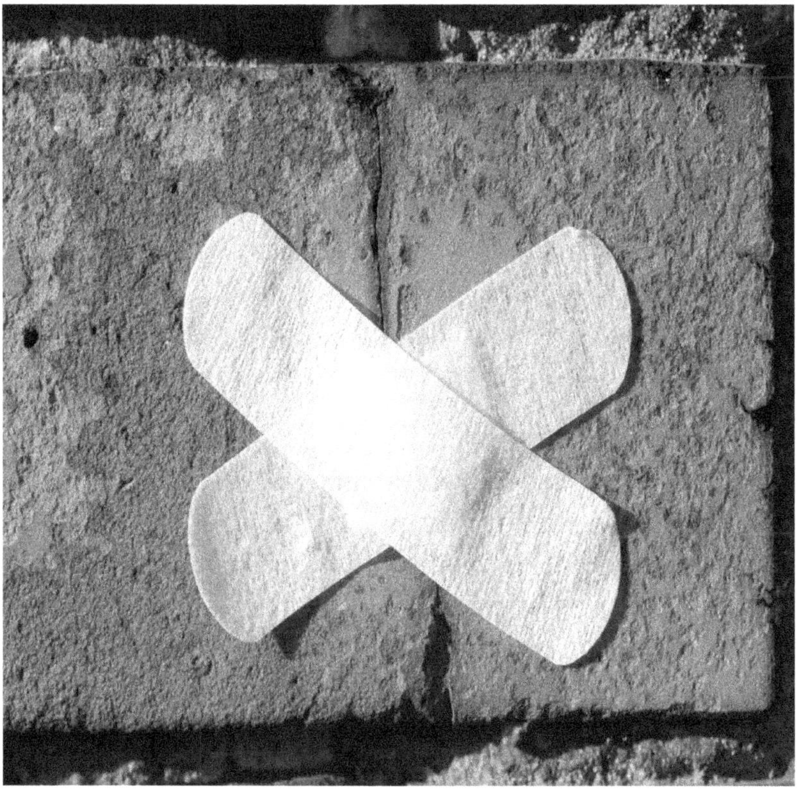

Conclusion

Anxiousness does not have to derail your life or the life of your partner. If you are in a relationship where anxiety is an issue, you should take comfort in knowing that anxious symptoms can be managed effectively in various ways, relieving the hold that anxious thoughts have on your relationship. One of the goals of this tome has been to teach the reader what worry is so that they can recognize it. Part of what makes anxiousness so difficult to manage in relationships is that many people do not have an accurate understanding of what anxiety is rendering the simple act of recognizing it a difficult one.

As the reader has learned in this volume, anxiousness impacts millions of people worldwide at any given time, with some estimating that as many ten percent of the population will experience an anxiety symptom in a given year. Anxiety can be defined as an emotion characterized by excessive worries or fears. It is this anxious emotion that allows a class of disorders referred to as anxiety disorders to be described. These disorders are all characterized by the experience of anxiousness, although how the feeling manifests may differ from one condition to the other.

Perhaps the most well-known anxiety disorder is what psychologists refer to as generalized anxiety disorder. This is the disorder that some people are referring to when they talk about anxiety, although it is estimated to account for slightly less than fifty percent of all cases of anxiousness. A common category of disorders characterized by anxiety is the specific phobias. Specific phobias are associated with excessive fear around a specific object or trigger, like crowds, spiders, or speaking publicly.

The first step to successfully dealing with anxiousness in the relationship setting is to educate yourself enough on the subject so that you can understand the condition and all the ways that it may surface in a relationship. The goal of the first part was to give you a thorough understanding of what anxiety is and why anxiety may be more common in certain parts of the world and certain groups. This allows you not only to approach the anxiety in your relationship from the standpoint of knowledge, but it also permits you to show sympathy for your partner's anxiety because you understand it better and have an idea of where it may be coming from.

Being fully educated about worry requires that you have a basic understanding of anxiety disorders. Although many relationships may be characterized by the general anxiety that is associated with generalized anxiety disorder, other conditions like panic disorder, specific phobias, obsessive-compulsive disorder, or post-traumatic stress disorder have unique symptoms which makes dealing with them a unique ordeal. The goal is not necessarily that the reader should know how each disorder should be managed, but at least to be able to recognize what type of anxiety their partner suffers from and to be aware that different types of anxiousness should be managed differently.

The question of where anxiety comes from is a loaded one. Although it has been observed that this condition does frequently run in families, it has also been found that anxiety appears to be more common in Western countries than developing countries (in addition to other notable demographic trends). A potentially important cause of anxiety is the dysfunctional relationships that some men and women may experience in their youth. This is the idea behind attachment theory: the model that shows how children learn how to interact with other people and their environment based on the relationship they have with their primary caregiver. As this is focusing on relationships, understanding the role that attachment plays as a possible cause of anxiety can allow the sympathy that a partner shows for their significant other to become true empathy another goal.

Anxiety can be treated successfully, providing relief for the millions of men and women in relationships and out of them that deal with anxiousness. Anxious symptoms can be treated with medication, but it can also be treated successfully with therapy, dietary changes, and natural remedies. These natural remedies include things like herbs found in the environment, inositol, and transcendental meditation. Although more research has to be done to show how effective these treatments are, they represent another option for people looking for alternatives to the more common medication and therapeutic options.

This would not be effective about dealing with anxiousness in relationships if it did not provide the reader with tips, they can follow to help them maintain their relationship in the face of worry. It is not easy dealing with anxiousness either as the individual suffering from it or as the partner of the anxious individual, and this is a concept that is being recognized. It is focused on providing the reader with tips they can use to support their partner through their anxiety, or to keep them from making their partner's anxiety worse.

An important fact to know about anxiety is that it usually does not go away on its own. If anxiety is left untreated, it will persist, potentially derailing the anxious individual's familial and romantic relationships and preventing them from forming new, enduring ones. The goal is to help the partner of the anxious person become more supportive, which may be so important for that person that it can change the course of their life. Anxiety can be beaten, but it will take effort and reading this is the first step in your accomplishment of this important work.

COUPLE THERAPY:

Change Your Bad Habits in Love Following This Effective Couples Therapy Guide. You Can Easily Improve Your Marriage, Rescue Broken Relationship, Solve Most Common Conflicts.

By Michelle Miller

MICHELLE MILLER

Introduction

Understanding of Couples therapy in all perspectives. You can also get the idea that how couples therapy work in the favor of couples. How couple therapy works as a beneficial source to reconnect couples and the whole phenomena behind it.

What is Couples therapy?

Counseling is for people who are married or are committed to each other. This is also referred to as a therapy for family. The purpose of couple therapy is to enhance and improve the relationship status of the couples. That form of counseling also help couples determine whether they should stay together or not. There are occasions when one or both parties need to discuss the psychological problems individually.

Understanding:

Therapy also involves sessions aimed at enhancing problem-solving, developing communication skills, and defining life goals and expectations for relationships. Many common problems include infidelity, financial difficulties, illness, and other changes in life, as well as frustration.

Counseling can be short-term or over a period of several months, depending on the extent of difficulties in relationship. If you and your wife are having problems because you end up in a big dispute any time you disagree, and fix absolutely nothing. The two of you are slowly growing apart due to the intense tension in the relationship. You have always thought about leaving your partner, but first, you want to try a couple therapy.

You are in counseling, and you understand that you both need guidance with the way you interact, and with your approach to problem-solving techniques. You also discover that you are simply continuing a form of behavior that was demonstrated by your parents: they yelled and accomplished nothing, and eventually fell apart and divorced. You can now change your actions with your newly gained awareness that part of the issue is that you follow what you have seen your parents do. You strengthen the relationship over time using constructive communication strategies and a workable issue solution. Positive feelings resurface for your partner, and you won't be able to believe that you had wanted to break the relationship.

Five Principles of Effective Couples therapy:

5 basic principles of effective couple's therapy are as follows:

1. Changes the views of the relationship:

Throughout the counseling process, the therapist tries to help both parties take a more realistic view of the relationship. They learn to avoid the "blame game" and look more at what happens to them in a cycle that includes both partner. You may also benefit from ensuring that their relationship exists in a specific context. For instance, couples who struggle financially may be put under different forms of situational stress than those who do not. Therapists begin this process by gathering "evidence" about the partners 'relationship by observing how they communicate. Therapists then formulate "hypotheses" about what factors could contribute to the problems in their relationship between the partners. Therapists share the knowledge with the couple according to the basic psychological perspective of the therapist and it also varies from couple to couple. With a range of methods, from clinical to insight-oriented, there is empirical support. Different therapists can use various approaches, but as long as they work on improving the perception of the relationship, the couple will begin to see each other and their experiences in a more constructive way.

2. Modifies dysfunctional behavior:

Good couple therapists try to improve the way the partners actually communicate with one another. In addition to helping them enhance their relationship, this means that therapists do need to ensure that their clients do not participate in behaviors that can cause physical, psychological, or economic damage. To do so, therapists must carry out a detailed evaluation to decide if their clients are genuinely at risk. For example, if possible, the therapist may recommend that one person be sent to a shelter for domestic violence, a specialist clinic for substance abuse, or anger management. It is also likely that if the risk isn't serious enough, the couple can benefit from "time-out" measures to avoid conflict escalation.

3. Decreases emotional avoidance:

Couples that refrain from sharing their private feelings are at greater risk of being emotionally isolated and growing apart. Efficient couple therapists help their clients put out the feelings and ideas they are unable to convey to others. Couple counseling based on intimacy helps couples to feel less anxious to communicate their desire for closeness. According to this view, some partners in childhood who have failed to build "free" emotional attachments have unmet needs that they bring into their adult relationships. They are afraid to show their partners how much they need them because they are afraid their partners are going to reject them. Behavioral therapists believe that adults may be unable to communicate their true feelings because they have not received "reinforcement" in the past. Either way, all psychological strategies recommend encouraging their clients to convey their true feelings in a way that would ultimately bring them back together.

4. Improves communication:

Intimacy is one of the "three C's" of being able to communicate. All positive couple therapies are geared towards helping the couples connect more effectively. Building on concepts 2 and 3, this contact should not be violent, nor will partners make one another crazy as they share their true feelings. Therefore, couples can need "coaching" in order to learn to talk to one another in a more supportive and understanding way. The therapist can also give instructional advice to the couple and provide them with the basis for understanding what forms of communication are successful and what forms would only create more tension. For example, they could learn how to listen more actively and empathetically. Just how to achieve this step, however, allows therapists to switch back to the tests they carried out early in care. Couples with a persistent history of mutual criticism can involve an approach different from those who seek to avoid confrontation at all costs.

5. Promote strengths:

Good couple therapists point out the strengths of the relationship and develop resilience, particularly when therapy is about to end. Since so much couple counseling includes concentrating on problem areas, it's easy to lose sight of the other areas where couple work effectively. Promoting strength is about helping the couple gain more satisfaction from their relationship. The behaviorally focused therapist can "prescribe" one partner to do something agreeable to another. Perhaps therapists from other orientations who concentrate more on feelings may help the couple create a more optimistic "plot" or narrative about their relationship. In this case, the therapist should stop trying to put his or her own perspective on what constitutes a strength and let the couple determine this.

We can see, then, that if their life seems hopeless, people in strained relationships need not give up in despair. In the same way, people who are reluctant to enter into long-term relationships will be motivated to learn how to repair problem relationships.

Looking at the other side, these five concepts of good counseling recommend strategies for partners to develop healthy close relationships and sustain them. Take an unbiased look at your relationship, seek assistance in eliminating unhealthy habits, feel like you can express your feelings, connect openly, and show what works. Most importantly, by ensuring that each partnership has its own specific challenges and strengths, you can give yours the best survival chances.

How does Couple therapy work?

Counseling will benefit couples with the use of the above approaches and more. For couple counseling to succeed, both people must be committed to enhancing their partnership while looking inwardly at their own strengths and weaknesses. Knowing their behaviors and habits that make your partner tick could have a positive impact on making improvements in both personal aspect and relationships. Couple's therapy is not intended to unload anger, frustration, and other negative actions against one spouse. It's about finding passion, commitment, and all the other approaches that lead a healthy relationship.

Does Marriage Counseling Work? That's a very big issue, but what people are really talking about is, "Will marriage therapy save my marriage? The response to that is very much based on a variety of variables beyond the counselor's office.

Although some of these points are highlighted below, some of the considerations to look for when seeking marital therapy are as follows:

1. Did you just wait too long? If you have been breaking each other apart for ten years, there is a very good risk that there is so much harm that it cannot be done to undo.

2. Need to save your marriage, really? People often go to therapy just to claim they've tried. They just don't want it to work. They save face just to assuage their remorse.

3. Is there harassment or aggression in the relationship? If there is a family, you're not trying to save it; you're trying to avoid the illegal activity. Abusers, whether physical or mental, are not "unhappy" in their marriage; they are often terrified and impotent people who feel helpless in their lives anywhere else.

4. Will the structure meet your needs? If saving your marriage means spending another 30 years doing away with everything you want to do, is that worth it? It takes a hard and truthful look at what every person needs to make sure you get exactly that what you need out of the relationship.

One of the most important factors in relationship counseling's success is the counselor. Nearly every counselor in the world claims they're doing marital therapy, but most never received any preparation. They also have a psychology or counseling degree and believe they should do it.

CHAPTER 1:

Understand Each Partners Inner World

When we are in a relationship, we desire to be heard, seen and understood. Understanding the other person is as important as being understood. We want to know that "we are being listened to, we are being understood". In fact, we want our spouse to say "Yes I hear you, yes I understand and yes I feel your pain. I am sorry that it hurts and know that I will be here for you." We desire that our partners are interested in us and what we are going through. These desires are basic human needs.

One of the key complaints raised by people in conflict is that they are not feeling understood or cared for. Feeling unheard, unseen and misunderstood is a killer of intimacy. if we do not feel understood, we feel rejected, more like it does matter. That will hinder relational growth and lead to fractures in the relationship in due time.

Being understanding is listed among the top qualities that facilitate a good relationship. Apart from allowing your partner to be him/herself in the relationship, it lets you see things from the perspective of other people without fear of being vulnerable. Most of us strive to be understanding to our partners.

There is an inaccurate belief that understanding a partner means that one has to agree with him/her. That is not true. You can understand someone and still disagree with him/her. Understanding simply means that you are listening to your partner objectively. It involves listening intently and fully to all the opinions of the other person and actually understood without interfering with your own opinions and judgments. In fact, you can check that what you heard is right by rephrasing the words of the partner. For instance, you can say, "I understand what you are saying but let me check, what you are saying is…"

Such fact-checking will reassure your partner that you are listening, understanding and also staying in touch with their words. Make sure that your partner feels so understood that he sees no reason to keep clarifying his/her perspective. Below are some of the procedures you can use to understand your partner better.

a. Understand first

When having a conversation, you do not have to give your opinion first. In fact, you do not have to start thinking of a solution before the person has finished talking. In most cases, our ability to understand something is affected by the thoughts running through our heads because we start thinking of a solution as soon as the other person starts to talk. Your main role in a conversation is to be a listening human being to your partner first. Be the pillar and shoulder they need. No matter how much you feel like sharing your opinion, reserve it. If your partner feels fully understood, he/she will reciprocate by giving you full attention and trying to understand your feelings, thoughts and perceptions.

b. Be fully present

Sometimes during a conversation, we are distracted by things such as our own thoughts, perceptions and even stresses. This only hinders us from understanding the other person fully. Be fully present. You can even use active listening skills to minimize the degree of distraction. You too will want to be understood fully when it is your turn to talk.

c. Avoid defensiveness and complaints

Complains are very toxic and defensiveness prevents us from truly understanding the perspectives of other people. In most cases, we avoid being vulnerable by being defensive. Intimacy requires openness and vulnerability. To avoid pushing your partner to the defense, do not use critiques. Instead of pointing out their mistakes aggressively, use the 'I statement' to explain how you felt. If you keep pointing at the faults of your partner, you are simply saying "It is your fault, not mine."

The trick to making sure that your partner feels understood is taking some of the blame. By sharing responsibility, you leave room for expression. You can say something positive like "I know I said …. And failed but …." It is also very important to tell your partner about your feelings and needs.

d. Understand yourself

If a person commits into a relationship without understanding his/herself first, it might brew trouble. Basically, before you start to involve another person in your problems, make sure that you know them yourself. That way, you will know what is bothering you at any one point.

It is very hard to help another person while we are burdened by our own problems. You will have trouble managing all the problems bubbling up in a relationship if you do not even know what is prickling at your heart. As such, it is very important to take some time and connect with yourself, connect with your feeling and acknowledge your emotions.

If you feel there are needs you need to heal in yourself, explain this to your partner. You can say "I want to understand you but first, I need some time with myself. Can you allow me time? That will make your partner to feel that you are trying and not being just selfish.

To understand yourself, tune in to your thoughts, feelings, and bodily sensations. This will help you to identify the things happening to you, which can be shared with your partner. Some of the physical signs that might help you understand yourself include, a racing heart, hair prickling up, the sensation in your mind, et cetera. Understanding a person requires patience. It means not interrupting our partners. It means listening without formulating premature responses. Understanding requires one to turn the full attention towards the other person. This is not easy, especially when you have personal baggage.

Understanding a person requires practice. Be patient and give your partner the special gift of being seen, heard and understood.

e. Do not impose your own beliefs and ideas

Regardless of the amount of experience, knowledge, maturity, and intellect you have, never impose ideas on your partner. Technically, this self-imposition feels like intimidation to a loved one. Doing this will hinder you from truly understanding the feelings of your partner.

To be an understating partner in a relationship, you need to acknowledge that no matter how much you know, your partner has his/her personality. He/she has ideas, feelings, thoughts, knowledge and beliefs. And you have to know and respect them even if you do not agree with them. This is necessary to keep a strong bond.

f. Allow your partner to live

Sometimes, we want our partner to leave everything else and live with us, that is, make the relationship the only thing in his/her life. In fact, many people crave to be the center of their partner's universe. Here is the thing, it is possible to have a partner make you the center of his/her world but, that will not last. Do not force your partner to drop most of their life choices and preferences for the relationship.

Ensure that you understand your partner and give him/she the freedom to have fun, just live, and enjoy life even without you. Besides, you need to respect your partner as a social being. It is unhealthy and selfish to limit your partner just because you are in a relationship. Let him/her go out with associates, spend time with family, travel on his/her own and live life to the fullest without your interference. Above all, let your partner pursue his/her goals and offer support.

MICHELLE MILLER

CHAPTER 2:

Strengthen Friendship and Intimacy

1. Start Trusting

Learn to get into the habit of trusting people more consciously. Choose a trusting disposition over a distrustful attitude. Unless you have concrete evidence about someone, take their word for it. Going around snooping, stalking your partner and behaving like a suspicious maniac only harms your relationship further. Rather, if there is no reason to be suspicious other than a feeling of insecurity or jealously, let it go.

2. Write Your Deepest Feelings and Thoughts

Journaling is well-known to be one of the most effective techniques for bringing to the fore your deepest feelings and emotions. It helps you discover multiple layers of your personality to achieve greater self-awareness. It also facilitates the process of an emotional catharsis for venting out pent up feelings. For instance, you may constantly harbor feelings of insecurity because neglectful parents raised you or you may never feel you are "good enough" because you were raised by parents who had extremely high and unreasonable expectations from you.

People who have been wronged in their childhood often feel they aren't worthy enough to be loved. This in turn causes them to reflect that their partner is seeking someone more worthy or deserving of love than them, which creates feelings of insecurity.

3. Regulate Your Negative Feelings and Emotions with Mindfulness

Mindfulness is a great way to calm your nerves and manage runaway emotions. Tune into your physical and mental self by identifying your feelings, thoughts and emotions by taking deep breaths. Try and detach yourself from overpowering negative emotions such as jealousy and insecurity. Every time you find yourself overcome with thoughts of jealousy or insecurity, practice mindful meditation.

4. Be Frank and Accepting About Your Feelings

Discussing your insecurities with your partner will help you create a frank and open communication channel. Rather than doing and saying crazy things to your partner, be upfront and share your feelings. Say something similar to "I apologize for bothering you regarding your friendship with ABC, but it is not my lack of trust in you. I simply feel insecure about it."

5. Avoid Suffocating Your Partner

Start relaxing a bit by letting go of your desire to imprison your partner. The harder you try to imprison someone against his/her own will, the more forcefully they'll try to escape your domineering behavior. Let your partner have the choice to spend time with his/her friends, talk to their attractive colleague or do other things that otherwise make you feel threatened. Once they realize how secure and confident you are about the relationship, they will automatically be drawn to you. A secure and self-assured partner can be extremely irresistible.

6. Create Boundaries as a Couple

Sometimes people act in a certain way without even being aware that their actions negatively impact loved ones. You may find your partner indulging in flirtatious behavior often, but he/she may believe it to be a part of their fun personality. They may not even be aware of the damage being caused to you or the relationship. For them it may be a harmless display of their charm and wit.

Setting boundaries early in the relationship will keep you both on the same page as to what is appropriate or acceptable behavior and where to draw the line. You both can mutually discuss and arrive at the "non-negotiable" in your relationship. Is harmless flirting alright with both of you? What about kissing on the cheek? Dancing with a member of the opposite sex? Once clear boundaries are established, your partner will be less likely to behave in a way that can upset your or incite feelings of insecurity. Talk issues through, look for a common ground and once everything is clear – learn to trust your partner unless there is compelling evidence to believe otherwise.

7. Go to the Bottom of Your Insecurity and Negative Emotions

It can be really hard to objective assess why you feel pangs of insecurity each time someone compliments your partner, or he/she speaks warmly with his/her colleagues. It can be highly tempting to blame another person for your emotions. However, getting to the root of your insecurity by being more self-aware is the foundation to free yourself from its shackles. Take a more compassionate and objective look at the origination of your insecurity. Think about the potential causes for feelings of insecure.

For instance, if you find yourself being increasingly insecure of your partner, know why you feel it. Is it because you don't want to lose him/her? Do you agonize from a false sense of self-entitlement that your partner's time belongs only to you? Do you feel what you feel because of a sense of inadequacy that constantly makes you think "you aren't good enough?" Once you identify the underlying reasons causing feelings of jealousy and insecurity, it becomes easier to deal with your behavior.

8. Switch Off from Envious and Insecure Mental Chatter

Tell yourself to mentally shut up when you find yourself engaging in self-defeating jealous self-speak. You can use several ways to achieve this. It can be using a stop or "x" sign whenever negative thoughts begin to pick momentum in your mind. Condition yourself to stop unexpected thoughts with practice sessions using visual and mental reinforcements. Try saying stop aloud when you find yourself embarking on a destructive insecurity self-talk journey. This way you will embarrass yourself more and realize how ridiculously you are behaving. The idea is to train your mind into thinking that it isn't alright to come up with insecure self-talk.

9. Avoid Judging Other People Based on Your Past

Ever notice how suspicious people are always suspicious of others? Or liars think everyone around them is lying? Our perception of people and their motives is often a reflection of who we are. Stop using your past or present behavior as a yardstick for perceiving your partner's actions. For instance, if you have a history of being involved with married men/women, do not assume that no married man/woman can ever be trusted and start mistrusting your spouse. Just because you did or are doing something does not mean he/she is indulging in it too.

10. Discard past Relationship Baggage

A strong reason why you are always paranoid about your current partner cheating on you can be traced back to an earlier relationship. You may have had an ex-partner cheat on you with your best friend. The betrayal may have had such a severe impact that you view every relationship in a similar distrustful light.

Painting everyone with the same brush can be a disastrous mistake in any relationship. There is a solid reason your earlier relationship did not last, and you should leave the garbage of your earlier relationship where it belongs – in the trash can.

11. Question Yourself Every Time

Each time you find yourself feeling even remotely jealous; question the underlying feeling behind the complex emotion of jealousy. Is the insecurity a consequence of my anger, anxiety or fear? What is it about this circumstances that makes me jealous? When you question your jealously critically, you are a few steps away from taking constructive steps to convert a cloud of negativity into a bundle of positivity.

12. Insecurity Is Not Always an Evil Monster

It may sound contradictory to everything we've been discussing about insecurity, but truth is insecurity may not always be harmful. Sometimes, a tiny amount of it may do your relationship a whole lot of good. How? It can sometimes motivate you or your partner to safeguard your relationship. If expressed in a productive and wholesome manner, insecurity gives you the much-needed impetus to protect your territory. Insecurity helps you assume the role of a protector for your loved one and relationship, and this can be good if it doesn't scale extreme heights. Be smart enough to realize when jealousy goes from being a relationship protector to a relationship destroyer. You choose whether it is a boon or bane for your relationship.

13. Remind Yourself of Your Strengths Periodically

Each of us possesses unique strengths that set us apart from others. Keep reinforcing to yourself how wonderful you are through positive affirmations and visualizations. You will find yourself feeling less insecure when you are aware of your positives. The more self-assured and confident you are, the less affected you will be by other people's actions. Know where your strengths lie, keep doing things that make you feel great about yourself and believe that you are worthy of true love.

14. Focus on Productive and Positive Ideas

Rather than obsessing over who your partner is cheating you with, try to develop interests outside of your relationship. Do not make it the nucleus of your existence even if it means a lot to you.

15. Imaginary Fears Do Not Necessarily Mean It Will Happen

We need to understand that our insecure hunches do not necessarily mean the act is occurring. Just because we fear something is going to happen doesn't mean it will happen. A majority of the times our fears are unfounded, and not even remotely close to coming true. Just because your partner is somewhere else, and you fear he/she is with someone else doesn't mean he/she is proposing relationship on a date. Understand the difference between thoughts and actual events. The make-believe imaginations of our destructive mind are often far from reality.

16. Be Generous

Spend more time giving and helping others. This will not just make you feel great about yourself but also help you develop a greater understanding of how you add value to others' lives and how they would be grateful to have what you have.

Volunteer within your local community by helping folks read and write English or preparing meals for the less fortunate or even assisting a friend who is struggling to finish college.

17. Stay Away from Insecurity Triggering Situations

Be aware of situations that trigger elements of jealousy and insecurity in your behavior and avoid these situations whenever you can. For instance, if you are a person who can't help experiencing pangs of insecurity each time your partner mingles with members of the opposite sex, avoid dating a person who generally hangs out with the opposite sex and is extremely popular with them. This will invariably lead to friction unless you work a common ground.

18. Focus on the Positives

So, you witnessed your partner flirting with one of his friends. Big deal? Not really. Keep in mind that you both have a history of intimacy and an incomparable closeness, which is why you are together in the first place. There's a unique spark about your togetherness that cannot be matched by others. Just because someone pays their friends a few compliments and displays warmth doesn't necessarily mean they want to be with him/her for life. Sometimes, people just flirt to lighten the mood or break the ice or make the other person feel good about himself/herself.

Remember the really positive and unusual things about your relationship every time you are overcome with feelings of insecurity/jealousy. Remind yourself of your beautiful moments, of everything your partner has told you about why he/she fell in love with you, and the loving things you have done for each other.

MICHELLE MILLER

CHAPTER 3:

Finding Each Other In New Ways

It's quick to get in a rut and continue to feel isolated from each other in these days of tight budgets, long working days, and jobs that keep us apart. Here are six separate ways you can make minimal effort or money every day that mutually influence your partner's attitude and can help to rekindle the spark in your relationship. The following list will help control your partner's opinion and keep him or her talking about you all day. This is such that the day to day they face their work doesn't preclude them from spending a beautiful night together when they get home.

- Tomorrow, add a cup of coffee and tea to your partner's room. There's no need to have just a hot meal. Easy toast or coffee cereal is the work.
- Ask them as you go, about how wonderful their companion feels, or how fine their hair or wardrobe looks today.
- Call your companion during the day just to let them know your feelings about them. Should not lament or say anything. Don't worry. Keep that for friends. Leave that for children. Depending on the work of your friend, you might need to be imaginative to find the right way to communicate without competing with your job. Two options to do that are to post messages to your personal cell phone, to immediately send an e-mail and, of course, to a fast phone call.
- If it is possible to meet your friend for lunch at least once a week.

- The minute you first see each other in the afternoon or after work, just hug them, kiss them, and tell them if you missed them before you say something.
- Seek not to get into a rut in the evening. Any night, mix up what you do. One night I go for dinner, rent a movie for one night, go for a walk, meet friends for one night and play the game for the weekend. Too many couples do their own thing every night in a rut of the same routine. Often work has to be done and time allocated to the task of making a living, but I believe you ought to diversify your post-work routine in order to avoid forming poor habits that mess with your connection. If you follow the above list sincerely and do it over and over for a long time, I guarantee that your relationship will start to feel different again.
- You both discover something entirely new for all of you is like joining unfamiliar waters together. In other words, this is an experience that almost always leads to pleasure, excitement, and laughter. If you pick a class where both of you are novices, you can, of course, rely on each other to find out details. Best of all, once you're doing it, you'll be "experts," you will have opportunities to talk about each other, your kids, and your social network.
- Record Your Happiness thought of the last shot you and your friend have shared together. When your relationship is ten years old, the latest proof, it is time to create new memories and record them. Take a mirror to your study; take brochures of the school. Save all the sheets of directions as well as other souvenirs. Using them to build a beautiful scrapbook for you and your friend. This is a perfect way to honor each other's new engagement.

CHAPTER 4:

Facing the Future Together

If you want your marriage to last a lifetime, you need to build your future together. Often, we come across couples who are so disconnected they hardly know what is going on in each other's lives. Staying invested in each other's goals, happiness, and dreams will keep you connected and reaching for the same future. When you are able to create a shared vision for your marriage it is easy to stay on track because you have a clear idea of what you are both aiming for.

Your spouse needs to be more than just someone you share a house or children with. You need to be partners in life. This means that even when you both have different passions and dreams your goals are aligned and you are working to achieving the same goals. You need to plan your future together so that you can work together to make it a reality.

One of the signs in any relationship is when you and your spouse do not talk about the future. When you have no idea of what you want your future to look like as a couple, it means that you are not really invested in that relationship. There is no guarantee that your marriage will last forever but if you are genuinely invested in your relationship you will have plans for the future.

The plans that you make will set the tone for your marriage and determine how you evolve both as individuals and as partners in a relationship. There is also a sense of stability and security that comes with knowing that you are building a future together. This security fosters trust and enables you to stay connected to your partner in the long term.

Strategies for building your future together

1. Be open about finances

In any marriage, your attitudes towards money will impact both of your futures. That is why having a conversation about money is crucial when trying to plan for your future. Conflicts about money are frequent in many marriages and the only way to get around this is to have a financial plan.

Agree on household budgets, saving plans, and your expenditure. This helps to lay down guidelines that both of you can live by in order to achieve your financial goals. A solid business plan helps to secure you a comfortable future and free you from constant financial worries.

If necessary, you can consult a professional to help you come up with a financial plan that works for both you and your partner. Being able to agree on money matters reduces conflict in your relationship and fosters trust.

2. Share responsibilities

A marriage is a partnership and this means you should be willing to share responsibilities. From house chores to parenting duties and all the commitments that come with running a family, sharing responsibilities creates a healthy balance in the relationship.

Sharing responsibilities will help to prevent the resentment that starts to creep up in relationships when one person feels like they are being taken advantage of. Come up with a list of duties and responsibilities and agree who is tasked with what. Of course, the duties can be switched between partners if need be but assigning creates some accountability in the marriage.

3) Build trust in your relationship

By being open and honest with each other about your goals, needs, and dreams, you can create trust in the relationship and forge stronger bonds. It is reassuring to know what your spouse is working toward and the things that are most important to them.

Being upfront about your expectations of each other will also help to avoid any feelings of disillusionment down the line. Do not keep your spouse in the dark about the things that you are planning for your future. When you know each other's plans, you can support each other and understand where you are both coming from as well as what your aspirations are.

4) Have fun together

Do not let your relationship become a dull affair. Inject some fun and romance by finding fun things to go together. Sign up for a dancing class, visit new places, or just find hobbies that appeal to you both. Spending time bonding and having fun helps to relieve pressure and build intimacy.

If you have date nights, make them fun by doing something different every time. Keeping things light-hearted and fun shows your partner that you can keep the relationship exciting and exciting. Being spontaneous and adventurous will help to keep your marriage feeling young no matter how old you are.

Remember just because you have been together for long, you do not have to turn into an old boring couple.

5) Give your partner space from time to time

Creating freedom in your relationship is excellent for ensuring the longevity of your marriage. Do not make your partner feel like you want to control them and monitor them all the time.

Have enough independence to give your partner space and room to breathe.

Giving each other space shows that you trust each other and that you are secure in your relationship. When your partner feels they still have the freedom to be themselves and pursue their passions, they will not be anxious about spending the rest of their life with you.

6) Embrace your differences

If you actually want to be together forever, you need to accept and embrace each other's differences. Stop the constant criticizing and judging. People want to know that their partner takes them, warts and all, in order to feel comfortable planning a future together.

When you feel tempted to attack or find fault in your partner, remember the bigger picture and consider whether you want to build animosity or intimacy. No matter who you end up with, there will always be things you differ on. Part of being emotionally intelligent is having enough self-awareness to accept not just yourself but your spouse.

There is no such thing as a perfect marriage, but with the right attitude and relationship skills, you can create a beautiful life for you and your spouse.

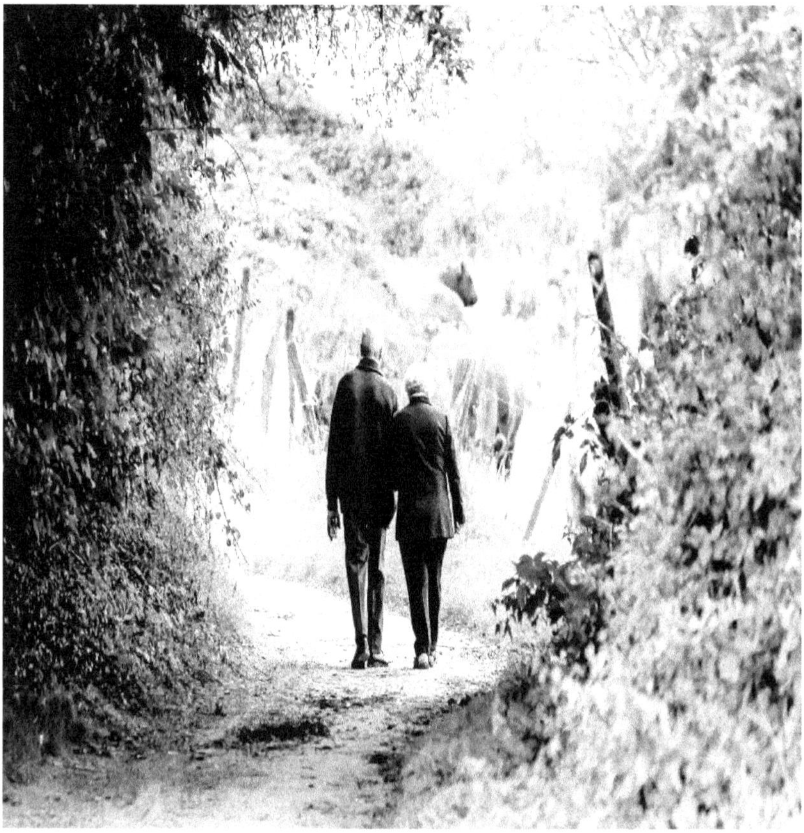

MICHELLE MILLER

CHAPTER 5:

How Emotions Affect Your Partner

Anger is a normal human emotion but a powerful one for that matter. It is essential to show frustration, hurt, disappointment, and annoyance with other people, including romantic partners. It is healthy for you to express anger when aggrieved by your partner, but you should do it in a controlled way.

When you express anger in unhealthy ways, you not only hurt your partner, but you also prevent yourself from conveying what exactly your problem with the situation you are in is. When you express anger in unhealthy ways, you also damage your relationship and make it impossible to salvage the once healthy, loving relationship you had with your partner.

Unmanaged anger also interferes with the quality of life that you lead as it affects your physical and mental health. To avoid all this, people can learn to control their anger. It is possible to manage anger in healthier ways. Here are a few ways to do so.

Once you're Calm, Express Your Anger

When your partner aggrieves you, it is crucial for you to let your anger subside before confronting him or her. This ensures that you do not say something that you cannot take back in the heat of an argument. If you cannot get away, try taking some deep breaths before you speak to the person.

Once you have your emotions under control, try to pinpoint exactly why you are upset or what exactly has set off the feelings that you are feeling. There are times when people get irritable because of other things that are happening in their lives.

You can begin by first telling the other person how difficult the situation is for you. By doing this, you disarm them and force them to show you empathy, which means that they also get distracted and forget about their anger.

Once both of you are calm, you can continue to explain the reason why you are upset and convey precisely what you are mad about. In the process, you should also talk about the emotions that you are feeling and how the other person's actions affect you. You should also focus on the current problem and not what mistakes your partner did in the past. If you, at any point, sense that your anger is beginning to rise, take a break. This gives you time to cool down and gather back your thoughts. You can also try counting one to ten as you practice some heavy breathing.

As you speak, be assertive but not hostile. Assertive communication involves stating only that which is factual without pointing accusations at the other person. As you point out an issue or issues, do not talk in a confrontational way, this can agitate the other party and cause them to react in anger. When you speak while calm, the other person is also able to listen and understand what you are saying.

Once you finish giving all your concerns, you should also provide the other party the same opportunity to state their case and the reason behind their actions. Try to see things from their perspective before you react in any way. Both of you should listen to one another keenly and repeat what you think the person means to gain a better understanding of each other.

Take A Timeout

Anger clouds people's judgment, so it is always a good idea to take time out of a confrontational situation to calm down. Timeout also gives the other person the same space to thinks about the issue at hand. Depending on the problem, the timeout can be as brief as a few minutes or can last even a few days. In a short timeout, people can practice some quick relaxing techniques. Some quiet time away, even in front of your partner, can give both of you time to cool down.

Counting to 100 can also help to take your mind off the situation and reset. After the timeout, you can begin to gather your thoughts calmly again. Anytime you sense like you are about to explode, you can get away and take a short walk outside or around the block to clear your head.

Exercise is also an excellent way to blow off steam. You can choose to go for a run or have an intense work out session at the gym. A high-energy consuming activity like boxing or martial arts, will distract and exhaust you to the point that you forget about your problem for a while.

Breathing exercises can also be beneficial, especially if coupled with an activity like yoga. However, you should look for something that you enjoy doing which you know can relax you.

You can also talk to a third party to vent out your anger and the frustrations you are undergoing in your relationship. This person can simply lend a listening ear, but they can also give a better perspective of the situation and reaffirm or try to change your perception of the case. The person can also help you to identify the exact cause of your feelings clearly.

Any activity that works to distract or calm you down like a shower, writing, listening to music is also worth a try.

Identify Possible Solutions

As you try to work out your issues with your partner, look for solutions to your problem instead of dwelling on the problem. If you find yourself always getting irritated with your partner because of a particular habit or situation, remove yourself from the trigger. Getting upset all the time does not help in dealing with life's frustrations.

You can decide to change your reaction towards other people's actions and in this case, your partner. Challenge your thinking and get down to the root cause of your anger. Identify the thought patterns that lead you to violence and change them. Make a decision to let go of situations that you cannot control as well as angry thoughts. You can also try to develop resilience in conditions that have the potential of making you angry.

Taking care of both your psychological and physical health on a daily basis also ensures that you are able to deal with people in the right way. People who are always stressed find themselves getting angry too often and too quickly. Daily exercises, even for a few minutes in a day, can help relax your body and burn out any stress that you might be experiencing. Meditation and deep breathing exercises also help in relaxing your body. Taking breaks to go for a holiday or enjoy a day out can help relax your mind.

Quality sleep also gives your body time to relax and rejuvenate in order to be able to handle any stressors or challenges that come your way. Experts advocate for at least 8 hours of sleep on a daily basis. Substance use and alcohol consumption also impair a person's ability to make sound decisions and reason, therefore avoid them if you can. You should also keep the consumption of high-energy drinks and caffeine at minimum levels to avoid being irritable.

Self-help books and self-help programs can also teach you anger management skills as well as healthier ways of expressing anger.

If you still find yourself incapable to control your anger with any of the above techniques and you keeping hurting your significant other, you can enroll for anger management classes to help you cope with your anger issues. Such levels advise and teach you healthier ways of managing your anger. Depending on how out of control your passion is, you can sign up for a one-off class, a weekend program, or a one-month program. Until you are able to manage your anger, you should seek all the possible help you can get.

Therapy is also an option. Psychologists can help people deal with other underlying issues that may contribute to them always feeling angry.

Do Not Hold a Grudge

Once you and your partner address a particular issue, you should close that chapter and move on. If you cannot agree with your partner, you can always agree to disagree and move on with life. You can also decide to ignore your partner's shortcomings and find a way of living with them. Another way to distract yourself is to focus on the good qualities your partner has. This takes your mind off things that irritate you.

Whatever way you choose to take, you should not keep dwelling on past issues, and neither should you keep bringing up past mistakes in future conversations or arguments with your partner. Holding grudges and reminding each other of one another's errors or listing each other wrongdoings will only escalate anger.

You should also practice forgiveness. Forgiveness has the power to heal you as well as the other party. When you forgive a person, they are likely to become conscious of their mistakes, and this can lead them to make a point of never repeating them again. Forgiveness also makes both parties let go of any negative feeling that they may have, which gives room for the healing process to begin.

Agreeing on healthy ways to resolve issues in your relationship also prevents couples from going at each other in the future. Couples should even know the difference between letting things go and suppressing their anger. Repressing anger is unhealthy in relationships. If you still feel resentment towards your partner, then chances are you are controlling some issues with your partner, and you need to be open about them to avoid exploding at your partner in the future.

Holding on to anger also affects the quality of life that you live and interferes with your physical, mental health, and overall well-being. Constant anger floods your body with stress hormones that increase heart rate and blood pressure. With time, recurrent passion can lead to heart disease, stroke, and psychological disorders.

Use Humor to Release Tension

You can use humor to change the mood in an otherwise tense room, but you should use it creatively, or it can end up doing more harm than good. You should never laugh at the other person's mistakes, their weakness, or their lack of sound judgment. Do not insult their intelligence or way of thinking. The other party may become upset and make a regrettable statement, which will only fuel the anger that both of you are currently dealing with.

You should avoid sarcasm or bad jokes that are insulting. Instead, try to direct most of the fun at yourself or at the situation. Self-deprecating humor, when dealing with anger, is used to remind the other people that everyone has flaws and can make mistakes, so they should not feel too bad about their wrongdoings.

When you use humor well, it can disarm the other party and bring his or her defenses down. Humor also prevents the two parties from hurting each other's feelings. It also reduces any tension between the two people, which creates a situation where both parties can begin to discuss the issue at hand and come to an agreement.

Silent humor can also help you cope with your anger. For example, you can draw a mental picture of your partner as a tiny mischievous cartoon devil with horns. You can choose to share the image with your partner or not, but in either case, the funny cartoon image can help distract you from your anger.

CHAPTER 6:

Fighting Less and Feeling Better

Ups and downs are part of relationship. Where there is love, there are conflicts, disagreement, and miscommunication as well. To minimize such events, try to avoid conflicts and do everything to gain your partner's love and attention. By doing so, you tend to bottle up your feelings and needs.

In this process, the bottle becomes full, and you realize that you are the only one in your relationship who is putting all the efforts to make the link right. When you feel alone and taken for granted, you will experience the hurt and tend to feel angry with your partner. This pattern will lead to more adverse circumstances and cannot make you happy. There is a better way for you to adopt.

With the help of compassionate self-awareness, you will be able to tolerate your emotions and learn to value yourself. You will become a positive person and will be able to take positive feedback from the caring and loving people in your life.

Consequently, you will be able to ignore the negative energy and will focus on the positive aspects of the relationship. This will help to maintain an intimate relationship with your partner. When you are expressive in a positive and enjoyable way, then healthy relationships are maintained. You will be able to know the coping mechanism to deal with the conflicts you face in the relationship.

Practices for support

Asking for support is the approach that helps to nurture the relationship. Asking what you want and need in a relationship helps to make the relationship stronger. Two basic practices help in this matter.

Always share your wants, needs, and feelings with your partner. Sharing thoughts makes both of you understand each other better. Ask concretely and directly to your partner what you need and want from them.

Sharing your thoughts and speculations with your partner is always a good idea. You both should know what you both are going through. When you both think and reason each other, you both will be on the same page, and resolve issues will be more comfortable.

If you don't like anything about your partner, then it's best to tell him rather than bottling up the feelings. There are specific tips and exercises that will help to resolve the issue and problems.

If you want to discuss some issues or problems, then pick a neutral time to time. Timing plays a vital part in the relationships. Dull time means that when you both are calm and relax. A problematic conversation will only go well when you both are ready to deal with it.

State and tell the problem shortly and succinctly. Get on the point, and explain how it does affect you. Cut out the unnecessary details.

Avoid the blame game. The blaming and pointing out the mistakes of your partner will make him/her defensive and emotionally distant. It only will make things complicated.

Show Empathy more

Other than sharing your feelings and desires, it is essential to understand your partner. Try to see the situation and interpret it according to the perspective of your partner. Empathize with your partner. In order to do this, you have to put your thinking and perspective sideline.

To minimize the conflicts, you and your partner need to share the feelings often and take them supportively and constructively. This approach promotes the sense of safety even in the times of vulnerable and personal conversations.

Whenever you need to do a difficult discussion, you need to prepare yourself to forgive and open up to compassion. For constructive results, you must talk to your partner with a strong intent of understanding him or her.

Always try to be a safe haven for your partner. Partners need to feel safe with each other to make the relationship successful. This can only take place when you try to focus on one partner at a time. When one partner is explaining the problem, then others should listen and understand it.

When your partner sees that you are listening and understanding it, then he/she will be less defensive and will able to tell you everything that is bugging him/her. Listen without interrupting your partner.

Try to stay on the same topic while discussing a difficult question. It is easy to jump from one topic to another and from example to the example but don't do it. This will lead to issues, and your partner will not be able to answer them coherently. When the subject tends to shift continuously, then problems are not usually solved.

Respect is the vital element of every relationship. Always be respectful to your partner when both are going through heated discussions. Work on your anger issues. Being angry and exploding on your partner will erode your relationship. Seek therapy to cope up with your anger issues.

Be more forgiving

Every relationship faces hard times. There always comes a point when one of the partners ends up hurting the other. It can happen in anger or in out of ignorance. Sometimes misunderstanding also becomes the reason for fights.

Feeling hurt is excruciating and is very difficult for people who have attachment-related anxiety. They tend to think that they are unworthy of love and are flawed. They flood their minds with sad and depressing.

This leads to self-criticism and makes the relationship destructive. When the person is hurt, he/she tends to recollect the bitter memories. If you are related to this, then let go of the past and learn to forgive. By adopting the habit of forgiveness, you will be able to overcome the anger that is hurting your heart and soul.

How to know that is your relationship really worth it?

If you are confused whether your relationship is healthy or not then you need to look into some aspects. Whether your partner is emotionally available or not? Is he/she is responsive towards your needs and wants? Are the care and value both sided?

Support and care are essential elements of a relationship. Is your partner supportive in difficult times? Is he/she there when you feel sad and upset? Encouraging each other to pursue interests is also very important. Is your partner there to support and appreciate you?

This not only implies to your partner, but you should also be there for your partner as well. It is not essential to have a perfect balance, but being comfortable with the balance you have is vital. If you want your needs and desires to be fulfilled, then be expressive.

But if the circumstances are bitter and suffocating and you decide you leave, then formulate a plan that will help you to walk away. There is some recommendation that will help you in this matter.

Construct a support system. Breakups are painful, and you eventually need someone to lean on and share your profound and sad feelings. Share your honest opinions and struggles with close people, so they completely understand you and support you when you decide to end your relationship.

One of the most challenging parts while leaving a relationship is that you need someone else to rely on and support you other than your partner. You use to count on your partner to lean on and for emotional support, but now you need new people. Having a support system will help to comfort you and will provide you with a secure and safe base.

It's okay to feel unhappy and even cry when you feel like. When you lose an essential person in your life, it is natural to feel sad and lonely. Do not push your feeling under the rug. It is terrible for you and will affect your mental health. Mourn and give yourself time. Time heals everything. There will be a time if that person will no longer matter to you.

Keeping reminding yourself that you are a valuable person. Always remember your strength and power. This can seem challenging to do in times of misery and sadness. Consider and pay attention to what your friends and family like and appreciate about you. They interact and socialize with you because they want you and like you..

Choose right and healthy ways of coping with your stress and sadness. When you are going through a problematic hard time, it is always an excellent option to take care of yourself. Make yourself busy with your favorite activities. You might want to go shopping, eat your favorite food or have sex. Then go for it. If doing such activities makes you less stressful, then do them right away.

You have to be smart and considerate about them. You can make the situation worse by buying Porsche or eating a lot of unhealthy food. Take part in the activities that will make you happy in longer terms. Eat healthy and fresh. Walk and exercise daily. Sleep and wake up the appropriate time. Perform spiritual rituals to cope up with negative thoughts and energy.

Do some meaningful work. Doing meaningful work brings a sense of engagement, and that is a beautiful cure when you feel disconnected. Volunteering work at shelters and schools bring a feeling of comfort and peace. Gardening is also beneficial in such cases. Helping others brings a sense of having value and connection. You feel happy and relaxed when you help others.

You should be prepared to go back to your partner. There are probabilities that at some point in your life, you will think about the idea of going back to your partner. The good times will appear in your mind, and you will think about the mistake as well. You might also think about doing things differently and better this time.

Before picking his calls or meeting him again, think about the difficult time you've faced while living with him. Remind yourself why you left him. Talk to your supportive friend and discuss the situation. Finally, when you conclude that leaving him was the right decision, then remind yourself that this weak moment will pass.

Forgive yourself if you try to go back to your partner. There are times when you feel sad and lonely, then you try to reach your old partner. You will see yourself in the arms of your partner before you realize what you've done. When you realize your mistake, then put an end to it. Everyone goes through weak moments, so try to forgive yourself.

Ending note

Hopefully, this has provided you with the guiding light to reshape your relationship. By making minor changes in your habits, you can create a path towards a healthy and happy relationship. Compassion and understanding each other is key to a successful relationship.

Consult a professional

The information provided that might not be enough for you. Maybe you still not able to cut off the patterns of the anxious attachment. In this scenario, consider couples therapy. If you are the one showing the toxic behavior then go for individual therapy.

Develop a secure base with your therapist so that you can share everything. Your therapist will guide you and assist you to cut off the problematic behaviors and negative self-perceptions. Find a therapist with whom you can emotionally connect because there will be a lot of heartfelt discussions that can only be done with the person you feel connected and safe.

MICHELLE MILLER

RELATIONSHIP THERAPY

CHAPTER 7:

Protecting Your Relationship from Affairs

Is your partnership descending? It is not easy to maintain a connection. Many couples face many bumps along the way to a healthy relationship. Until previously understood, these bumps may cause couples to step in the wrong direction leading to breakdowns or divorce. To avoid further harm, it is essential to understand many such relationship psychos beforehand. There are reasons why relationships fail, and when you know these causes in advance, you have a greater chance to save your troubled relationship. Although nobody can mention most the particular reason for the failure of relationships, we have listed the main reasons. So, what are these victims in relationships? Loss in contact or lack of coordination. One way to connect is to have good, regular communication between couples. Couples continue to fall away because of inadequate contact or loss of touch. Many issues with relationships begin with the lack of contact. Assuming you care what, your husband or wife feels that your partnership is dangerous. Misunderstandings and disagreements are often the product of your wife or girlfriend, not talking. If this occurs in your relationship, you will realize that this is one of the reasons that relationships fail and that you have to do something to improve communication. Not respectful of the aspirations, interests, and careers of each other. One of the reasons why marriages are collapsing is the difficulties between couples with jobs and aspirations. If two parties have conflicting interests and goals in a relationship and cannot agree or accept each other, the relationship will eventually fail. That is that two people have different goals and professions to seek, of course, so it is better to respect one another's desire or occupations to prevent pressure on the relationship in a relationship. It is safer for a husband or wife who trusts and respects the career of his or her wife or girlfriend to work with. Where it is not possible to achieve 100 percent appreciation, approval, and support, a friend or a girlfriend would at least be able to adapt and find a role with both their jobs and families. Sacrifices and sacrifices are inevitable. Obviously, they all will learn how to navigate their love-life careers. It's better to say than to do but not unlikely. There are couples who both excel in their careers while keeping a stable and healthy friendship.

Don't get along with friends and families of your girlfriend.

The friction with those nearest to the family or friend is one of the reasons why marriages collapse. Let's face it. You and your friend don't revolve around the world alone. You and your family can not exist without people like friends and relatives around you. Your friendship can not be compromised by not being close to your friend. If you and your partner's mother or best friend can't tolerate each other or live in a single room, the friendship can be difficult. Holiday meals and family gatherings will be unpleasant if the families and friends of your wife are not on good terms. It is best to get together with people important to your partner because you wish to build a healthy friendship with your partner. Things of life and luggage. Life baggage occurs, and complications as a relationship are formed may cause harm. A residual ex can spark envy, distrust, and resentment that will weaken your relationship today, so it's best to be sure that this is now in the past, and you are adamant about your relationship today. This is, therefore, inappropriate and damaging to equate your current relationship with your past relationships. Children and past marital complications can be daunting and can also influence your relationship, and you need to know how to handle with these issues to make the present relationship succeed. Another cause of relationship loss is the inability to manage issues and baggage in your life. Issues of capital. One explanation of why marriages collapse is financial problems. If not properly handled, money issues will ruin your relationship. Economic instability and hardship will eventually destroy a relationship. People or people who are overwhelmed by financial difficulties may become irritable, angry, violent, and cold towards their wives or friends, and they can eventually ruin a relationship. It is best to be frank about your financial situation from the outset, be open to discussing each other's investment patterns, money-sharing, and expenditures. With good and honest conversations, plans, and financial concessions, a tough couple can iron out problems and save their marriage.

Infidelity

Infidelity. It is difficult to sustain a relationship between two men, but involving a third person or abusing a girlfriend is a grenade that can ruin a relationship immediately. Infidelity is the greatest killer of marriages, and certain marriages cannot survive. Betraying your partner's trust is one of the key reasons why marriages collapse. There is no simple feeling to be replaced or cheated, which means that the cheated spouse or friend also leaves the relationship. Though there are people who can endure and make the relationship work again, it's best not to be infidel if you want a long-term partnership.

Disgusting behavior and behaviors.

While it is true that loving someone requires embracing all his or her flaws, there are also behaviors that can get irritating over time and may cause your partner one day to wake up and decide he or she needs to end the engagement. Only small issues like not putting the toothpaste cap on, not cleaning the bed, not putting the ground washing in the laundry, or getting the shoes and boots filthy in the house will be picked up because issues do not go well and your wife will break the relationship. Nagging, being a battle, arguing openly, insulting your wife or husband, calling or shouting disputes, hanging on to rancor, punching your spouse or partner when you're angry, tossing away too much or unfair anger, ignoring conversations about issues in your partnership, deception or dishonesty to your spouse or partner is a bad thing! Being in a relationship should help partners to be happier people and not get worse because it is easier to improve and create a good relationship than to have negative habits that will ruin the relationship in the end.

Things are a ritual in your relationship.

The fire and the desire in the relationship could die because you were too relaxed or content to have a routine rather than an act of love. You're looking more like family or friends than like lovers. Very relaxed with one another extracts suspense and passion from the relationship and makes it predictable and repetitive. When partners do the same thing over and again, as people and as friends, they stopped through. Shake your routine and spice you up. You can do different things and desires to evolve as an individual, and there are things that you can do to bind together. It is important to encourage your husband or companion to do his own thing or to enjoy the company of his or her mates, but it is also important to spend time alone with each other on frequent occasions or holidays in order to interact and build new enjoyable memories.

Intimacy and sex are absent.

Life can be too chaotic and difficult for partners to end up being too distracted or depressed for love or sex that is not appropriate in a relationship. Couples have to interact closely mentally and physically, and sex is the perfect way to do that. During a long-term relationship, sex will dry up, and partners appear to have fewer sex over the years. Couples are meant to discourage this. One of the causes why marriages fail is lack of affection or sexual dissatisfaction. When people avoid having sex, they appear to be isolated and withdrawn and are vulnerable to unfaithfulness. It is best for couples to lead a healthy sex life to keep the relationship alive and exciting. Although having your partner closely with you through daily sex is vital, couples should be aware of the pressure on your wife or girlfriend not to participate in frequent intercourse. There are studies that suggest that having daily intercourse once a week is acceptable and enough to sustain the romantic relationship between partners. There are many barriers to doing this, such as job pressures, pressures of your daily life, caring for children, and the situation in which you are not sexually mood yet, like all other problems in your relationship, the amount and scheduling of sex should be addressed and prepared. Intimate sexual connections are important in any marital interaction, and if partners do not have enough sex links, they have to do something to address this issue in order to save the relationship.

CHAPTER 8:

Rescue Broken Relationship

As time passes by, you and your partner might go through many difficult moments. The fact that you are still together proves that you both learned to navigate the difficult waters of commitment. But now, after so long, you feel you have fallen into a rut. You feel the relationship is pretty monotonous. It's not that you have unresolved issues, it's just that the routine has finally set in.

So, what can you do to preserve the flame of love alive? How can you help your partner be excited about the relationship again? Is there anything that you can learn to turn love back on?

Like the First Time

Do you still recall how the relationship used to be in the past? Do you have fond memories of when you began dating? Then use that to your favor. Treat your spouse the same way you treated him when you began dating. You may still remember how many details were involved in a date.

You were kind and loving with him. Why don't you attempt to talk to him with that same energy and excitement you had when you first got together? You liked showering with presents and letters. Why don't you bring back all of those special actions again? You liked hanging out together alone or even with friends. Why not try to do the same again?

Letters and presents help your partner realize that you still care about the relationship and him after so much time. Don't think that they are too cheesy! They might be just what your partner needs. You don't need to make them so elaborate. You only need to have him in mind.

Going out on a date in itself is an exciting idea. You can plan a date at the same place you had your first date. If that's not possible, you can think of a restaurant, park, or any other place that your partner might enjoy. Planning something together will also help you be united. Teaming with some friends will make it even more exciting and funny.

Don't limit your thoughts to just what you used to do. You can also try something new that you've been thinking about for a while. Even if it seems something that your partner might not like, why not inviting him to see if he's also interested in joining with you?

Affection Is Still Important

Stress is still an issue that many of us have to deal with on a daily basis. Affection can relieve that stress. Showing affection is still important as it was during the first days of the relationship.

Show consideration for your partner's good qualities. Notice how your partner displays his perseverance when going to work, his effort when helping in the home, his determination to commit to the relationship. His good qualities are what endeared him to you.

Strive to show how much you value his good qualities by telling him how you feel about them. Men also need to be told how valued they are in a relationship. You can have his good qualities in mind when congratulating him. The point is that you need to acknowledge these good qualities and be truly grateful for them. Be observant.

In the coming week, you can try to put effort into noticing what your partner does to add positively to the relationship. Even things that you may possibly take for granted. After much time, there's the risk of you taking your partner for granted or the other way around. You can easily start to focus, not on what he's doing, but on what he's not. Never underestimate how words of appreciation can have an effect on your partner. If you don't start feeling appreciation for your partner, it's easier for him to feel drawn to someone who does.

Take the Initiative

You should also be willing to take the first step towards keeping love alive. You may think that your partner also has to show some initiative since he's also part of the relationship. But your partner might be thinking the same!

Take the initiative by communicating how you really care about the relationship and your partner. Do nice things for him. Your partner might react in a very pleasant way. But even if at first, he may not seem to react in the way you expected, don't give up. It might take a little bit extra effort or consistency for him to see that you really want their love to turn back on.

One issue that refrains many people from taking the initiative is infidelity. If this has occurred to you, you know how difficult it is to regain trust. You may have felt his unfaithfulness was blown to the relationship. But there are ways you can take if you feel you want to give the relationship a second chance.

MICHELLE MILLER

CHAPTER 9:

Some Example of Conversation and Dialogue in Different Day Moments

What does a relationship defined by good communication look like? Here are eight habits that couples who communicate well practice all the time. We'll give examples of the habits in action when relevant:

They express their appreciation for each other

Good communication is about staying in sync not only about hard things and conflicts, but also about positive feelings. Couples who communicate well are always showing their love and appreciation for each other. This can include thoughtful texts, little love notes, compliments, and nice gestures. Even on busy days when distractions abound, an emotionally-healthy couple always remembers to show each other some love, even if it seems small. This habit nurtures the security of the relationship, and both people never feel underappreciated or neglected.

Examples:

Text your partner "I love you" in the morning, so it's the first thing they see when they wake up.

Bring your partner flowers, their favorite snack, or a movie when you know they've had a bad day.

When your significant other does something around the house like cooking dinner, doing the dishes, or putting the kids to bed, say, "Thank you."

Send your partner a song that makes you think of them.

Tell your partner, "You look really good today."

Learn your partner's love language, and work on expressing your feelings towards them in a way they really connect with.

They make positivity a priority

Studies support the idea that intentionally working on positive thinking and reducing negative self-talk can actually make a person happier. The same applies to relationships. Couples, who actively make the effort to say positive things, especially during arguments, are happier and enjoy stronger relationships. A relationship with lots of negative energy is bound to make one or both of the people depressed, cynical, and frustrated. Instead of a source of happiness, the relationship becomes a source of stress. If the couple commits to being more positive, seeing the silver lining as much as possible, and expressing it out loud, both people get a boost and feel more secure.

They physically connect

Physical connection doesn't mean sex, though regular sex is often a sign of a healthy relationship. Besides that, other physical contact is a sign of good communication and can help improve communication. Whether it's hand-holding, back rubs, kissing, etc., physically connecting allows a couple to communicate without words. They get to know each other's nonverbal language on a deeper level.

Examples:

When you're watching a movie with your partner, sit with your legs touching.

Be physically close, like cuddling, without expecting sex.

When you're going for a walk, hold hands.

If your partner had a hard day and doesn't want to talk about it, offer to give them a back rub, foot rub, etc. instead.

When you're lying in bed relaxing, give your partner a head rub.

Always kiss and hug "Hello" and "Goodbye."

They listen to each other

We've talked a lot about active listening, especially in arguments, but listening outside of conflicts is a sign that a couple is communicating well. A couple who listens to each other will remember what their partner likes and doesn't like what they've asked them to do, and how they feel in certain situations. Neither feels like they always have to remind their partner about things, like chores or schedules. The same applies to body language; both people make an effort to notice nonverbal cues, so their partner doesn't feel that they always need to vocalize a feeling. They understand each other with a simple look or a touch, or at least pick up that their partner is trying to tell them something.

They validate each other's feelings

In a relationship built on empathy, the two people will make validation of the other's feelings a top priority. This means not getting defensive and making excuses for behavior or words they don't like. Instead, there's a lot of active listening, putting themselves in their partner's shoes, and respecting what they feel. Even if they don't completely understand where their partner is coming from or feel what they're feeling, they never dismiss those emotions. The mere fact that their partner is feeling something is enough. In healthy relationships with good communication, this validating is a two-way street.

Examples:

While your partner is talking, maintain eye contact and give encouraging sounds or words, like "Hmm mm," "I see," and "I get that."

Direct your body towards them, instead of away, and keep it open, so they feel like you are really there in the moment with them. If your partner likes physical touch, hold their hand or rub their shoulder while they're talking about something that makes them emotional.

Ask follow-up questions, so your partner knows you're still interested and committed to really understanding what they're saying.

If you notice your partner acting differently, take the time to ask them if something is wrong, and if they want to talk about it. This shows you are observant and not dismissing what you see.

If they seem insecure or embarrassed about their feelings, validate them by saying something like, "Of course you feel that way" or "I would feel the exact same way, too."

They aren't afraid to be honest and vulnerable

Honesty and vulnerability are essential in a healthy relationship. With couples who have good communication, opening up to each other isn't scary. The relationship is a place of safety, not judgment, so both people feel comfortable talking about anything and being themselves. The significance of being honest and vulnerable with one's identity can't be overstated. This gets to the root of good communication and the positive power it can have over a relationship. When communication includes empathy, validation, and no judgment, both people in the couple feel secure in them as well as in the actual relationship. This manifests as honesty and vulnerability.

They are flexible and willing to compromise

Seeing conflicts as puzzles to be solved together is huge for a relationship. When communication is good, both people are more flexible and willing to compromise. They aren't stuck on a specific resolution they believe is the best one; they're open to their partner's input and finding a solution that makes both people happy. Arguments are much less likely to get really heated and emotional when this is a priority.

They are able to take accountability for themselves

Couples who communicate well are not afraid to say two simple words: "I'm sorry." This phrase is short, but incredibly powerful. It's a manifestation of an ability to take responsibility for one's own actions and mistakes. It takes humility, which is a vital trait in any relationship. People able to recognize when they're wrong and apologize have let go of the need to always be in the right, or always "win." They can humble themselves before their partner and themselves. This type of "I'm sorry" isn't just skin-deep, either; it's a true apology that means the person is committing to being better in the future. A relationship between people willing to apologize and really mean it will last way longer and be much stronger than relationships where that isn't a practice.

Examples:

When your partner points out something that annoys them, say something like, "Oh, I didn't know you felt that way, I'm sorry."

If you say something during an argument that you regret, come back to your partner and apologize, saying something like, "I feel really bad about what I said earlier, and I want to say I'm sorry. Next time we're arguing, I'm going to try really hard not to let that happen again."

If you can, be specific about the mistake(s) you made, saying something like, "I wasn't being respectful of your feelings, and I'm sorry;" "I know you don't like it when I raise my voice, so I'm sorry for doing that;" and "I'm sorry I forgot to take out the trash this morning, I'll be sure to remember tomorrow."

CHAPTER 10:

Significant Habits of Good Relationships

Habits have a significant effect on your relationship. When it comes to having a good relationship, there are certain behaviors that can have a strong and positive impact. It's essential for you to be conciseness when forming routines, especially for your relationship.

Significant Habits of Good Relationships

You need to make an effort every single day to perform them, so they become part of the routine to you.

Always show respect

Showing respect for your partner is a habit worth making, as it is an ingredient necessary to create a happy, safe, and long-lasting relationship. You express your affection, appreciation, and comfort when you show respect for your partner. If you show contempt, you convey that your spouse is not acknowledged. Respecting your partner, despite variations, is all about valuing them for who they are. You may have a other view on life, but that doesn't mean you can neglect and put down your friend.

If experiencing conflicts, make sure you respect the disagreements between your spouses. This does not allow you to offend your partner in front of friends and family or in public. Also, show respect, especially when you're in disagreement. There will be moments when you disagree on a topic, and it's going to be how you approach this problem as a team that's going to make the world difference.

Go for a stroll with your friend

This is a ritual formed by a husband and where they find a deeper connection in their relationship. If you love nature and spend time with your mate, make it a habit to walk— either in the mornings before beginning your day, or at night. For example, husband and wife walk on Sunday mornings and in the evenings. It's a mental decision which they make to go out together every day. It encourages communication, fresh air access, and quality time. Once you develop this routine, the body may actually want to go out. It is noticed this with couples when they made it a habit to walk at night, and on Sunday mornings, their bodies became ready to spend the quality of time. Walking with your partner also promotes good fitness, and can be as easy as walking up and down the block. Decide how long and how often you'd like to walk with your partner; the major thing is to being on the same page and making sure you make the mental decision to build this routine together.

In the night time turn off the television and be with your friend

How can you relate to your partner when there's always television? There is no bond established when you both look at the television screen endlessly in the evenings. Take the mental decision to turn off the television at night, and spend time together in quality. You may be able to snuggle and watch a movie sometimes but avoid watching TV most evenings.

Take the time to chat with your friends about their day and how they're doing. The behavior causes love and attachment.

Snuggle up and chat on the sofa with your partner; talk to each other and what you two can do to strengthen your relationship. Whether it's preparing for the next holiday or your next date night, there'll always be something to consider. Focus on developing your relationship and discuss issues you need to tackle.

In the morning, take some tea with your friend. This simple gesture indicates a great deal to my husband. He loves drinking coffee and shows morning love and affection to get it to him. If your partner likes to drink tea in the morning, and through this act of service, create that habit, Express love. When you bring a cup of tea to him, it shows you care, and this is one way you can show love to him. Wake up a few minutes earlier so you can spend some quality time together with your partner before going on the job. This is an easy yet powerful habit of happy relationships.

Share positive attributes about your partner to others

'Habit of sharing positive attributes about your partner can help the relationship deepen. Alternatively, sharing negative attributes about your partner will only build a tall wall between you two. Would you know a couple who always argue with friends in public and show negative characteristics about each other? This is a bad habit that inevitably wrecks a friendship. This destructive behavioral pattern causes distrust, disconnection, and disrespect. Get used to projecting positive attributes for others. An optimistic behavioral trend produces respect, appreciation, and devotion.

Scroll down to read the article Are you reaching your full potential?

Take the life-potential evaluation of Life hack and get a personalized report based on your unique strengths, and find out how to start living your entire life and achieve your full potential.

Reconnect throughout the day

We have such busy routines that it can be the last priority to communicate with your partner throughout the day, but if you want a healthy, long-lasting relationship, reconnecting-connecting-connecting with your partner throughout the day is important. It is as easy as sending a romantic text or calling your partner on the way home during your lunch break. This habitude is meant to keep your partner linked and focused. You can still take the time to send a text message or send your friend a phone call, even if you have a hectic schedule. Render yourself artistic. Think about ways you can reconnect-connected-connect with your partner all day.

Take time to think

Take time to think out how you feel loved most and how your partner feels the most affection by looking at these 5 love languages. Imagine having a tank of love inside of you. Your love tank is filled up each time your partner speaks your love language. Your love tank runs low each time your partner doesn't convey your love language. When it comes to important behaviors of happy relationships, establishing the habit of speaking the love language of your partner on a daily basis creates in your relationship, passion, affection, and warmth.

Cooking and cleaning

The cooking with your partner is always much more fun. I know when John helps me; I enjoy cooking a lot more.

Cooking together builds intimacy, communication, and love; creating and eating food when you are with your partner becomes an intimate act. I express my love by cooking and eating with my husband (with TV off), which creates a deeper bond between us. This is a big opportunity to spend time together in quality. If you prefer cooking or your partner, make it a habit that the other person cleans. John and I have a habit of cleaning up afterward whenever I cook, and vice versa. It shows appreciation for my cooking when John cleans after I cook and that he values me. It is important that you always love and respect your spouse, even if the cleaning of the dishes is as easy as that. It's nice to know John appreciates the love I put in my cooking, and it's a sign of love-affection to want to do the dishes Become mentally stronger!

Become Stronger

Every day shows love for your partner welcomes to your partner! It is just as simple as this. Whatever love you want to show in your relationship, do it. Do this on a single day. It's about showing your gratitude to your partner when it comes to important traditions of happy relationships. This can be leaving a love note at the end of the day before going to work or taking flowers home. It goes back to the love language of your mate. Find the language of love for your partner and show your gratitude for your partner through their language of love. If your partner feels valued by quality of time, make sure "turn off" and focus your attention on your partner when you get back home from work. Sit down on the couch, and be with your partner. Whichever language your partner loves, make sure you speak the same language. Make it a habit of showing your partner appreciation every single day.

Working together as a team towards objectives (short-and long-term)

A happy relationship focuses on short-and long-term objectives. Unhappy couples have nothing in their lives to look forward to. Focus on creating, establishing, and attaining goals within your relationship. Happy couples have ambitions, small as well as large. Follow this template setting target, and start cultivating your partner link.

Spend quality time

In the morning to show and be with a partner before beginning the day. Surely this practice starts to rob your relationship and the bond you have with your partner. We have such hectic schedules that it is even more important to take the time to talk with your partner in the mornings. Reflect and understand what brought you two together. It's easy to allow tension, anger, and distractions to get in the way of a happy relationship, but when you take the morning time to love and appreciate your partner, you're building a routine that's filled with comfort, affection, and care.

RELATIONSHIP THERAPY

CHAPTER 11:

Cultivating New and Healthy Relationships

Allow Vulnerability

One of the first thing of being in love is when you become suddenly very vulnerable. This vulnerability is present in your feelings, longings, and fear. When you start to fall in love, your heart will open to your partner. You begin to entrust your heart to your partner and show yourself to them, as you do only with very close people.

You may be worried about being vulnerable, especially if you've had bad experiences in relationships. When you are open and vulnerable, those issues that were otherwise suppressed by you can come into your consciousness in new relationships. Therein lies the fear that is often justified - but don't allow it to scare you away. New relationships are just that - new. Judging them based on past experience isn't fair to you or them.

True Beauty Comes from Within

A different sure sign of falling in love is the capacity to see the inner beauty of a person. At the beginning of a romantic relationship, much attention is paid to the exterior.

Over time, as the feelings of love blossom, you will see the true personality of your counterpart - their true inner beauty. At this thought, the saying "love makes you blind" is confirmed.

The Family

If you are committed with someone who one day asks you if they can meet your family, you can be sure that the person is falling in love with you or even deeply in love with you. The family is very important and getting to know the family of your partner makes the seriousness of the relationship clear. If you have been introduced to both the family and the circle of friends, you can be sure that the feelings of your partner are genuine.

Selflessness

The last and clearest sign of falling in love is pure selflessness. This happens when you or your partner put the needs of both of you in the foreground and subordinate your own needs.

A one-sided relationship does not help you. Even if you feel that you cannot live without your partner and love them beyond measure, if both of you aren't on the same page, the relationship will go nowhere. Here are some ways to cultivate meaningful and healthy relationships in the early stages:

1. Be clear about what you need

On your first date, before your entrées have even touched the table, the both of you should examine what you truly want for from a relationship. Be clear about what you are looking for. In this way, you will both be on the same page from the get-go. The idea of this can be alarming, but in any case, learn to expect the unexpected. They just might disclose similar wishes.

2. Talk about your dreams and wants

Would you like to build a small home and live off the grid? Take a year off to travel the far reaches of the planet? Share these dreams with a potential partner. Discover whether your objectives compliment another person's and if you have overlapping interests. It's extreme more fun to find out about someone when discussing dreams rather than general hobbies.

3. Have wide open communication

If something is disturbing you, do not hold it inside because of a paranoid fear of what may occur if you bring it up. Address the issues and have quiet, caring discussions to see the two points of view. It's such a much-needed refresher to know you both want to cooperate to discuss anything before something turns into a major issue. It's not about being right or wrong — it's about the two individuals working together.

4. Accept each aspect of yourself

If you don't accept yourself for who you are, why should someone else? There may be aspects of yourself that you don't like or would change if you could, but they aren't important. The sooner you can look at yourself and be happy with everything you see, the better of you'll be in life and in love.

5. Manage stress together

Stress will never leave — it's the means with which we handle it that matters. When your partner is disturbed or stressed, be there for them to vent to. Don't attempt to fix it all; rather, allow them to work through the problem as they wish to. All they want is to know that you're there.

6. Offer thanks regularly

Having a mutual appreciation for each other is massively beneficial. It's also important to give thanks for other aspects of your life. Grateful people are happy people, and a couple that is grateful for each other is better able to build a healthy relationship.

7. Talk about the big things

Talk about everything, from moving in together to building a home, from children to funds and family travels. Don't wait until these events are here - get a head start and begin discussing your expectations early. Many couples dread this sort of talk for fear that their partner will not agree with them. But the sooner you uncover differences, the sooner you can begin working to come to a compromise.

8. Have dinner together

People bond over shared food, so make the most of it! Put on some romantic music, dress nicely, and connect. The meal almost doesn't matter as much as the full, undivided attention of the both of you.

9. Be available

When you need your partner, do you want them to be available, or will you be able to deal with them prioritizing something else over you? If you wish to be put first, start by putting them first. Be ready to come to their aid if they need you. You don't have to drop everything on a whim, but ensure you know what you're going to do if they ever let you know that they're going through a crisis and could use your support. Your actions in their time of need set the tone for the future.

10. Work toward being a better partner

If you're like most people, there are things you wish to change about yourself. Some of these desired changes can positively affect your relationship. By striving to be the best person you can be for the one you love, you're also becoming better for yourself.

A solid relationship is two people cooperating to build a life together. A solid relationship is somewhat similar to a trinity, two people make something more profound and superior to themselves, yet they are still themselves. For a relationship to develop, you should likewise develop as an individual and not lose yourself.

Enjoy Being in Love

Are you newly in love? Then you are probably feeling great right now! I have a few good tips for you to help you get the most out of your love and keep it strong for a long time.

Additionally, talks should not be neglected despite the romance. Celebrate your shared romance, because it gives strength for less good times and creates a great common ground. Conversations are just as important as experiences, though. Share your feelings with your partner and give them the opportunity to get to know you as well.

Tips for a Long and Happy Relationship

The following tips will help keep your relationship healthy for a long time.

Avoid nagging

Any kind of criticism of your partner's idiosyncrasies either leads to quarrels or makes you feel annoyed. Psychologists are of the opinion that criticizing your partner in many cases is a projection of your own shortcomings.

Rather than frustrating your partner with complaints, you might think about what makes you uncomfortable about their traits, and work on reframing your viewpoint.

Understand that your partner is their own personality

You must accept the fact that your partner is an individual with a unique personality. Nevertheless, we subconsciously and sometimes consciously treat our partner as if they are an extension of ourselves. Accept that your partner is a being with a character of their own with appropriate feelings and perceptions, opinions, and experiences.

Accept your partner's mistakes

To err is human. Your partner is not an angel, so they are bound to make mistakes. When that happens, learn to forgive and do not capitalize on the mistakes of your partner.

Above all, there are lots of things we cannot change about our partner, so rather than grumbling or nagging, why not learn to live with them? Small mistakes are not a matter of life and death. If you find it difficult to cope with your partner's idiosyncrasies, call their attention to it, and explain yourself in a polite manner. Don't blame or accuse, simply discuss.

Do Not Tolerate Destructive Behavior

Learn to tolerate your partner as long as their behavior is not destructive or life threatening. If you discover that your spouse or partner is very aggressive, don't paint over the situation and learn to "cope." Your safety is important. If you ever feel threatened, don't stick around to try to keep the peace. Get out.

Take Emotional Time Out

Our skin needs sunlight for the production of vitamin D. However, prolonged and frequent sunbathing can cause life-threatening skin cancer.

So, the right dosage is important. This applies to relationships, as well.

Of course, we need each other to fill our lives with happiness. But we also need emotional time-outs in which one does not think of the other person or is involved in the planning of joint activities.

Meet alone with friends or join a club alone to develop yourself as a person. If both partners experience something different from each other, there is also something to talk about at the dinner table.

Be Faithful and Sincere

Unless you have made other arrangements, share a duvet exclusively with your romantic partner and no one else. To be deceived and cheated on by a close person is one of the cruelest experiences that can happen to anyone. If you really love your partner, you will spare them that experience. Ultimately, faithfulness builds such deep trust that you can't replace or fix it once broken.

Address Problems

No partnership is in complete harmony. You are two different personalities with thoughts and feelings. A relationship, no matter how much love and dedication you feel for each other, is always the result of many compromises. Therefore, face critical matters head on rather than waiting for the other to address the problem. Couples therapists unanimously agree that communication is the key to a long, healthy, and fulfilling relationship.

Appreciate What You See in Your Partner

The first infatuation does not disappear forever, most of the time it gives way only to another feeling, that of deep attachment and love.

You have found that you can rely on your partner, that they think of you, and in so many ways suit you perfectly. That you as a couple harmonize and like to be with one another.

MICHELLE MILLER

CHAPTER 12:

How Do We Work Together

It might seem impossible to work together at this specific point in time, but you can start answering this question by remembering when you last worked together.

Look at the timeline you made and recall the ways you worked together to resolve problems. That should tell you what you should do now.

The ways you worked together need not be deep. For instance, it could be as simple as the time you two worked on a garden together. It could be the way you each do your part for Thanksgiving every year.

It will you figure out how you can work together on some of the specific problems in your relationship.

When you worked together for Thanksgiving, who did what? What problems did you run into while you did this task together, and how did it turn out? What did you two do to make things work out the way they did, for better or for worse?

From here, expand to more everyday ways you already work together without even thinking about it as working together. That includes chores, financial planning, and the like. As you found out in the "How do we relate to each other?" question, we don't always work together in ways that we acknowledge in marriage, because all the things we do together are so intertwined into our daily lives that it just feels normal. But the more you reflect, the more in touch you will be with how you are already working together.

The problem is, when we are working with our partner on more challenging tasks, we are more aware of the fact that we have to work together. If we aren't aware of that, we will make a lot of mistakes.

We like to think that in a previous life, we've been very good at showing our partner how to do something even though in this one, we have to do a lot of things in a row that we aren't very good at. Sometimes we know what we are doing, but other times we don't. It is the problems that we do not see coming that make it harder to work together in a productive way.

We want our significant other to admit to their crimes — and part of starting again is admitting fault and apologizing. We may want to think that we couldn't have done anything wrong. As we've been trying to be more aware of throughout, though, none of us are perfect, neither you nor your spouse.

You won't abruptly become more perfect because you are pretending to be. All you are doing is being dishonest with yourself in a way that is extremely counterproductive to working through your issues together. You are better off being yourself in all of your flaws, so you can both at least be open about your flaws and work with them.

Now that you have thought of a time that you two worked together for Thanksgiving and times you work together every day; the next exercise will be about practicing working together right now.

It may be an exceedingly simple task, but it will test how well the two of you can work together so you can (1) get the task done and (2) do it without bickering too much.

Together, find a new meal that you can eat tomorrow. The catch is that it does have to be new, so you can't just say you'll make one of the dishes you cook all the time and be done with it. You need to find a new recipe in a cookbook or somewhere else and then make a plan to get all the ingredients, determine who will do what, and come to an agreement about all of this.

As an extra challenge, I want the two of you to try to get this done in just fifteen minutes. Start a timer as soon as you can, and then get started. When you are done, come back to the workbook so you can have a discussion.

Read on only after you have already done the exercise. Then, ask yourselves some quick questions. What went wrong? What went right?

You should also ask yourselves if you met the two requirements, which were to get the task done and to do it amicably.

Start off by each telling the other what you did right. You want this to be a positive exchange before a negative one. They want to hear good things from you first, and that's a principle that you should apply throughout these exercises: whenever possible, try to let the positive come before the negative.

Only after you cover the positive should you move on to what could improve. Take note of how I didn't say what went wrong, but what could improve. This way, even the negative things sound more positive. It may not seem like it would make a big difference, but it really does, because negative and positive attitudes are contagious.

When you and your spouse learn that you can each work through your disputes without it being filled with negative emotions, you will stop dreading it so much, and you'll get excited to work through things together because you'll know that it doesn't have to be so bad.

It might sound like this couldn't possibly be the case right now, but if you give the methods outlined in this workbook a real shot, you'll see that they really work. It's just that you need to be able to imagine how things could be different.

Sometimes, we lose sight of why we even try to work with our spouse. We may even have thoughts like it isn't worth the pain to work with someone else.

But remember that everything in life comes with benefits and drawbacks. It might sound like it would be better to be alone, and it might seem like everything would be easier. Of course, in some respects, everything would be easier just for not having to work with someone else anymore. But there is more to it than that.

When we have the opportunity to have a spouse who will be there for times that would be difficult alone, we shouldn't take that for granted.

No one can deny that sharing and working with other people can be harder than doing things on our own sometimes. When we get frustrated working through the same problems every day with our spouse, we can't help but think that we would be able to handle it better alone.

Try this. We have issues that we don't think are serious, but affect every aspect of our relationship. What do we think is important to us in our relationship? What do we believe is critical in creating a strong marriage?

But how can we achieve this understanding of what really matters to each of us? By taking the same observations that we used, to begin with. The same questions that we asked before. To turn on the kind of self-talk that will improve our relationship, we must see ourselves through the eyes of our spouse.

But the truth is, you don't even appreciate all the things that are having someone there for you helps with, not the least of which being sheer emotional support. On the surface, it may seem like a small thing, but having someone there for you feels much different from when you are going through hard life experiences such as job loss, the passing of someone we love, and so on all by ourselves.

We don't even think to appreciate having our spouse there when these things happen, because, by their very nature, these things are still so rough to go through.

But try to remember that it would be harder without them there. Try to remember that the most important thing they do for you is just being there. Do all you can to be there for them, too?

MICHELLE MILLER

CHAPTER 13:

Practice Empathy

The heart of a romantic relationship is empathy, according to Carin Goldstein, a licensed marriage and family therapist. It is the heart of all human relationships, but we have a bias towards romantic relationships.

It is through empathy that we can understand and maintain the relationships that we build. Compassion, or in the words of the Dalai Lama, Emotional Awareness, is our ability to recognize the emotion not only within ourselves but also in other people. When you are empathetic, you may get to experience emotional resonance. Emotional resonance is when you encounter another person's emotions as your own, to the extent that you feel their pain and pleasure.

When you and your partner get comfortable around each other after dating for a long time, you will find that, with time, familiarity sets in. So, you begin not to take their emotions as seriously as you did at the start of the relationship. Familiarity breeds contempt, they say. When you stay with someone for so long, you tend to become accustomed to their presence. So, you no longer put effort into understanding them. Because of this, you then grow distant from your partner. You do not put effort into communicating with them, and as such, intimacy suffers, you break the trust, love becomes an illusion. All this is the result of a lack of empathy. And it is what breaks a lot of relationships.

According to psychologists, we will often experience different types of empathy;

Affective Empathy. This type of empathy involves us understanding the other person's feelings and then responding appropriately.

Somatic Empathy. Somatic empathy is the kind of compassion that is more pervasive. When someone experiences somatic empathy, the individual gets to feel, physically, the distress the other person is going through. If the other person feels pain, you also feel pain.

Cognitive empathy. This kind of understanding involves you understanding the other person's state of mind and what is going through their mind when they act the way they do. You can put yourself into their minds and understand what would make them make the choice they do. You may not agree with how they react, but you put yourself in their shoes for a better perspective.

To be a better empath, you need to have a great understanding of all three and know how to experience them with regards to the situation.

So, how do you build empathy in your relationship?

How to Build Empathy for a Happy Relationship

Become More Self Aware

As with any other situation that relates to how we can improve our relationships, self-awareness is the top priority. When you are open with yourself about your emotions and feelings, you will then become more in tune with who you are as a person and how you deal with these emotions. When you come to terms with how you deal with your feelings and work to improve them, you will then begin to feel the emotional resonances of others around you.

So, to become more empathetic, begin by going deep within yourself. This understanding of who you are helps you become intimate with who you are and then work on how you build intimacy and trust with others.

Be Vulnerable

We are all scared of being vulnerable. Have you ever gotten into a relationship, but because you are afraid of the other person hurting you, you hold back. Since you view the other person as being capable of destroying you, you also become cold and callous. These are defensive measures we often take when we do not want to be vulnerable. When you put a wall around yourself so that you are not sensitive, what happens is that you also do not consider other people's feelings. In this case, you become cold and distant to your partner, thus breaking down communication between the two of you.

But when you begin to make yourself open up about yourself emotionally deliberately, you will find that you also become more receptive to other people's emotions. In this case, when you take the time to open yourself up to your partner, you give clear indications that you trust them. In return, they will also share their feelings with you intimately, bringing the two of you closer. Even if they do not reciprocate and hurt you, you come to understand that it has nothing to do with you but with them. So, you let go, knowing that you are doing your best to become a more emotionally intelligent person.

Listen to Understand

Active listening is one marker of empathy and emotional intelligence. It is what brings you closer to others and helps you build a rapport with others.

When you listen, you gain a deeper understanding of what other people are going through. You learn about their emotional state of being. What they feel and how they feel about things becomes your issue too. You do not need to agree with what they are saying, but you understand where they are coming from. Active listening is how you develop emotional resonance, which is what leads to a growth of intimacy with your partner.

When you are empathetic, you do not center your feelings if your partner is talking about their passion. Here, you sit back and listen. You try to understand them, and they, in turn, will make the same effort to follow you.

Consider Your Partner's Emotional Truth

Sometimes, your partner might not express how they feel directly to you. But to be empathetic is to be emotionally intelligent. You should contact their emotional resonances, either through reading their body language or their tonal variations and choice of words. Then, show that you understand them by expressing the feeling that they are having a hard time communicating. 'I take this to mean that you are angry/saddened/hurt by what I've said.' When they affirm, do not be defensive. Apologize and make a point of taking into consideration their desire for you to change.

When you do this consistently, you will find it become easier to feel your partner's pain. Empathy takes time, but when you make deliberate efforts to building it, you will improve the dynamics of your relationship.

Ways in Which Empathy Improves Your Relationship

You Humanize Your Partner

When you practice empathy deliberately, you take note of your partner's humanity. When you stay with someone for long, you tend to overlook their humanity. Dehumanizing the other person is why many relationships crumble; because the couple forgets about each other's humanity.

But when you begin to practice empathy, you never let go of the knowledge that your partner is a person that deserves your compassion and understanding. This way, you communicate better with them, you listen to them better and learn from them too. You also provide them with love and intimacy, which we all need.

You Learn to Regulate Your Emotions

When you develop empathy, the first thing you learn is self-awareness. Self-awareness then allows you to create the understanding that your emotions are not more important than other people's feelings. Have you ever come across a person who feels as though their opinions are more important than others? It's annoying.

When you become more empathetic, you begin to learn how to limit your emotions and take note of your partner's feelings. You learn to deal better with your emotions without feeling overwhelmed, and in turn, help your partner deal with theirs.

Better Conflict Resolution

Building empathy is building a connection. When you and your partner are more empathetic to each other, you bear each other's emotions. Thus, when you disagree, you will often go through the conflict with a desire to see out the disagreement without letting your emotions get the better of you.

Rather than blame each other for the different views, emotional intelligence, the basis of empathy, allows you to look at the situation, not your partner, as the problem. Rather than direct your dissatisfaction at your partner, you direct it to the issue.

Improved Intimacy

Your partners' feelings become your feelings and vice versa. Empathy develops an understanding of your feelings as well as those of your partner. You develop affective empathy. You relate intimately to how they feel. This affective empathy then grows into somatic empathy and then cognitive empathy. This empathetic intimacy allows you to grow beyond just being in love. You become each other's place of refuge. This closeness improves your intimacy and will enable you to grow closer still.

Empathy is what will determine whether you and your partner will get along when you follow any other related advice. It is empathy that will allow you to listen to your partner actively. It is empathy that will make you trust them, and they, you. This understanding then guides you to make the right choices to manage a crisis.

CHAPTER 14:

Couples and Compromise

The basis of a good relationship depends upon your skill in being able to compromise. Two people can be deeply, intensely, passionately in love and yet not be able to live together. For living together demands the capacity and will to compromise—not just once, or now and then, but continuously in a thousand little ways, all day long.

At night in bed, do you want one blanket, two blankets, or none? Is this a good time for sex or not?

If it is time to eat, are you both hungry? Do you want to eat the same thing? What movie do you want to see? On and on, when you live with another person, both trivial and major life events demand continual compromise.

If all is going well, the process of adjusting is so easy it almost goes unnoticed. On the contrary, if it is not going well, every moment, every trivial issue has the potential to become a major conflict.

The Meaning of Compromise

Compromise can mean different things to different people.

What is compromise?

Perhaps you think compromise means having to give in. Or, on the contrary, perhaps you think it means your partner should have to give in.

Not so.

Compromise is a process whereby each of you gives a little, in turn, until a mutually satisfactory agreement is reached. For each act of giving, something must be given in return. It is like balancing a seesaw.

The further apart you are, the more difficult it will be to reach a compromise. For example, you may have little difficulty resolving which movie you want to see, but it is a decision of another magnitude to decide where you want to live, or whether or not you want to have children. In some cases, keeping the relationship may demand major sacrifices for both partners.

Sometimes Compromise Can Bring Rewards of Its Own

Mary and Tom had come to see me because of conflicts over money, but then, during one of the sessions, issues came up in regard to their vacations. Tom was a surfer who loved the ocean. He really didn't like the desert at all. Mary, on the other hand, loved the desert but couldn't care less about the ocean. This difference caused constant bickering. Neither wanted to go on a vacation separately; after all, the fun of vacationing was really the pleasure of being together.

What to do?

"Why not compromise," I asked. "One time try the desert; the next time, the ocean?"

They were reluctant—particularly Tom, who said, "I hate the desert; too hot!" Nevertheless, they agreed to compromise. Tom would try to put up with the desert if Mary would accompany him to Hawaii and watch him surf.

Following the end of their sessions, I didn't see them for several months, until I happened to run into Mary in the grocery store.

Guess what?

They had followed through on the compromise. They had gone to Palm Springs for the desert vacation, and Tom had had a wonderful time at the music festival. And Mary had loved Hawaii, even though she didn't want to go in the water, just sit on the beach and watch Tom surf. Compromise had not only improved their relationship but had enriched their lives.

And then there is the story of Francis and Scott, whose compromises were more difficult to make but that made a big difference in their relationship.

Frances and Scott had been married about ten years. They had had a good marriage, but bickering between them had increased to a point where they were feeling chronically angry with each other.

Frances was somewhat overweight—twenty pounds—and Scott would make an occasional comment such as, "I see the cookies disappeared," or, "I thought we were going to skip dessert." Comments Frances didn't respond to but that stayed with her and were upsetting. Yes, she had eaten the cookies, and yes, she had meant to skip dessert, but no, she didn't need to be reminded of this.

And then Scott, who had been a fairly heavy drinker for years, had increased his cocktails from two martinis before dinner to three. Frances would say each time, "Do you really need that third drink?" and he would say nothing but would go ahead and have the drink anyway. Then they both would feel irritated.

When these interactions and the bad feelings associated with them came out in the session, both Frances and Scott wanted to change them. They agreed to try to reach a compromise. Francis would talk to her physician about her weight and begin exercising, and Scott would save the third drink for special occasions.

An important part of their agreement was that they would be responsible only for their part of the compromise—they would not criticize each other for failing to carry out their part. They would be as supportive as possible.

This was not easy for either one of them. Despite good intentions over the next few months, they each had relapses. Frances still occasionally ate cookies or dessert when she shouldn't have, and Scott still occasionally had that third drink when he shouldn't have. However, Frances had seen her doctor and begun exercising, and Scott had taken seriously her request to keep the cocktails at two rather than three. They were quite supportive of each other, praising each other when they were successful and remaining quiet when they were not. When I saw them a year later, Frances had lost ten pounds, and Scott had (for the most part) kept the cocktails at two.

Frances and Scott were lucky. Although compromise is always worth a try, certain problems, such as weight and addictions, are difficult to handle on one's own and can require outside help.

Sometimes a compromise is asking too much. If you feel you cannot go that far, you have to say to your partner, "I'm sorry, I can't do that. You are asking more than I can give."

For example, if one of you lives in Alaska and the other in Florida, and neither one of you is willing to move, your differences are too great. A compromise is not possible, and you will have to say to each other, "We love each other, but we cannot live together."

Sometimes one partner will make immense sacrifices to adjust to the other, but this may well lead to grief. A compromise needs to be mutually satisfactory, otherwise the decision rankles beneath the surface until it finally comes to a head.

Staying with another for years while swallowing one's own wishes may be an unwise decision. Painful as it may be, it is far better to be open and honest as to one's feelings. Putting the cards on the table, where they can be talked about and worked with, is far better than the seemingly easier "going along with it" and having the hope things will eventually change on their own.

MICHELLE MILLER

CHAPTER 15:

Know Your Partner

The more you know and are willing to learn about your partner, the closer you will become and at a much faster pace. Finding a few bits of information to identify with will help offer you reassurance that you've found your forever mate. You don't want to be identical twins about everything, but a few things in common gives you an instant bond. Some areas such as goals and values are important to be on the same page for relationship success.

Know the History of Your Partner

Knowing a few of the basics in the history of your partner and openly sharing your history will give each of you a foundation to begin exploring more in-depth. You can't be expected to remember everything in the beginning but build on information as time goes by. A few of the things to start with could be:

- Where they were born.
- Where they grew up.
- The size of their family.
- Where their family is located.
- Education level.
- Profession and job experiences.
- Any past serious relationships/marriages.

- Any children and where they are located.

A small amount of information to start will allow you to initiate conversations that lead you to learn even more. It's important to have enough information to feel comfortable that you are making a great choice in partners.

Discuss Life Ambitions and Goals

What are your goals in life? Are you wanting to live in a big city or have dreams of a small cottage near the woods? Do you like fancy cars, or is an old 4X4 pickup all you'll ever want and need? What are your ambitions with career, home ownership, salary, retirement plans, and savings? You can find out the same information in return. It's vital to ensure you and your partner have ambitions and goals that line up with one another or you will end up a miserable person.

Know their Core Values and whether they Line up with Your Own

Core values are the value you place on things like honesty, integrity, work ethic, compassion, and more. It would be difficult to establish a long-term relationship with someone that did a little shoplifting or found lying to be no big deal if those are not your values as well. It's a recipe for immediate disaster. Most core values are established before the age of six, although it doesn't mean that values can't be added to and expanded over the course of your life. It's good to know where you're starting at and see where things align and where there are potential problems.

What are their Tastes in Music, Movies, Books, Food?

Great conversations require a good supply of basic interests and knowing what their tastes are in music, movies, books, food, fashion, and all things current or trendy. The better you share the intricate likes and dislikes of basics in life, the wider the arena is for powerful conversations. It's also nice to know areas you may differ, at least slightly. It can help expose you to something different you might end up loving just as much. Every person that loves Mexican food never realized it until giving it a try. Sharing new experiences forces you to look at your favorites in a new light. It can breathe new life into what had become stagnant.

What is their Favorite Color, Animal, Car, and More?

Keep it going! You aren't finished in the learning process if you are going to become a true expert in your partner. You still need to discover important things like what is their favorite color, favorite car, favorite animal, and whether they prefer gold or silver. It's almost as if a floodgate opens and the conversations become powerful and filled with vital information. It also provides plenty of clues on what you can get for birthdays, holidays, and anniversaries. The sky is the limit in asking the question but try and spread out the questioning over a long period of time.

Are they a Deep Thinker or Impulsive by Nature?

How a person communicates can have a lot to do with their baseline personality. You'll be able to make observations as easily as they can see where you sit on the spectrum. More reserved, deep-thinking individuals often seem to have fewer words to say. They tend to place a lot of emphasis on the words used, however. It could be that they are introverted. It doesn't mean they are shy but more deliberate and selective in action.

A more impulsive person is generally considered an extrovert. Although it may appear to be all over the map, the tasks and conversations are skillful and done in their own special way.

You'll find that the more impulsive personalities hardly ever run out of conversational topics. Most are upbeat and highly energetic. Making these simple observations can point you in the best directions for starting and continuing a conversation.

What are some of their Basic Habits?

Learning a few of their basic habits will help make you an expert on your partner. Do they go jogging every Monday and Wednesday morning? Is there a show they have to watch on Friday evenings? Do they prefer to drink coffee out on the patio on their day off? Do they have an irritating twitch to their eye if you leave a dirty dish in the sin after a midnight snack? Studying and understanding the habits of your partner will help you work more in unison and help create a happy home environment

What do they need from a Relationship?

All parts of information you gather culminate in showing you what they are looking for and need from a relationship. Ask the important questions, assimilate the information, and use it to help create a smoother transition into the relationship. (See figure 5)

Figure 5 – The process of discovery and learning about your partner.

Learning about your partner should be something you look forward to on a daily basis. Most successful relationships are not based on a perfect fit. It's finding ways to fit together in the uneven areas that make the difference. Finding ways to grow together is the ultimate goal.

CHAPTER 16:

Couples Therapy Exercises for Improving Communication

Viable communication is the lifeblood of any relationship. For some couples, merely figuring out how to convey emotions, resolve conflicts, and offer with one another is a challenging endeavor. Utilizing a couple of basic couple's therapy practices for communication can do miracles to support you and your accomplice manage issues and develop nearer. Learning communication skills that can allow you to appreciate the marriage or relationship you have wanted continuously is significant. By setting up a superior discourse with your accomplice and figuring out how to share your sentiments and address issues with less conflict, it will be conceivable to make a relationship that is healthier, stronger, and all the more emotionally satisfying.

Using Positive Language

Couples therapy activities can extend your emotional bond and allow you to manage muddled circumstances and issues without lashing out or contending. Utilizing positive language when you speak with your accomplice might be the absolute best approach to make an increasingly successful emotional discourse. It is all too easy to wind up baffled, especially if your relationship has hit an unpleasant time. Bending over backward to embrace a positive and empowering tone during your discussions can turn what might have generally turned into a warmed contention into an open door for positive development and progress. Being excessively basic or receiving a negative tone might cost you numerous chances to sustain and strong. This activity, when polished after some time, can allow you and your accomplice to develop nearer.

Communication Exercises to Build a Lasting Relationship

Learning and applying couples therapy practices for communication can do a lot to reinforce your relationship. Managing touchy issues and sensitive issues can be a strenuous endeavor. Tools and activities that will allow you and your accomplice to more readily share and convey what needs be can demonstrate to be an essential piece of making a healthier and all the more satisfying relationship. Poor communication might do unmistakably something other than restricting your capacity to manage common issues. Activities that have been intended to make communication quality as opposed to risk can help guarantee a more drawn out and more joyful relationship. Figuring out how to improve as an audience and rehearsing the skills that will allow you and your accomplice to develop nearer makes it feasible for you to appreciate another degree of understanding and gratefulness for one another.

Active Listening

Numerous couple's therapy activities are based around rehearsing skills that will improve you and your accomplice audience members. Undivided attention is intended not just to make it easier to banter about touchy issues but also actually to develop your understanding and valuation for your accomplice. When rehearsing undivided attention, it is significant for the speaker to stay focused on a single idea or point. For the audience, focusing on sharing their accomplice's point of view while endeavoring to find new bits of knowledge about how the person thinks and feels can be of incredible advantage. Regardless of what subject is being examined, the most significant piece of undivided attention is to do it with persistence and love. Tending to how your accomplice feels as opposed to merely responding to what your accomplice says is essential for successful communication.

Learning to Grow Closer

Individuals change and develop after some time, regularly in manners that are amazing or startling. Being in a long haul relationship can make it easy to ignore new features and aspects of your accomplice's character. Couples who think that it's challenging to acknowledge who their accomplice has developed into will likely experience difficulty imparting. Couples therapy works out, for example, learning undivided attention skills and sharing emotions uninhibitedly, can enable you to build up a superior feeling of who your accomplice is. Indeed, even the most agreeable endeavors could be bound to disappointment if you can't understand and identify with how your accomplice's advantages and passions may have changed after some time.

Sharing Emotions Freely

Numerous couple's therapy practices for communication are intended to diminish conflict and make a progressively successful path for you and your accomplice to share what you are feeling. When it is challenging to examine emotions without starting a contention or causing a battle, working through issues and differences may also be unimaginable. Talking about what you need to have a sense of security when sharing how you both feel can be useful. For some, couples, having a specific time or spot to examine significant issues or to take a shot at the structure, better communication may have any kind of effect. Set aside the effort to ask your accomplice what might make that person feel progressively useful when sharing your emotions. At that point, put these ideas energetically to help guarantee that your future endeavors to improve your relationship are as successful as conceivable.

Taking a Trip Together

Keeping up relationships requires a great deal of diligent work, which is the reason it is significant for you and your accomplice to unwind and loosen up. Masterminding an outing with your accomplice can give chances to you to take a shot at structure excellent communication while having some good times. Following a similar everyday practice or remaining in a safe environment can eventually cause a relationship to stagnate. Sharing time together in another condition will allow you and your accomplice to make new recollections while alleviating the pressure that could be making communication unquestionably progressively tricky. It's also regular for couples to go on couples withdraws where the very purpose of your outing is to improve your relationship.

I Feel

Expressing your sentiments in a manner that is easy to understand can be a precarious endeavor. Starting your announcements with "I feel" can give couples a progressively powerful approach to organize their considerations while offering the audience data that is easier to grasp. This is one of the numerous couple's therapy practices that can be used to handle sensitive issues that can prompt contentions. By isolating the manner in which you feel from the original conditions and occasions being examined, you can support your accomplice feel not so much guarded but rather more ready to tune in.

RELATIONSHIP THERAPY

MICHELLE MILLER

CHAPTER 17:

Steps to Set Relationship Goals

About Setting Relationship Goals

Did you know that the laws of motion can be applied to your relationship? Yes, I am not joking, and it is true! The first law of motion states that an object will not move until an external force is applied. The second law states that an object will accelerate only when an external force is applied. The third law of motion states that every action has an equal and opposite reaction. These are three simple laws and can be easily applied to any relationship. By applying the first law of motion, you will realize that your relationship will continue to exist the way it is and will not change unless you make any changes. This applies to things both good as well as bad. For instance, if you are tired of the way you both deal with arguments, then this pattern will not change unless you both make a conscious effort to make the change. According to the second law of motion, you cannot make any changes unless you make a conscious decision to do so and put in the necessary effort. The third law of motion is perhaps the most easily explainable one. The way you act influences the way your partner reacts. Now, the same concepts can be used for setting goals in your relationship as well. When you set goals, it gives your relationship the required momentum to keep going. When you and your partner come up with certain mutually agreeable goals to improve your relationship, you can create an assignment that is conducive to your relationship's growth. The goals you set will help avoid your relationship getting stagnant. Setting goals is quite easy, and the chances of success in attaining these goals increase when you set simple goals. The relationship goals you come up with will help you and your partner concentrate on your relationship even when you hit a rough patch. Once you come up with goals, you must make sure that you are both willing to put in the necessary effort to attain them. Establish goals yourself and allow your partner to do the same. You can sit down together, brainstorm, and come up with relationship goals for your relationship together.

Make it a point to set goals about communication, love, compromise, commitment, sexual intimacy, household chores, and support. These are the main aspects that influence the quality and strength of your relationship. Once you cover these areas and come up with attainable goals, you can improve and strengthen your relationship.

It is quintessential that you and your partner both work on improving the way you communicate with each other. While setting goals in this area, think about ways in which you can improve your communication.

I am certain you love your partner, but how expressive are you? If you don't express your love, how will your partner ever know? How often do you express your thoughts? I'm not suggesting that you need to keep telling your partner over and over again that you love them, but there are little things you can do which convey your love for them. For instance, sharing in on any household responsibilities, cooking their favorite meal, or giving them a hug as soon as you wake up in the morning are all ways in which you can show your love for them. In a long-term relationship, it is quintessential that you express your love and affection for your partner.

A relationship will not last if there are no compromises. My way or the highway kind of thinking can quickly shatter any relationship. Instead, learn to compromise. It is okay if you don't always get your way, and it is okay if you are not always right. Start making an effort to understand your partner's perspective. Learn to negotiate and understand the importance of coming to compromises. When you compromise, it doesn't mean that you are wrong while your partner is right, it merely means that you love your partner more and are willing to concentrate on the relationship instead of any other petty issues or problems.

Emotional intimacy is as important as physical intimacy in a relationship. So, make a conscious effort and set certain goals for physical intimacy in your relationship. Be a responsive and caring lover to your partner. Spend some time and discuss with your partner about all the various things you want to try and be open with them. Learn to cater to not just your needs, but the needs of your partner as well.

A common problem a lot of couples run into is related to household responsibilities. I believe in the equality of partners, and therefore partners must share all responsibilities. After all, you are living together, so why not share the responsibilities? Spend some time and come up with a schedule to divide responsibilities between the two of you so that one partner doesn't always feel burdened with household work. This is quintessential, especially if you and your partner have day jobs to attend to as well.

Tips To Keep In Mind

Happiness doesn't always come from getting what you want, but it can come from moving toward what you desire. When it comes to relationships, it essentially means that couples must have a couple of goals they are moving toward together. So, how can couples support and motivate each other to achieve their individual goals along with the relationship goals? Well, here are some simple steps you can follow to ensure that you and your partner reach your goals while maintaining the health of your relationship.

The first step is to ensure that your individual goals are in perfect alignment with your relationship goals. This alignment is quintessential to create a sense of harmony, which allows you both to attain your personal goals. Once this harmony is present, there is no limit to the things you can both achieve together as a team.

It is time to make two plans - a six-month plan and a two-year plan. Think of this as short and long-term goals for your relationship. Have a discussion about what you plan on doing, where you want to be, and how you want to be within these two timeframes. The next step is to visualize and think about where you want your life to be in the next five, 10, 15, and 20 years. Ensure that you both maintain a positive attitude, and don't casually write off any ideas until you have both had a chance to express yourself first. Don't judge your partner, and don't allow your partner to judge you. Keep an open mind toward each other and attentively listen to what the other person has to say.

Spend some time and make a list of all your personal goals. You and your partner must do this individually and then spend some time together to discuss the lists you both made. You can take all the time you need, and carefully note down everything you wish to attain in life. Include short-term as well as long-term goals and discuss this if you feel like you're getting stuck while making this list.

Whenever you are setting any goals, the goals must be such that they make you feel good about yourself. If the goal you are setting for yourself or for your relationship goes against everything you believe in, you will not be able to achieve it. The goals you set for yourself must not only be good for you but must be good for your relationship as well. When you have shared goals, it not only becomes easier to achieve them, but the health of your relationship also improves along the way.

Regardless of the goal you set, make sure that the goals are specific, realistic, and attainable. If a goal doesn't fulfill even one of these conditions, then you are merely setting yourself up for failure. People often think that setting lofty goals for themselves is a good idea. They seem to stand by the age-old adage of, "If you shoot for the stars, you will land on the moon." Well, I don't think this is the right way to go about setting goals. After all, if you don't attain your goals, it will be a source of massive disappointment and discontent. To avoid this, ensure that the goals you are setting are realistic, attainable, and quite specific. You and your partner must come up with an arrangement that helps you stay focused and accountable for any commitments you make to each other. The relationship you share with your partner is quite sacred, and you must cherish and nourish it. The arrangements you create must support you and your partner along with your relationship. It's not about getting rewards or punishments to create accountability. It is about coming up with a mutually beneficial plan to create accountability to each other.

It is okay to concentrate on your goals, but it is not okay to overlook any victories you attain along the way. Attaining your goals is seldom a sprint and is always a marathon. So, the journey to your goals matters as much as the goal itself. You and your partner must be appreciative of each other and each other's accomplishments. Rejoice in all the small wins that happen in your lives. Celebrate each other's successes. By doing this, you are naturally cementing the bond you share. If you celebrate every milestone you cross, it will give you the motivation to keep going.

You must be supportive and understanding. Support and encourage your partner to achieve their goals, and your partner will reciprocate these gestures towards you. Give your partner the room they need to attain their goals and don't become a hurdle. Keep a conscious check on any criticism you dole out. If your partner is making a mistake, feel free to correct them, but do so gently.

Be each other's support system. There will be days when you or your partner simply don't have the motivation to keep going. In such instances, be each other's cheerleaders. Your relationship will be happier and more satisfactory when you know you have your partner's support, and the same applies to your partner too. In fact, make it a point to seek feedback from your partner to see how they are doing. By asking for their feedback, you are not only making them feel important but are also giving yourself a chance to view things from a fresh perspective. Spend some time and make a note of all your goals. Keep reviewing these goals as you go about your daily life. Your goals can change, or the way you want to achieve them might change. You might also need to tweak your goals occasionally. So, don't forget to include a weekly review session of your goals.

The final step is quite simple - always remember you are a team. Achieving goals becomes easier when you are doing it together. You don't have to do everything by yourself, and you can count on your partner for additional help or support.

Once you have accomplished your dreams or goals, don't forget to come up with new goals. Goals give you the motivation to keep going!

CHAPTER 18:

The Importance of Having Fun to Couples

A strong, healthy, happy, and long-lasting relationship does not just happen. It is a conscious effort by both parties, where each partner sees to the betterment of the relationship and each other in all ramifications. Dull, droll, lazy, boring, and annoying are definitely what you'd want your relationship to be described as. Fun-filled, interesting, happy, and joyful are better words you would want your relationship to be described with. It is understandable that things change in a relationship, and things move from how they were at the very beginning where you both met to become more mundane. With increased meetings, house chores, jobs, children, and other impromptu activities that spring up here and there in a relationship, it is only important that couples find a way to balance every part of their lives. The importance of being spontaneous and playful in your relationship cannot be overemphasized. It takes away the burden of having to constantly sit down and speak you mind and painstakingly explain certain things to your partner because when having downtime, there is a bond that is fostered. Your partner knows you more and can figure out your boundaries. Having fun with each other in a relationship helps increase your affection for each other. Imagine saying something and having the other person laugh so hard and then noticing that they have a particular trait about them you never noticed. The relationship is strengthened when you are reminded that the source of the other person's laughter and joy is you. The implication of this is that the possibility of you both getting a divorce anytime soon is very low if at all existent. Couples who have fun are happy and tend to spread this happiness around even beyond their relationship. It rubs off on the kids, in the church, at the office, and even amongst the people in the neighborhood. While it might be easy to fake that you have it all rosy at home, or that you dread going home every time it is mentioned, having to pretend is not healthy.

In a relationship, there is nothing more important than being united. Your ability to stand for your partner, come what may, is often as a result of coming to know them through constantly interacting and having fun with them. Having fun with your partner breeds unity; you learn to forgive quickly, you learn to overlook certain acts of the other person even before they apologize. It does not mean you should allow your partner to take you for granted or be manipulative. Ensure that being playful with your partner does not rob you both of communication and the other necessary factors for a healthy relationship. If your partner is one who constantly gets you angry without seeing the need to apologize (or if their apology never sounds like they are sorry), then you might want to sit and work that out before allowing it to slide and perhaps breed more negativity in your relationship. Don't allow constant fun between yourself and your partner take the place of real apology in your relationship when your partner has done something wrong. An apology is appropriate, and it could be done playfully so long as they mean their apology, and you do not feel shortchanged in your relationship. Another benefit of being playful with your partner is that it breeds hope. Hope for better things to come in the future. It is not unusual to see people in marriages as if they cannot wait for it to end (even after saying 'till death do us part'). It should not be that way. Many times, the reason for this feeling is that couples have lost hope in the marriage - they feel they are merely passengers in the marriage instead of the drivers of their marriage who take charge. What hope does for you is that it assures you of the future even when you do not know what that future holds for you two. Having fun with your partner reassures you and keeps you optimistic about the relationship. There's just that joy when you rough and tumble, and laugh with your partner that assures you everything will be alright between you guys. This is what hope is all about; you are positive in fun times with your partner that the future will be better and that whatever hurdles are present can be overcome. Being playful in your marriage rubs off on your children as they grow and your children are the best legacy you can leave the world with. No one wants to have annoying, angry, and sad children around them. Statistics have shown that nurturing kids in a happy environment tends to boost their positive outlook and helps them strive for better things in life. Children who grow up in a happy and playful environment tend to be more optimistic, and they approach failure as a stepping stone rather than a setback. Your playfulness as a couple also rubs off on your family at times. There are stories of marriages that have survived the hostility of family members (perhaps because the couples are from different countries or religions and the family members did not support the marriage) simply by being constantly happy in their marriage.

What then does it mean for couples to enjoy some recreation time in their relationship? Having fun with your partner could be described as a pleasurable manner of having fun at a discretionary time. Of course, our definitions of what is pleasurable in a relationship may differ. But, taking from the analogy of cake, fun time with your partner is the icing which should not be sacrificed. Research has shown that having fun and bonding in a relationship is not only a pleasurable activity but also a form of developmental activity. Just like the way children, while growing, learn a lot from interacting with their peers and playing games and having conversations, we also learn a lot about our partner from playing with them. It was Plato, a Greek philosopher, who said that what could you learn about a person in one hour of laughing and having fun with them, might not be even be understood about that person in one year of conversation. So, in having fun with your partner, you learn a lot about them and yourself. For example, how your partner reacts to losing a game played with you might just be the way they would react when they are let go from a job or lose someone dear to them. The manner your partner behaves during certain moments might just be indicative of what they would do in the real world. It will show if they are the type that takes responsibility for their actions, if they laugh at and look down on others who have experienced failure with pride, or if they treat people like they are part of the same team. Recreation time with a partner reveals to you a lot about your partner, and this knowledge can be garnered covertly, as opposed to typical dialogues.

Some persons see recreation time as childish. There is a video on the internet of a groom who had slapped the bride on their wedding day, simply because she had tried to be playfully mischievous with their wedding cake as she attempted to feed him. The point is, playful activities in relationships are not taboo. We should not be ashamed of them. You probably shouldn't say things like this to your partner: "lower your voice and stop laughing like a kid, the neighbors will hear us." While every relationship does not function in the same way, how about loosening up a bit? Nothing positive, good, or healthy comes out of a relationship unless the partners have consciously worked towards making it happen. An interesting fact here is that many people, before agreeing to be in a relationship with someone, may not mind the fun and games. There is a possibility that this all changes upon entering a relationship. By this time, it becomes immature to laugh in a certain way or behave in a playful manner. It's quite funny when people see or interpret playfulness in relationships as an act of childishness. The advantages of being happy in a relationship are not debatable, and neither are the advantages of being playful. It's important to state here that being playful in a relationship does not guarantee everything that has been explained above in the form of advantages, but the possibilities of these advantages coming forth are quite high. Here are some tips you should consider to spice up your relationship.

Schedule time for fun

Most couples intend to have fun but never really get around their business schedule or household chores or dealing with kids to really have fun. Fix a time for recreation on the calendar. If some time is allotted for you both to have fun, then you would get around having done so one way or the other.

Spontaneity

You should not make having fun bureaucratic or mandatory. Make your relationship as spontaneous as is reasonable considering what both of you are used to and can adjust to. Having fun should not be a do or die affair, it should be something that you do because you want to enjoy each other's company and not because the calendar says so. It's important that you find time for downtime at some point in your relationship. The reason why a calendar is important is for situations when you have been so busy for too long that (though you are not quarreling or drifting apart from your partner) you no longer have time to throw funny jabs at each other.

Variety

Having fun should be pleasurable and could and should include playing games, going to the movies together, having sex, looking at old pictures together, etc., so long as it involves something pleasurable that keeps you both happy and promotes intimacy. To help you and your partner spend more time having fun, it is important you learn healthy habits and try to exude positive energy all the time.

Loosen Up

Give yourself the opportunity to be a kid once in a while in your relationship. Be open to new things, and don't let your relationship make you lose your wonder. Look forward to new things and be ever ready to learn, especially when it has to do with new and untried ways of having fun with your partner. Be willing to speak to your partner about anything. Communicate your fears and concerns about things to them. This is wisdom about communication that can be learned from little kids. Most times, we get so caught up in being perfect adults that we forget how to be kids or begin to see being playful as being childish. It's not childish to tickle your partner out of the blue when tickling them makes them laugh. Learn to confide in your partner. It's easier to find the voice to tell your partner uncomfortable things when you both are out having a good old playtime.

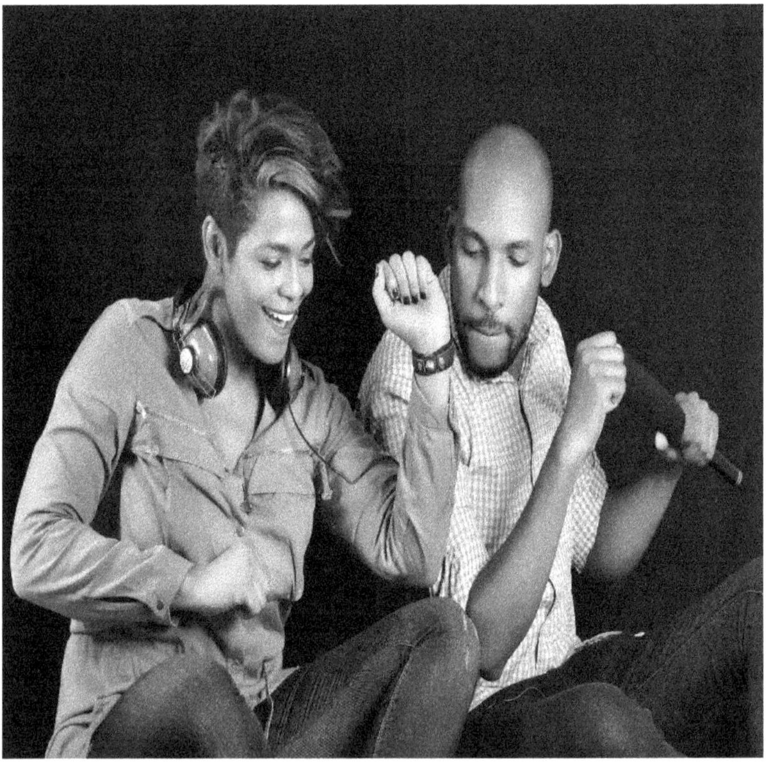

MICHELLE MILLER

CHAPTER 19:

Learn How to Apologize

One critical way to build trust, rekindle intimacy, and connect emotionally with your partner is to learn to apologize when you hurt them. In the long-life journey of love as a couple, there will be moments of arguments and broken promises, which will result in hurting each other's feelings. At such times, learning to say "sorry" can save your relationship. Learning to apologize to your partner is a crucial life and marriage skill. It is difficult to say sorry or apologizes to your partner, especially if you belong to the class of individuals who view that as a sign of weakness.

Sometimes, neither of the partners is willing to apologize or admit their mistakes when they are wrong. This is a sign of pride and selfishness and only serves to make the situation worse. Let's say that you have had a heated argument or fight with your partner. Such an argument tends to make you feel awful. You find yourselves caught up in power struggle and a lousy tradition of waiting for the other person to admit their faults first creeps into your marriage.

You should learn to take the initiative, admit, and accept your faults, especially when you know you have made a mistake or when you are wrong. Sometimes, you don't even have to be wrong to apologize. As you will learn with time, it is usually not a matter of being wrong or right in the marriage, but just a difference of opinion. At such times when you feel that both of you are wrong, and you are wondering whether you should apologize to your partner, just do it! This is not a sign of weakness but a path that helps you become a better spouse.

When you understand what it means to you and your spouse, offering an apology becomes easier. Apologizing is one way to show that you are selfless, and you care for your partner's feelings. It shows that you are treating your partner the way you wish to be treated when you are hurt. It is a simple way to admit your faults, and that you are willing to correct yourself and try to do better next time. It is a way to own up your mistakes by acknowledging that you are an imperfect human being, and you can be wrong sometimes. It shows that you are willing to make an effort to grow from your mistakes and become a better partner.

When you make an apology, you learn to strike a balance between your pride and struggle for power in your relationship. By learning to put your ego aside and embracing selflessness, you can become one with your spouse and grow together, appreciating each other's mistakes and weaknesses. You can save your marriage or relationship by learning to apologize. But how do you learn to say that you are sorry and mean it? Let us look at some of the ways through which you can master the art of saying sorry so that you can save yourself and your spouse a lot of marriage or relationship woes.

Admit your mistakes

The first essential step in learning to apologize to your husband or wife is to admit that you a human being, and you are eligible for making a mistake. This makes it easier for you to accept that you have a problem, and you are wrong in one way or another. Unless you accept that you are wrong, your apology cannot be genuine, sincere, or meaningful. You will just say it for the sake of avoiding a further argument, and it may not reflect your actual position, attitude, or facial expression. So the first thing is learning to admit and accept your mistakes. Show that you are willing to be fully responsible for what you did and take the necessary corrective measures going forward.

Learn to respect the emotions of your partner

When our partners do something wrong, we get hurt. Anyone who has been in a relationship knows this to be true, and it is a rule with no exceptions. All of us feel hurt when it happens. As you approach your partner for an apology, after doing something wrong, it is good to keep this in mind. Show that it wasn't intentional and put yourself into your partner's shoes. This will show that you respect how they are feeling, and you will do your best to avoid making them feel the same next time.

Be sincere with your apology.

Listen to your partner as they vent out, and do not interfere until they have finished explaining how they feel. This will help you understand their perspective and the extent to which your actions have hurt them. That way, you will be able to offer a sincere and honest apology that reflects your true feelings and attitude towards how they feel. Don't begin to give explanations as to why you did what you did or start to give excuses. This will be a sign that you don't care, because you will be trying to justify your deeds. Be as specific as possible in your apology and just focus on that one issue at hand, which your partner has raised. Don't go outside the topic and bring a mix of other past problems into the picture. The bottom line is that you should never say you are sorry for the sake of pleasing your partner. You should be sincere and honest by being specific with your apology. This enables your partner to know how sorry you are, and will help you strengthen your intimacy, rebuild trust, and enhance how you communicate as a couple.

Humble yourself and ask for forgiveness

It shows how humble and caring you are to your spouse when you present yourself in person and offer a face-to-face apology. You may want to write a letter, send an email, or a text message, but that should come as a way to emphasize what you have already verbalized. If you find it hard to face your spouse and verbalize the apology, then you need to dig deep and unearth what is preventing you from doing the same. Don't be that kind of a spouse who gathers the courage to communicate face to face only when they are fighting. Master the courage to face your partner and offer an apology. After making an apology, take it one step further and ask your spouse to forgive you.

Forgive yourself

To show compassion to your partner, you must be able to be compassionate with yourself first. To be able to welcome and accept your partner's forgiveness, you must be ready to forgive yourself too. It may not be easy to forgive yourself, especially after realizing the severity, or the extent of the emotional damage you have caused your partner. Forgiving yourself gives you the confidence to work on yourself and make critical changes that will help you rise above your mistakes. Failure to forgive yourself can make you begin to play the victim. You may end up with inward resentment, which can make it hard for you to forgive or accept forgiveness from your spouse. This can limit your chances of becoming better.

Create an action plan

You don't want to keep on apologizing all the time for doing the same things. The best way to avoid the same issues from cropping up all the time is to come up with an action plan. You need to come up with a list of things or steps you will follow to avoid repeating mistakes. It makes no sense to your partner when you keep on repeating mistakes and apologizing every time you do so. If it was a communication mishap, focus on improving your communication skills. If it was delayed payment of some bills, come up with a way to remind yourself of such responsibilities. You can set a reminder on your phone or the calendar.

In other words, tell your partner the measures you are going to put in place to prevent the same from happening. Don't do this alone, but seek the feedback or the input of your partner while devising your action plan. This shows that you value their views and opinion, and they can see the effort you intend to make to turn things around and change for better.

Put your action plan into practice

Take bold steps to practice your action plan. There is no amount of rhetoric which can take the place of what you do. As they say, action speaks louder than words. Let your actions from that point on, reflect your commitment into making sure that the same issues don't arise again by acting your words. Change your behavior by putting the requisite effort to make up for your faults. This will eliminate any fears or doubts your spouse might have developed as a result of your mistakes. They will begin to rebuild their trust and intimacy once they see that you are putting a lot of effort into becoming better.

CHAPTER 20:

Accepting and Sharing Opinions

Some people, when they start dating, think that having differences in opinions about politics, religion, values, or morality means they will always be fighting over things from day one. This is far from reality and only becomes a problem when both parties refuse to take into account each other's viewpoints. Instead of accepting them or viewing them as a new perspective, they perceive it as something negative and thus, are always trying to change them. Opinions can be changed, but they don't always have to. If we take things back to the day you two met, was it not your differences that attracted you to each other in the first place? There is a strong backing behind opposites attract – proven both by science and psychological experts.

Having a different opinion does indeed complicate things slightly in a relationship but there are many ways to deal with it.

In this, not only shall be looking at these, but we shall also learn about why people have different opinions, why they should be accepted and appreciated.

I Have Something to Tell You?

The moment couples start living together, they are bound to come across diverse opinions – most of which may not match yours. This can lead to misunderstandings as well as arguments over even the smallest of issues such as what to dress your kid as on Christmas. If you come from a Jewish family and your partner is a hardcore Christian, this argument may seem quite valid as Christmas isn't a celebrated holiday according to the Jewish tradition. They celebrate Hanukkah instead. The same differences can also be seen in how the money is spent in the house, who gets to make the final call, who gets to discipline the kids, who is responsible for housekeeping and raising the kids, etc.

But where do these differences come from?

For starters, we all come from different households, neighborhoods or different sides of the country. Partners may have been raised in a certain way that conflicts with the other's way of living. In some houses, it is considered bad to talk back to your husband; whereas, in some homes, nearly all the major decisions are taken mutually after thorough discussions. This diversification of environments and early childhood experiences play a crucial role in personality development. Your partner may come from a family that spent every summer vacation out in the woods, but you may have never experienced anything as outdoorsy. Therefore, when it comes to taking the kids to someplace, your partner may insist on renting an RV and heading for the woods while you might be more interested in visiting the entertainment hub of the country for some family time together.

Then, we also have different educations, different exposures, different jobs, and different perspectives about life. All of these can easily become problematic when going unheard or unresolved.

However, these differences don't mean that your partner is right and you aren't or in any way demean you. Accepting others' opinions is a crucial aspect of every marriage. A relationship can be fostered with unity and understanding where every different idea gets discussed with an open mind.

Why You Should Listen to What Your Partner Has to Say

We believe everyone should see the world as we do. We think of it as the right way and are rarely keen on changing our minds about it. When we are paired in a relationship with a partner who has a completely different point of view than yours, it is so easy to blame them for being misinformed or living with a distorted opinion about reality.

But they think the same about your views too. So how to go on living with them when you constantly feel that they are wrong and vice versa?

First off, each individual is entitled to their opinions. Opinions are formed based on real events and make the individual who they are.

They aren't wrong, just different.

When you two are journeying together, keep in mind that it is never going to be easy or simple as a straight line. You both chose to be together and thus must provide each other with some space and understanding about the things they solely believe in. Having a partner with a different opinion is also a healthy thing for many reasons. For starters, it will enrich and broaden your vision about reality. Next, it allows you to question your own beliefs and opinions and see if you are wrong. A different opinion can also give you the chance to ask them what made them think that way or why do they believe what they believe in. The newfound information can help you two understand each other better and strengthen your relationship, as then you will be more considerate when discussing important issues with them.

Thirdly, when you acknowledge and accept your partner's opinions, they will feel more valued and understood. When they feel that, they will be more open with you and feel safe sharing their deepest thoughts and ideas with you without feeling judged. The level of trust between you two will blossom, and your partner won't need to amplify their views just to be heard.

It also helps to bridge the gap between you two as you learn to respect each other's viewpoints. Moreover, there may be times when one of your decisions may require more thinking on your part and your partner may help you see it. For instance, you are thinking to get a new job. You are thinking of a good pay raise and fewer working hours. However, you might overlook aspects like long commute hours and heavy traffic. If your partner knows how frustrated you get when you drive for long hours, they may ask you to reconsider. You might feel a little taken aback by their idea and believe that they don't want to see you succeed. But when you two sit down to discuss why you think it's a great idea and why they think otherwise, a different point of view may change your mind. You may come to realize that their worry wasn't about you earning more but rather about your mood and health. So a different point of view can help you see past all the glittery stuff.

You can also visualize the long-term impacts of your decisions. For instance, if we follow-up with the same example as above, your primary objective was short-term goals. You just wanted to work a few hours less and get paid more. However, your partner's concern was more about your health. Who knows, ten days into the new job and you are back to hating your life again and regretting ever leaving your previous job.

A difference of opinion can also help you overcome your weaknesses. As humans, we have the habit of underestimating our skills and talents. We always think that we aren't good enough. That is your opinion of yourself. Chances are, you may have backed down on some good potential opportunities in the past due to the same fear. Now enter a partner into this situation who thinks no one can beat you at the skill you are good at. This positive and refreshing boost of an entirely different opinion of yourself will improve your self-confidence.

How to Resolve Contradictory Opinions without Fighting?

Differing opinions will arise between partners – that's a given! How you are going to resolve them is the more important question. Sometimes, these differences in views can become the reason for fights and arguments between couples. So how can they move past that and accept and respect each other's opinions without breaking into a fight?

We have some great advice to offer. Take a look!

Negotiation

Negotiation or compromise is a suitable way to come out of a difference in opinions during complex situations. When you two want to do something your way and the partner intervenes with their methodologies, opt to compromise. Find a way in which neither one of you feels left out or disrespected. If you two can't reach a consensus and aren't; willing to give up on your stance, it is best to avoid attempting it at all. After all, nothing can be more important than your relationship, right? Don't be hell-bent on proving yourself right all the time.

Don't Argue

Sometimes, it can be very hard to change someone's perspective about things because they are very personal to them. In that case, it is unfair on your part to expect them to give it up. You must understand where they are coming from and why they think a certain way. If no mutual ground can be found, you must retreat.

Be Sensible

What your partner is saying might be rational, and you know it, but if you continue to argue, then that is just egoistic on your part. Try placing yourself in your partner's shoes and look at the world from their eyes for once. If you know that they are right and you keep fighting for the sake of being right, then you need to back up and accept it as a mature individual.

Don't Force It

It is unhealthy to impose your beliefs on someone and expect them to abide by them fully. No one ever said that differences of opinions are a bad thing. Forcing someone to think a certain way because you think it is right isn't justifiable. That would be acting childish. Express your mind and let the other person decide if they think it is right or not. Don't force it upon them.

Act Mature

Could they be right? Hey, we all can be wrong at times. At least, accepting it will let your partner feel valued and also leave you with some newfound knowledge. You are totally not too old to learn something new.

CHAPTER 21:

How Couples Therapy Helps

Couples therapy is intended to explain the personality discrepancies between people in a relationship to more efficiently solve problems. Couple therapy is a fast, solution-centric approach that describes and takes the outcomes into account clear and achievable recovery objectives. Couples therapy allows couples to develop relationship enhancement approaches.

The pair therapy approaches teach you how to take constructive chances in establishing a romantic relationship. Opportunities for personal development persist throughout the lifespan. Individual development contributes to healthy, engaged ties. Couple therapy encourages relational development that allows people to feel more connected. People gain trust when they feel confident to expose to their partners the darkest, most private self. The best way of obtaining a successful outcome is to partner with an accomplished specialist including a licensed marriage counselor and a family therapist.

Which kinds of issues are dealt with in the consultation of couples?

Psychotherapy for couples deals with common issues in relationships, including inadequate communication, difficulties getting along, and boundary conflicts with other family members such as parents or grandparents, parental disputes or financial stress. Couple counseling teaches couples a more caring and compassionate way of living.

Employment or job, financial and child and family problems are the pressures that modern society imposes on a relationship. Through marriage therapy, people learn how to cope with daily challenges without damaging their relationship. Through psychotherapy, couples understand that we are all imperfect and that we all have human flaws. Couples in counseling gain an awareness that we are both capable of harming one another and learning strategies to avoid it as much as possible. Partners in the therapy process feel that they have a safe place to identify negative behavior. People learn good communication skills in relationships to apologize for and to express sorrow.

How long do people live in pairs?

Counseling for couples is structured to deal with unique issues. In 10 to 12 sessions, problems should be detected on average and effective behavioral approaches start to take effect. The number of sessions is adjusted according to the couple involved and their specific problems.

Many couples want to work with the therapist to develop new skills and successful approaches. They know that cognitive instruments that lead to a more productive partnership can be taught. When a few put into practice what is learned during the original sessions, they are inspired to "learn more," because they see that they have a happy life with their partner. Couples frequently initiate marital counseling in a situation of crisis. If heavy emotions begin to withdraw, the psychotherapist and the couple will begin the real learning work and develop other skills and strategies to strengthen marriage or relationship.

Why do you use a marriage and family therapist (MFT) for counselling and psychotherapy for couples?

Marriage and family care practitioners, who have a certificate in marriages, family dynamics and psychotherapy, are specially trained. These experts diagnose and treat a broad variety of emotional and psychological problems among people in a relationship.

A marital therapist is professionally trained to listen and unbiasedly examine the problems posed by partners. The couple's friends and family are always caring and want to help, but their deep emotional involvement in one or both partners leaves them unable to consider the dynamics of the relationship critically. Just after the first session with a successful marriage therapist, it is very normal for couples to have "hope" in their relationship that they do something good.

Can I become a better listener by offering advice to couples?

During couples' therapy, people learn different methods of responding to the needs of their spouse. Effective listening strategies enable people to build their partner's empathy, helping them to understand better and strengthen their relationship with their partner. Relationships and relationships are improved and cherished when people learn to listen to each other.

Psychotherapy for couples includes instruction in dispute management, the removal of miscommunication and painfully hurt emotions. Any unavoidable partnership causes issues. You should listen entirely to your partner's needs through counseling. An accomplished marriage therapist, a family and couples may help people to develop their communication skills in a special way.

The therapist will help you keep track of a question while working on it. You learn to avoid "making a case" by carrying insignificances that can only cause suffering to others. Couple counseling can help establish dialogue surrounding a difference of opinion that leads everyone to a suitable solution.

Why is counseling couples going to help me overcome my marital conflicts?

Next, for both parties, the therapist should help develop a secure, warm and trustworthy relationship. So you meet with the therapist to grasp the conflict's existence. Conflicts also occur when partners vary in intent or expectation in a relationship. The therapist helps you and your partner to consider each other's needs and to learn new ways of interacting to overcome the conflict.

An experienced couple therapist may help couples to build communication skills to strengthen dispute resolution techniques that can be developed over time. People develop an improved willingness to listen to the views of the other person, although they may not agree to the specific question. In a non-critical and non-confrontational manner, the marriage therapist will demonstrate successful and reliable ways of communicating negative emotions like hurt and rage. Efficient resolution of disputes leads to couples becoming stronger and more secure, strengthening their marriage.

Is therapy for couples really effective?

Many studies indicate the importance of therapy for couples. The vast majority of people in pair counseling show a change in their understanding and relationship.

Couple therapy does not only allow people to remain together very effectively. Nevertheless, as each person in the relationship continues to grow and evolve, they progress to more efficient, constructive contact and successful conflict resolution outcomes outside their relationships in their lives. Person therapy is not a passive "done" for a person, but a "service" with the psycho-therapist. The counselor and the couple have positive communion in order to achieve positive outcomes.

Couple counseling is an efficient way of recognizing the relationship's actions of spouses and allows an effective resolution of relationship problems. A couple counselor deals with a number of different problems and helps couples learn to work together more lovingly. Couple counseling varies in length to provide ample room for different issues in connection. Professional marriage and family therapists are highly qualified professionals who can promote impartial and comprehensive care for a couple. Those attending marriage therapy learn some skills for better listening and dispute resolution. Overall, people find that couples therapy is successful and that their well-being and relationships are strengthened overall.

MICHELLE MILLER

CHAPTER 22:

Things You Should Do Before Marriage

You have reached a place where you know who is the one you want to spend the rest of your life with. You popped the question and now you are preparing for the big day. However, there are a few things you should consider doing before starting officially your lives together. Let us take a better look at what are those things.

Before getting married, you should clarify which are the career goals of you and your partner. You must talk about the different things you wish to accomplish in your life and how those things will affect your relationship. Supporting the dreams of your partner and your partner supporting your goals is an essential part of having a sild marriage. Besides, what a better motivator to succeed than the support of the one you love?

The next thing you must talk about is money and the spending habits each of you has. This discussion includes any debt you or your partner may have as well as your saving plans. However, if you have different spending habits it doesn't mean that your marriage is going to fail as long as your responsibilities are taken care of and there is money left for you to be comfortable.

Another discussion you need to have before tying the knot is whether you want children or no as well as when you should have them. Starting a family should be a common decision and a general plan should be discussed before marriage. By getting married it doesn't necessarily mean that your partner wants to have children, so before making more wedding plans keep in the back of your mind that you should also pop up this question too. Also, you shouldn't have to agree on how many children you want just yet.

You should also talk about the past each of you had and the important things that affected your life. Like it or not, your past played a big role on who you are today and the same principle applies to your partner too. It doesn't matter that there are things in your past you are ashamed of. Your partner surely has some too and it will not hinder him or her from telling you about it. This discussion should include the existence of any previous spouses or children that may come from this previous marriage.

Also, you should talk about how each other response to stressful situations. Your partner may have seen how you react to stress since they have lived with you for a while, but hearing you talk about it as well as giving away some useful tips will be an added bonus to building your solid marriage. Many marriages end up in divorce because stressful situations have not been dealt with effectiveness that comes from effective communication.

It would be good to discover how to talk to each other. Not through emails, phones, or texts because your most important conversations as a married couple will occur through face to face contact. Any uncomfortable conversations you will have will be dealt with accordingly and with effectiveness if you have cleared beforehand how each partner faces various serious problems. You don't only have to talk about how you should speak to each other through difficult situations, you could only talk about the various habits you have when communicating that gets on each other's nerves or love.

Another thing you should do before getting married to the one you love is to live with him or her. This way you will be able to see which are the habits your partner has that will annoy you the most and deal with them before things get out of hand. There are many traits your partner will have that you will find out during that time and may annoy you too much for you to be able to handle. There have been many reports of couples constantly arguing about small habits that have been an integral part of their partner's lives when they lived alone. The key here is compromise. When we live with someone else, we should take into consideration the things that annoy him or her and try to fix them. Just like your partner should do about the things that will annoy you.

If you re both working, then it should be wise to have a discussion about dividing up the chores of your house. You wouldn't want your house to be constantly a mess because neither partner will be too tired to tide up the place. Even if you think that dividing the chores is not a serious matter, you will find out that there will be arguments later because you didn't take out the trash and your house smells. So, try to fair and help each other out when it comes to house chores because this could potentially be a source of argument.

Another thing you should do before getting married is to plan a big trip together. Whether you believe it or not this trip will be a source of stress for both of you since you will have to book a hotel room and plane tickets as well as organize your budget for this trip. This will be a perfect exercise that will somewhat show you how to handle your future shared responsibility. Also, when you reach your destination, you will have to make various decisions on where to go, what to do while you are there, and where you should spend your money. A trip will be a true eye opener.

When you are getting married to someone the most essential thing you will need to accept and realize is that you will share a future you will create together, you will have a common purpose. If you want different things, you will never be able to unite so as to achieve this common purpose.

However, if you have successfully managed to plan a future together, you will have to make compromises, deal effectively with the various problems that will arise through effective communication and share your thoughts with your partner. Be honest and true to your significant other and do not take advantage of his or her love for you. A solid marriage will make you the happiest person in the world if it is treated with the respect it deserves.

CHAPTER 23:

Creating a Higher Sense of Intimacy with Your Partner

Now, when we are talking about intimacy here, we need to understand that we are not talking just about sex. While sex is an vital part of a healthy relationship, and should be something that you can discuss comfortably, and consider with your partner on a regular basis as your sexual desires and needs change over time, it is important to remember that there are other forms of intimacy that need to be focused on in order to help your relationship grow stronger and your relationship to stay around.

By the way, it's important that we speak to a large extent on sexual communication, how it helps to build your relationship and avoid insincerity from any party. Partners in a relationship who fail to bring up matters on sex may be due to them seeing it as a lesser topic for deliberation, or it doesn't seem pleasant to them, is at a risk of some kind. It is important to question your partner of your lapses and where you've to make amends. It shouldn't piss you off or cause a disagreement. It is a route to building a reliable and lasting relationship.

Sexual communication is expected to be at the peak of topics for discussion in every relationship that aims to grow stronger and longer. This creates a balancing ground for partners and shaves off distrust of any kind. It is no doubt that a huge number of persons find it absurd or, less important to discuss sex with their partners whenever they feel sober or unsatisfied. They feel the best is to consult a third party, whether through books, findings made through the internet or their friends or relatives, they find comfort from this discussion and sought remedies, this is done with the total exclusion and awareness of their partner.

Why should there even be a sexual communication in the first place? Sexual communication is so cogent that it must not be sidelined in any relationship. It has a way of building the sensation that creates a strong bond, it makes partners share the innermost part of themselves which invariably makes them share other parts of themselves, intrinsic or extrinsic troubles. You should not be ashamed of letting your partner know where he needs to make amend. "Oh, the styles are cool, do make a readjustment here", the mode at which this discussion should be made must be on a polite and frank note, you can do the jokes but with a sincere face, let them know what bothers pertaining their sexual activities.

Therefore, how then do we make this sexual communication on a simple note, concise, conservative and with honesty? The steps are as follows:

1. Do not bring up this topic after having sex: You know that moment when the truth hurts, when it might not be so easy to bear, that is the period. You should not bring up matters related to the sex you made abruptly, it demeans your partner sense of humor and it could result into a misunderstanding. When is suitable to bring up the matter for ironing? It could come later during your bedtime or when there's an outing involving just the two of you but not immediately after the sex.

2. Do not make your conversation on sex seem like a shock to the partner: This is very much important, there are times to convey your message and it will be swiftly understood. You

should try to present these matters in a happy atmosphere. You should endeavor not to speak the truth that may destabilize your partner when you unleash his shortfalls. The conversation that has deepened the interest of your partner is an open space to let them know. It'll make them know of the need to fill the loopholes and connect those pleasures you want to feel during your sexual intercourse.

3. A quiet place far from home: There is a possible case of not having a quiet time with your partner. Tight work schedule, children frolicking, and the chores at home gives you no time for your partner. Make a quiet time. Maybe somewhere far from home where the children are far from earshot. This quiet place is an opportunity for both partners to reminisce on their sexual life. You can talk on when you both first had sex, this will then extend into discussing your present situation. Do you feel the warmth as much as you felt during your first night? Do you feel that absolute pleasure during sex or has it deflated? Do you feel that wondrous sensation that looks unquenchable or it has started to fade? These and many more are what you can talk on during this quiet time.

4. Present it in the form of a suggestion: The erratic behavior of people to when sexual discourse is brought for discussion that nails them to a fault makes it so difficult for partners to anger their beloved. This is why you must present it in the form of a suggestion. This won't all the time sound embarrassing or seen as a means to belittle him. Your choice of words must be cautiously chosen so as not to arouse their anger.

If you adhere to the enlisted ways, it will help you enormously in bringing up sexual matters with your partner. If you feel you are enclosed in thoughts pertaining to your sex life because you're trying to maintain the relationship, the harbored thoughts will further lessen your strength and leave you in shatters. Therefore, ponder on every word herein, muster that heart to bring up matters of your sexual life with your relationship and you shall have more than one cause to enjoy a lasting relationship. To reiterate, relationship that sidelines sexual communication is open to seismic disruption. Love them but most importantly talk about your sexual life with your partner.

How do you control your partner if they react badly?

Sexual communication should not sprout any bit of quarrel, but it should rather be a basis to build a comforting relationship lay on honesty, understanding, openness, and love. The above phase that talked on when and the appropriate time and place to bring up matters that relate to your sexual life with you partner will also tremendously help us in treating reaction too. For example, the quiet place that was proposed, if they react disorderly, you are in the position to put them in order. Make them know the importance of your sexual life and why they need to give ears to your suggestion.

Sex can't be completely separated from a relationship and a relationship that never bothers on the pleasure derived by the partners is most likely not last long. You must be able to bring joy to yourself if you can face your partner and let them know the importance of sex in modifying the mightiness of your union.

In building your intimacy through other means, to start with, we are going to talk about the five methods that you need to follow in order to create some more emotional intimacy with your partner. Emotional intimacy allows you and your partner a way to not only look good on paper, and to the outside world, but also to look good on the inside. It allows you both to know each other deeply, in a way that no one else should know you or your partner.

The good news is that this intimacy can be obtainable, no matter how long you have been in the relationship. Provided that both of you are willing to invest the time being vulnerable, and you are willing to talk to each other, you can make this work. Some of the steps that you can follow to create a deeper sense of intimacy between you and your partner includes:

When you start the conversation, pick out safer topics

When you first get started, you don't want to just jump into the tough stuff. Even if you have been into the relationship for a long time, jumping into the deep stuff can be intimidating, and can make one or both of you feel nervous and unsure of how you should proceed. Starting with some of the safer topics, the ones that you are both pretty sure how the other one is going to respond can be a much better option. This allows you to feel more comfortable, to get the hang of the process, and can build up some confidence for when you get deeper into this process.

So, to start, you need to focus your conversation. You can choose to do this for a few months or any length of time that you would like. Make sure that you set aside a good 30 minutes a day to talk and work on this. And when you start, you want to make sure that you are working with some comfortable topics so that this activity is more enjoyable, and you will be more willing to stick with it for the long term.

There are a lot of questions that you can talk to your partner about with this in mind. You can ask them about some of the memories that they remember back from when you were dating and ask why that memory is so important to them. Ask if there is something that they would love to be able to go back and do again.

Make it clear that both partners can share anything

When you are working on these conversations, make sure that both parties know that anything is safe to say or share during this time. Starting out with these conversations can be hard, but when everyone knows that they are in a safe space then they may be more willing to go along with it. You and your partner both want what is best for one another, so why try to make the other one feels bad or feels worried about what is going on when they tell you something?

This isn't an excuse for one or the other to be mean to each other. You can't go into this and say all of the bad things that your partner has ever done wrong in the relationship. This isn't going to be productive, and can make it almost impossible for them to feel good or open up to you. This is supposed to be a time for the two of you to learn more about each other, and to gain a fuller knowledge about one another. If one of the partners feels like they are being attacked, then they aren't going to open up, and they will probably try to get out of doing this again.

The point here is for the conversation to be a good way for you and your partner to become vulnerable with each other. This is the only way that the two of you are going to become more intimate with each other in this sense of the word. If you aren't opening up the floor as a safe space, then it is going to be almost impossible to get any further.

CHAPTER 24:

Marriage Secrets

When it comes to getting married, there are only a few people who are certain what they are getting themselves into. The truth is that we all have an idea of what marriage is about. What we have are hopes, expectations, and dreams of what marriage truly looks like. When we watch some of the movies starts we like, we think that the kind of marriages they show on Tv is what it is like in real life.

Well, let me tell you something, you have no idea what marriage is until you are there!

When I was getting married to my wife, there are things that I thought I knew, but once I got in, that is when I got the real deal! Getting married does not also mean that you will know everything. However, you will get to learn new things as you get by.

Here are some of the secrets I can tell you will strengthen your marriage if you pay attention to them;

Secret 1 Marriage is more about intimacy than sex

If you ask anyone that is single and planning to get married what marriage is about, they will tell you it is about sex. While there is so much value you draw from getting married to your partner as far as your sexual relationship, the truth is that a good marriage is built on intimacy. This is the only way you are going to enjoy good sex and not the other way around.

When I got married, I was excited that we were finally going to enjoy all the sex we want with my partner, and we do! However, I never quite understood the concept of real intimacy until I committed to spending the rest of my life with my lovely wife. What I have come to learn and understand is that marriage is a brilliant opportunity in which you allow your partner to look right inside your life, heart, and mind. That is what true intimacy is about!

Secret 2 Marriage uncovers self-centeredness but also cultivates selflessness

Confessions, I didn't realize how selfish I was until I got married to my wife. One year down the line, my selfishness was out in the light. I could choose what restaurant we would eat, who gets to clean up, what movie we will watch, and who gets the remote. What was even shocking was that each time we argued, my wife would apologize first even if I was the one at fault.

One thing you need to realize about marriage is that if you are going to make it last, you have to learn to place the needs of your spouse before your own. This is how you start learning the true meaning of being selfless. Trust me, even though this is a hard lesson to learn, it is a beautiful reminder of God's selflessness when He gave His all so that you and I can have it all in abundance.

Secret 3 Oneness means being ONE

Have you taken a time to think about the spiritual and physical benefits of oneness? The truth is that most people fail to consider the part where it is slightly inconveniencing, living in one house, sleeping on one bed, sharing the same bathroom, working with the same budget, and operating one bank account, among others.

The truth is, when we get into marriage, we stop being "me" and become "us." We stop having things that are "mine," and we view everything as "ours." To build a healthy relationship, you have to care for everything as though they were not just yours but also belonged to the person that you love most.

Secret 4 At certain points, you will be disappointed

This is one of the most tough realities that most couples find it hard to believe. You must be aware of your spouse's humanity and yours too. However, it is interesting that this reality does not hit home sooner until you are disappointed.

My wife and I have always loved each other deeply. This does not mean that we have not hurt each other a few times in our relationship. One thing you have to set in mind is that when you marry someone, you are choosing to bury your heart in theirs, and theirs in yours.

What you need to be ready for is that there will come a day when you will feel an ache. This agony can come in the form of an unkind word, a selfish moment, or even a thoughtless action. However, you must choose to embrace the grace of God so that every hurt and wound pave the way for forgiveness and restoration. Each wound should serve as a constant reminder of our need to love deeply and better each time.

Secret 5 You must learn the meaning of forgiveness whether you like it or not

The fact that you are going to get hurt means that you have to embrace the reality of learning the essence of forgiveness. One lesson that you must learn is that forgiveness comes not just because your partner deserves it, but because it whelms from a heart that understands how much forgiveness we had received even when we least deserved it.

Secret 6 Marriage will cost you

When you are in the glory of marriage, the truth is that you will lose a part of yourself. In other words, you exchange a portion of who you are for the sake of taking up a little bit of who your partner is. In short, you learn the essence of giving and taking. In marriage, you will know to let go of the things that do not matter to you at all. What you realize eventually is that what you have given is far much less than what you receive ultimately.

Trust me; love is good, just like that!

Secret 7 Love is a series of decision and not a feeling

Before you got married, the chances are that you did not understand the strong feelings that you felt. And then, suddenly, you start realizing that you cannot trust your feelings because there are days when you don't like your spouse, and most days, you just can't let him go.

Note that feelings are temporary. They come and go. They are more like a compass, and in other instances, they serve as a guide, but the truth is that you cannot follow them because they don't lead anywhere specific.

The true test of love is what you do when you feel that you don't like your spouse. Understand that marriage is about choosing to love your partner even when you don't want to. You are choosing to give your all into serving them because you committed to them, the world, and God that you would love them "for better or for worse." It is about you constantly choosing your spouse instead of yourself.

That is what true life means!

Secret 8 Marriage requires that you learn how to communicate

We have mentioned before that one of the most important building blocks of marriage is effective, clear, and honest communication with each other. It does not matter what it is that you are fighting about with your spouse. What matters the most is what you would do about it. How you will choose to communicate to them how you feel.

In short, marriage is about you constantly communicating with your spouse, your values, beliefs, opinions, and feelings. It is about not fearing to ask the tough questions, tell the hard truth, or even respond to difficult questions. It serves as a lifeline between you and your spouse. Trust me; there is no other way around it. You have to be ready to take responsibility for what you say, how you say it, and how you react to your partner's response.

Watch your tone, sarcasm, and body language! It speaks a lot.

Secret 9 Marriage is not the end of your destination

When you are still dating, it is often easy to look at marriage as your grand finale! It is that thing that you have been dreaming about since you were a little girl or boy. It is what you have lived for all your life, and finally, it is here. The next thing you think of when you get married is, "Now what?"

What you need to discern is that the relationship and marriage God has blessed you with is just a small portion of the grand scheme he has set for your life. The truth is that your purpose and passion will supersede the relationship you have with your partner. God will use your relationship and the love between you and your spouse for the glory of His name.

Your marriage is not the end of everything. Instead, it is just the beginning of the many more blessings he has in store for you.

So, quit giving up and fixing your mind on an ending. He has so much up his sleeve, and you have not seen anything yet!

Secret 10 Marriage offers you a glimpse of so much more

Aside from the fact that you already know God has so much more in store for you, there is a lot you have to learn about God as you interact with other people regularly. Realize that there is a reason why God uses the institution of marriage when talking about the love He has for the church.

There is no single relationship you are going to have that will compare to that intimacy that is exchanged through marriage here on earth. The love that God has for us is magnified through the lens of a strong, healthy, and long-lasting marriage. But the best part is that he uses the institution of marriage to teach us, mold us, refine us, and laid us through the test. In other words, it is through marriage that God keeps making us be more of Him.

When we reflect on the love of God in the way we love our spouse, we honor Him, and that is exactly what He uses to keep our marriages alive. What you need to understand is that there are so many ways you can achieve holiness, and marriage is one of them. Note that you are a different person because of the relationship he has given you and realize that he is not yet finished with you. Always purpose to expect from Him every single day.

CHAPTER 25:

Dealing with Temptations

Every day we are faced with temptations. They can be anything from getting a new motorcycle to cheating. Anytime we are tempted to do something we know, we should not do it is a temptation.

For me, my biggest temptation is chocolate. Even though chocolate is not a serious offense in a marriage. Yet, it is still a temptation. The problem is, the way we deal with our temptations. If you have a chocolate temptation, let your spouse help you kick it. They will gladly hide it from you, so you cannot find it.

I remembered a few years ago, and I was craving chocolate. My wife does not allow me to have much, and so the craving is always here. I went to the store to get groceries and picked up some chocolate. I snuck it home and hid it under the bed. Little did I know she was cleaning the bedroom that day. The chocolate that was hiding was found. What a sad and depressing day. Chocolate is one thing, but what about temptations in your marriage? There are some severe temptations that you must avoid. I realize that you cannot stop your urge of attractions. The best solution is to run away.

The history of temptation goes back during pre-historic times. It is as old as, back to the Garden of Eden. The devil, in the form of a serpent, tempted the first humans, Adam and Eve. They fell for the lies the serpent told them. The Bible says a lot of stories about the temptation. It has always been a part of human nature to be tempted. Temptations are brought our curiosity; we indulge in things that entice us, gratify us, and makes us feel emotions we have not thought for a long time. Temptations come in several different ways, such as eating healthy foods, maintaining a good lifestyle, managing finances, and attraction to someone. There is a lot of ways to be tempted. In some context, the temptation is connected to sin for those who sinned are those that cannot resist temptation. The temptation may be used to the state of being satisfied without following moral standards.

The attraction is one way to be tempted, and perhaps the reason is why affairs and sexual intimacy to someone other than your partner are happening. Although it is reasonable to be attracted to other people, what matters is how you act on those feelings and how you stop it before it creates sin in the marriage.

In marriage, every affair begins with a temptation of an attraction. Marriages break up because one partner loses themselves in fascination and thinks they can get away with it. One selfish act can wipe out your relationship and vanish the years of integrity. Most families are broken caused by one of the parents having an affair and not thinking about what effects it may have.

In some cases, the notion of a marital affair will always lead to blaming the husband. In every cheating husband, there must also be a cheating woman. Extramarital relations outside marriage where an illicit romance or sexual relationship, romantic friendship or intimate attachment occurs are being done by two persons. An affair that carries on in one form or another for years will eventually lead to separation and divorce.

In a marriage concept, temptation often builds up when one partner started looking for someone who treats them better than their spouse. A marriage becomes weak when facing problems; for example, a wife becomes attracted to a man who empathizes and listens to her more. Both partners are susceptible to committing a mistake. Marital problems were existing between partners, and it has become easy to look for others who will give them the attention they are not getting from their spouse. It is a human weakness to fall for someone who gives them more attention and affection. Eventually, confiding their problems to that person will lead to closeness resulting in an affair.

The temptation is one of the challenges married couples are facing. Together, we will learn how to identify various ways on how to deal with temptation. You will learn the underlying factors that cause temptation to exist in your marriage and its consequences if it continues to exist. Each topic will provide you with solutions that refrain you from being tempted. However, this will only serve as a guide for married couples that are currently facing temptation as a challenge but not to the extent that would provide an exact solution to the matters at hand. Spouses need to keep an open mind when working out a marriage, it is not suitable for judging your spouse if they committed a mistake, but rather it will be helpful if you keep an open ear and trust them to be honest about their confession. Marriage is hard work, and making it successful takes a lifetime. It is only common for couples to experience temptation along the way; the important thing is to have both partners to be determined to drive against it.

Take the time to go over the list of ways on how to battle temptation. It will provide insights that can assist couples in determining ideas on how to overcome temptation. It is better to discuss this with your partner to be able to come up with a solution that could help you resolve your situation.

The Courage to Resist Temptation

Temptation can be described as an immediate pleasurable urge and impulse to fill the void of something lacking. It exists because something is lacking in a married couple's life. Some say affairs happen because the love of each spouse was no longer alive. It involves a romance that brings back those memories of being pursued, excitement, and sexually intimate. It makes you feel young and being wanted again.

One way to avoid temptation is to fill the void of whatever you feel is lacking in your relationship. Sometimes we compare our married life to others, and nowadays, with the use of technology, we often see the gaps in our relationship. We long for consistency of love, touch, romance, and the desire brought about by our insecurities, making ourselves more vulnerable to temptations. We try to think of scenarios of "what ifs." What if our husband is more compassionate than he is now, practices romance, and remembers all the special occasion? Then maybe we wouldn't be tempted to look for others in the first place. You try to picture a different person out of your husband throughout your marriage. You no longer admire the one you signed up for through marriage. We often believe that it is our husband's fault that you came looking for others, but it's not. Signing up for marriage is nothing like a membership club; you pay the fee and use it all you want. In marriage, you must make all the effort to keep your membership, or otherwise, you'll be taken out.

The critical thing to remember in resisting temptation is to have the "courage" to resist temptation. For instance, thinking of others through your thoughts during your marriage chaos, such as leaving your spouse or involving in an affair, will feel desirable at the moment; however, in the long run, it bears undesirable results. Exercising self-control is also essential; it makes us feel superior to our desires. Once we thought we are walking on the wrong path, we need to take a detour and regain control of ourselves. We need to paint the 'what will happen" if we succumb to temptation. Fixates ourselves to the aftereffects if we divulge on our selfish desires. We cannot sacrifice the well-being of our family. Giving in to temptation will result in a broken marriage and interfere with your long-term goals. We were making it easier to deal with temptation if you were avoiding what tempts you.

Do not Be Surprised When It Happens

Do not be afraid, but rather be prepared. Make it a habit dealing with temptation, for it's always there. Temptation can come in any form; for instance, your eating habits, sleeping routine, and managing your finances. Let us acknowledge that we will be tempted in all kinds somehow, but the upper hand of letting it happen is in our hands. You were born with the wisdom of differentiating what is wrong from right, and through this, we will be able to determine what is better.

You need to be prepared. Like commencing a "fire drill" in a school to make students and staff prepare in case, a real incident will happen. You must equip yourselves with the knowledge that is beneficial for you in dealing with temptations. For example, exposing yourself to healthy foods through the process of not buying processed or carb-filled food will take you to your goals of achieving a healthy lifestyle. You need to have the determination to continue what you are starting.

Giving in to temptation is only one part of the journey, but do not be surprised if you see yourself on the verge of losing it. Be prepared and regain your self-control.

Ask for help

People with a strong sense of independence are not fond of asking for help in times of trouble. They believe it is their responsibility to resolve problems on their own without asking for help. Most people think of a notion that temptation often leads to marital affairs. These stereotypes suppress people from talking about attractions. They don't want to be judged and make their family look as if they're breaking apart; therefore, keeping it from others. For some, the word temptation alone carries the burden history of a broken marriage and family. Most often, marital affairs are caused by temptation, such as husbands cheating on their wives or wives cheating on their husbands. The attraction had done its part in creating chaos in the married world. It is good to be aware of another way of dealing with temptation is to ask for help. It is significant to have someone that you can consult with the same experiences you have. Realizing that someone has gone through what you are also going through is like a breath of fresh air. Through your friends, you can ask for help. For example, the way you resist temptation in a particular situation. It's better to have someone who can understand where you are coming from and who will pay attention to your thoughts without judgment. Asking for help can have many benefits, such as helping you progress better and faster. Asking for help makes you feel more grateful, you develop your sense of trust, and strengthen your relationship to the people you confide in. You are bound to live with companions, which is where the famous saying "No man is an island" comes from. Everybody needs a companion or friend. It is not weakness to ask for help. If you choose to accept support from someone you can trust, they might teach you something new and provide you with more useful knowledge that you can use in your marriage.

RELATIONSHIP THERAPY

CHAPTER 26:

How to Live a Happy Relationship

Relationships require maintenance and constant work for it to succeed and turn into a long, loving, and happy relationship. People are often taught that love just happens, and sometimes they are even told that for a relationship to be successful, love is all that is needed. However, relationships are much more than that and love is not enough. Love can be the first spark that ignites the relationship and is how it came to exist. To build a long-lasting connection with another person, you need to think in more realistic terms when it comes to defining love. Expanding on the simplistic view, or fairytale, you dreamt of when you were young is the first step.

For a happy relationship, you have to actively work on it and make the best of everything you encounter on your path to happiness. Having a happy relationship means making conscious choices that will work towards that happiness, even if sometimes the decisions you make seem difficult and challenging.

Everyone makes mistakes when it comes to relationships, and we aren't referring to solely romantic ones. Even with friends, our behavior might influence how much they trust us, rely on us, and how much we will connect with them, and on what level. The fact we all make mistakes doesn't mean there is nothing you can do about it. There is actually a lot! There are procedures both you and your partner can take to avoid mistakes, manage them if they already happened, and bring happiness to your relationship:

1.   Your partner is your equal: This is something people often forget when they are bossing each other around. Do you recognize yourself or your partner while reading this? Instead of being the leader of the relationship, try collaboration. Work together, listen to your partner, and be as supportive as possible.

2.   Be respectful: Spending a lot of time with one person can be indeed exhausting, especially if you live with your partner. Once in a while, it may seem like your partner is triggering your nerves or anxiety, and you may feel anger or resentment building up. You may end up lashing out even if he or she isn't entirely at fault. No matter how you feel, how mad you are, your partner needs to learn about such emotions respectively. Communication plays an significant role here as well as self-control. Practice both of these even outside of your relationship, and you will see only the positive influence it leaves on people.

3.   Spend quality time with your partner: Back when your relationship was fresh and new, you spent so much time together, and you did everything together. Where did all of that go? Well, life happens, children come, people focus on their jobs and careers, home, chores, and so on. Some may lose all of their free time that they used to devote to their partners. Even so, for a relationship to succeed, you need to make that time even when it's scarce. Happy relationships demand you to push yourself and your partner and do something together. It is not enough to talk to each other at the end of the day about work or various problems. Quality time means getting to work together on a project. For instance, you can repaint your home, build a dollhouse for

your kids, go hiking or exercising together, volunteer in an animal shelter, and so on. By working together on something that you are both interested in, you will reconnect and even learn new things about each other. It is a satisfying and enriching experience.

4. Learn how to forgive: It is essential to know how to forgive your partner's mistakes, but you also have to be ready to forgive yourself. Empathy plays a significant role in forgiveness. It helps you feel your partner's emotions, understand their behavior, and make room in your heart for real and unconditional forgiveness. Be the same towards yourself. Learn self-compassion and practice it. It is a great skill that will not just heal wounds created by mistakes, but also teach you not to repeat them.

Confidence, Honesty and Loyalty

The three most desirable traits people seek in their love interests are confidence, honesty, and loyalty. But they do not come easily to everyone. Some gain them during their childhood, while others have to learn them and stay true to them to build a healthy, stable relationship.

Confidence

We quickly develop low self-esteem if you are hurt in a previous relationship. It may be hard to win back your trust, but it is not impossible. Confidence should be strong yet yielding, as overconfident people can be inflexible and bad listeners. However, the right amount will improve your relationship, the way you react in stressful situations, and it will positively affect your health. There is a series of exercises you could do every day to build your confidence, such as the following:

1.   Imagine what you want to be: Visualizing your goals is a fantastic technique to build motivation. It will keep you moving and remind you of your aspirations and goals. Don't be afraid to talk about what you want with friends, family, and especially with your partner. They can help you get there, with proper advice or with support.

2.   Affirm yourself: It means you need to vocalize positive statements and opinions regarding yourself. It may sound meaningless at first, but hearing it, even hearing yourself saying it out loud, will help you believe it. The human brain tends to accept statements more quickly if they are in the form of a question. Instead of saying, "I am good with money," try asking yourself, "why am I so good with money?"

3.   Challenge yourself: Once a day, do something that scares you. In most cases, the best way to overcome fear is to face it. Anxieties often stop people from performing simple, everyday tasks like making a phone call, going to the bank, or meeting new people. Doing things that scare you will push you to realize that you can improve yourself. Going through the challenge may even boost your self-confidence and in time help you get over some of your anxieties. Just be sure to make a ritual of it and challenge yourself every day.

Honesty

Being honest is so much more than telling the truth. It also means not keeping any secrets from your partner, caring for others, and having integrity. Being honest means your partner can fully rely on you, trust you with his whole heart, and be proud of you. Take note, that even small "white" lies can generate relationship problems, mistrust, and anxiety, for yourself as well as your partner once he or she learns the truth. If you find yourself telling small lies due to your stress, you may need to practice honesty. Here are the steps you can take to learn how to be completely honest without being anxious:

1. Understand why you lied: Did you fabricate things to make yourself look better? Or to avoid embarrassment? Understanding why you lied is a big step forward to changing the things about you for the better. People lie for various reasons but being aware of those reasons will help you deal with them in other ways. Perhaps you need to work on your confidence, or you think you deserve more respect. Try to earn it with honesty instead of making up stories about yourself. People often lie out of shame or out of a lack of confidence and self-esteem. For instance, if you did something you aren't proud of, you may be tempted to cover it up with lies. Many people even lie to themselves in an attempt to get rid of that feeling of shame. Instead, be responsible and accept your bad behavior because acceptance allows you to take the steps needed to correct it. This way, you will show others that you can be honest and possibly someone to trust and rely on.

2. Change your behavior: Guilt is a powerful feeling, and any behavior that has led you to experience it will cause anxiety. When you are found guilty by others, you may also lose their respect. Being guilty and admitting it will more often bring understanding instead of judgment, especially when it comes to your partner who loves you. However, you should not rely on knowledge alone. Try to change bad habits and behaviors and avoid putting yourself in a situation that will make you feel guilty and that will make you lie to your loved ones.

3. Don't compare yourself to others: In our attempt to be better and earn respect, we often lie about who we are. You need to recognize who you are and to learn to live with it, even if you see yourself in a negative light. Don't forget that anxiety

often makes people overly critical of themselves, and you might not be as faulty as you think. Improve yourself, work on your personality, and become who you want to be instead of lying about it. Instead of making up things about yourself to impress your partner, let your honesty impress him. It will build a connection between the two of you, and it will make your relationship stronger.

4. Avoid lying for others: Sometimes, our friends and family will put us in stressful situations and ask us to lie for them. Let them know this is not an option for you and that you are an honest person. If they want you to keep a secret for them, be sure you can do it, and don't dive in to the temptation of gossip.

Loyalty

When we think about loyalty in a relationship, it usually means as not cheating. But, loyalty also implies devotion to your partner, being faithful, committed, and honest. Loyalty is so much more than just fidelity. It means opening yourself to your partner and sharing all of your emotions, thoughts, and opinions. Here's what you can do to show and prove your loyalty to your partner:

1. If you want to be truly loyal to your partner, you have to be honest with yourself. Practice transparency, get to know yourself and be aware of who you are. We often have the wrong image of ourselves, and if you don't know yourself, how could you offer to be connected to someone else. How can you share yourself, and commit?

2. Be open with your partner. Not just honest but let them read you. Share your emotions and opinions at the end of your day. Sit down with your partner and spend time talking about

your day. Include all the events and express how it made you feel and how it has influenced you.

3. Don't put yourself in the position that will make you hide something from your partner. Don't hide events, experiences, and don't hide your emotions. Keeping secrets is postponing the inevitable. Secrets will somehow come out one way or another and your attempt to hide them will just cause pain for you and your partner.

4. Be supportive. Be present for your partner through the good and bad. We all have our moments when even the slightest tantrum will trigger anxiety. Don't judge your partner. Don't tell him or her how to behave or what to do. Support them with understanding and care. Don't say things like "There is no reason to be angry", say it "I understand why that would make you angry."

MICHELLE MILLER

CHAPTER 27:

Overcoming Negative Thinking

All sorts of things can ruin a perfectly successful relationship. For example, money and incompatibility are the two big ones. But according to professionals there is one thing that can destroy a relationship more than anything else. Nicole Issa Psy. D., a Bustle certified psychologist calls it "the ultimate relationship killer", that is, negative thinking! There's a very close feedback loop between the thoughts, emotions, and actions of a person. And getting negative thoughts will take you down the rabbit hole." It's important to realize that your habits of thinking will contribute to major relationship issues. Early childhood encounters with your parents, for example, can lead you to believe you're unworthy of love. Because of that, you may go into a relationship believing that at some point, your partner will abandon you, and you may be afraid to speak up.

The truth is we're making our own truth. When we assume we have a good relationship, then we work through things hoping everything will always be fine. But when you enter a relationship with pessimistic feelings, you always expect the worst not only of your partner but of the result of your relationship.

You'd like to think twice before you let yourself down or place an over-negative and frustrating relationship if you're looking for love (like most of us). When you are trying to find true friendship or the right relationship, you're going to want to be more optimistic about your approach. Meaning: you're going to have to be more optimistic about your spouse, particularly if it's fresh, and you're going to want to be more open-minded to love and be real, when you know how much you value. If you start to put in fear, doubt, hesitation, and a false character, you'll probably lose out on something that could be awesome down the road.

Will negative thinking ever harm you? You know some signs firsthand whether you're harshly critical or trapped in concern, stress, anxiety, depression or low self-worth. Negative thinking can affect our relationships, our health and our jobs, our lives, intensely and often devastatingly.

I think everyone can break free from negativity for good with the four keys mentioned below. Why do I think so? And if I can (and I have) from the dark place in which I used to be, I believe those resources will also work for you — wherever you are.

People also seek and get rid of their negative ideas in several different ways including distraction. They 'drink their sorrows' and later and punish themselves emotionally for still being trapped in their misery. It could feel like a true inner struggle. These are common policies that seek in the short run to stop the thoughts and relieve the pain, but which only exacerbate things in the long term. The question at its root is not solved.

The work shows that challenging, contending, attempting to overwhelm or push unhelpful thoughts just amplifies and worsens issues.

I work with clients to find satisfaction in their relationships as a professional wellness coach, of course, you must express the good and evil in terms of thoughts and feelings while you are honest so that your partner is better equipped to do all that.

But it might be too much to deal with if you're ever bitter or pissed off, particularly if you know it's too long or too lengthy.

Moreover, you should not only be thinking negative thoughts about a potential relationship but also the negative thoughts that might keep you from putting yourself in the first place. You will not give yourself a reasonable chance to find love and match with someone when there are too much strain and doubt. The crap? Know when to hold negative feelings in order to boost mental wellbeing and when to make those unpleasant thoughts constructive.

Think of other times they've taken some time to react or prove. This shows that they're still interested. The alternative idea here could be straighter than just because I haven't even heard of them yet, that doesn't mean they're not interested.

Recall that controlling your goals is important to your relationship's success. In the world of relationships, discord and conflict are inevitable, just note this is normal and all right. What is most important is how you and your partner manage and develop in tough times.

Recall that your partner is also a person. Not all your partner does will be "right" or "good," but you do not feel frustrated to put your critical lens on. Say your needs and do not want to spread the word when the entire relationship is hurt. Find the partner deliberately in a favorable light. Thank your partner for their little acts and deeds of love and kindness. Say thank you. This perpetuates your relationship with a supportive and caring loop.

Don't actually take it all. Poor dates, challenges, rough talks and times can be frustrating at the time. Don't add these experiences to the negative stack, but then find the life lessons that are aligned with your goals. Engage yourself to be happy on the journey to love.

Break up is not a viable option, whatever your toxic thinking is, it typically comes from the same position – fear. Fear of your partner quitting, in particular. When you [commit], I use an example, you burn the ship. You so honestly do not have a way to reach the island when you burn the ships, and you need to work together to survive. You should often see the positivity in every condition when there is no other choice. You will enable your relationship to come from a position of love rather than misery if you take the possibility of breaking out of the equation (i.e. 'burning your ship.'). It is easier for you to remain optimistic when your words and acts come from a position of affection. A thought is just thinking at the end of the day. It's not the truth, actually. Your connection will be a much stronger one if you don't allow it to overtake you.

Dr. Natalie Feinblatt, a licensed clinical psychologist, explains via email with Bustle, that he only need someone that's complete. You must love yourself and feel whole as if you want to open up to someone else. You are already done! There are two half-ways to form a whole, and there are two whole communities together to create a beautiful couple that is the basis for a lasting stable relationship.

This attitude generates a strong assumption that an individual is right for you. You certainly do not want anything to lose, this idea places incredible pressure on yourself to find the one thing and protect it. This might also make people choose partners who do not suit their wishes, since they are too overwhelming to release someone who may be one.

It's not going to work out. Don't get upset without understanding first even your date. In a new partnership, assuming it's like the last one (which obviously was a failure) gives the new relationship a ticking time bomb. This new relationship. Fear it and be hopeful instead.

It isn't like my husband. No similarities with a husband-boyfriend in your relationship or your spouse. Just don't do it. Just don't do it. Such things obviously aren't fit for you two anyway, they're different men. If you equate your relationship with one that has not been established in the past, then the relationship you are creating may be a failure. So sit tight and enjoy the magic and joy oozing out from your relationship. Give your partner an open and equal chance.

You can limit your chance of happiness by defining the ideal partner based on assumptions or personal preferences. He or she may prove to be the most affectionate and marvelous companion. It's not my kids. You might be shocked at the kind of person you ultimately fall in love with. Allow yourself to learn from someone you know and understand that there is no "kind" here.

You're going to cheat on me, is one way these thoughts could be fused in your head. If you've been lied on in the past, you may develop a presumption that all people cheat. This induces anxiety, leading to behaviors that stress and strain those involved. We should prevent mistrust, lack of contact and anxiety of involvement.

If this is the right guy, your true self will never get rid of it. "I'll mess this connection up." It just implies that it didn't work out and you're both not compatible. Breakdowns, as they arise, are the reason for new development. If the relationship is not meant to go on, it will become obvious. Do not repress the real and genuine self because it will only come out later anyway. Be safe. Be confident. Make moves.

"You're out of my own league." If you're constantly questioning your own values, you could ruin a relationship that is great. There wouldn't be any truthful partner left for you due to your lack of self-confidence. It also brings into question their decision by being with you first and foremost. Moreover, a poor partner sees this as a chance to step all over you.

You cannot change the people; instead, while in some areas, such as communication, you could create some improvements, you should take your partner for their core values. (They're not going anywhere.) Nobody wants to be a pet project. You're going to find that the next person that embraces them as they are is taking the whole job that you've done to make them the person you'd want to be. On the other hand, if they've never changed, you're frustrated with no reason.

If you constantly think that you are used for your money, power, or access, it's hard to know the real person, because you are likely to put up emotional walls to shield yourself and avoid an actual link. It protects you from getting hurt by putting up emotional walls, but it also protects you from getting love.

Some couples bring this into their marriages or relationships. "You would have done this or that if I meant anything to you." However, the truth is, don't expect too much from your relationship. Of course, empathy and consideration will be required when appropriate but you can ruin everything if you are too protective and demanding if it's not appropriate and you force others to be there too much for your every need. Taking it seriously is the end of the relationship. This also doesn't mean they don't value you if your loved one doesn't respond in the way you think you're supposed to or do something you won't do.

Don't worry about the ex of your partner. This doesn't matter. While it's in human nature to be curious about who our partners dated and even compete with them, it doesn't do anything positive just to waste time. Their ex is for a reason — it doesn't work! Forget about the past because it's not important at all today, the more time you waste thinking about their past relationships, the less time you have to make sure your present relationships work out. The most frustrating thing about this is that it sparks up insecurity in your mind and nothing is just enough to make you happy.

MICHELLE MILLER

CHAPTER 28:

Tips and Strategies to Maintain Your Emotional Wellbeing

Reminders of Your Own Mental Health

There's no five-step program of fixing depression or your relationship. Depression is common in the short term, inevitable, and impacts everyone differently. You are likely to come across problems linked to it. Your outlook does, however, influence both your partnership and your ability to support your partner.

You are not their therapist. It's really important to show your love and support for your friend, but it is never equal to counseling or professional help for mental wellness. Don't put pressure on yourself to repair your partner's depression, because it's not your job. You are not liable for their hardships, and feeling as though you were places undue pressure on your relationship. Just do anything you need to support them, as would any committed friend.

You need self-care, and you may know that you are exhausted from constant high emotions. It's vital to care for your mental health. Many partners will overplay the needs of their significant others who are distressed. This may deplete your mental resources, and may even physically tax you. Take a step back and ensure you still have the support you need.

Empathy and open communication are important in all relationships, but when coping with depression, extra effort is needed. Depression in your relationship allows you to develop a new vocabulary of emotion with your partner.

Be transparent with how you feel, and realize that they can struggle to put their feelings into words. Validate what they're doing, even though you may not personally understand what they mean.

It's difficult to negotiate a relationship with a depressed partner. Depression will show relationship's defects and make them even more difficult to surmount. Many of the abilities needed, such as empathy, can, therefore, enhance any relationship.

How to help your partner when their anxiety is out of balance

1) Ask questions and do the best to understand what they are going through; it can be different for everyone. Some people will experience painful body reactions like a churning stomach or a heart rate out of control.

Although you can read articles online about what it is like to deal with anxiety, you won't get the full picture of your partner's reality.

It is a personal and profoundly subjective experience.

If you want to comprehend what it's like for them, you need to talk about it with them.

It's easier to have the conversation in a quiet room while you're home. After all, the friend needs to feel comfortable thinking about something that puts them in distress.

Here are three relevant questions you can ask:

a) Is there something about your anxiety you want me to know?

b) Is there something I can do that will help if you feel anxious?

c) Is there anything you might not like me to do?

As someone who has spent my entire life coping with anxiety, I can assure you it is not easy to talk about anxiety.

So be patient, and take your time talking with your partner about this difficult subject.

Note, you don't have to understand everything there is to know about your partner's anxiety, in one conversation. It'll take quite some time.

Also, if you've just started dating, it will probably take time to build the trust and understanding required to be completely truthful with each other about these kinds of things.

2) Do not underestimate the power of insight.

It is very normal for most anxious people not to want to speak about it.

If this is the case, even though they aren't transparent about it, by watching them in various circumstances, you can still learn a lot about your partner.

See how they are responding to other issues. Remember how awkward or relaxed they feel.

When you are closely watching, you will be able to grasp what is causing their fear, and what is not.

This is an immense support to your friend because they may not be able to communicate their fear.

The more you appreciate your mate, the more support they experience in the relationship.

This is what it takes to build a satisfying and long-lasting relationship.

3) Have patience.

Patience, when you're dating someone with anxiety, is a very important quality. Feeling antsy and trying to always be "in the know" will make things worse.

Unfortunately, being cautious often is the only option, particularly if your partner then experiences anxiety. Anxiety requires time to pass.

The important thing about anxiety that you need to realize is that it can't be "fixed."

Sure, some strategies and medications can help manage anxiety, but no one can be magically cured of their anxiety.

Instead of trying to save the day when your friend feels distressed, it's best to be patient and reassure them that everything is all right.

In reality, rushing to act will intensify your partner's anxiety. This is going to demonstrate to them that there is a major issue that will make their anxiety worse.

The best you can do is be cool, compassionate, and let them know you're with them.

4) Communicate with your partner clearly. Not being truthful with your partner will make matters worse. It will lead them to doubt what is going on and to see themselves second-hand.

That is not what an anxious person wants.

You need to communicate clearly and be sure in yourself.

This also means you should not be playing games. After you have seen it, don't take 4 hours to answer a message.

Be prompt and truthful, and respond when you see it.

It's about getting rid of unknowns.

Most anxiety is fear of what will happen in the future, so you can help your partner from second-guessing the future and themselves by being transparent and optimistic about what is going to happen.

5) Calm down. This one is very clear. If you get frustrated, nervous, or impatient, it won't support anyone with anxiousness.

Trust me when I say a person with anxiety likes to be around calm people.

You should aim to maintain your composure, particularly in moments of anxiety that your partner experiences.

It's also significant to note that anxiety can make you feel a little angry or rude to your partner. Sometimes, they do not want to speak with you. You must remain cool, calm, and composed in these situations.

Now, of course, if your partner abuses you while they feel anxiety, it shouldn't be accepted, and you need to talk about it with them.

But if they only want time to have space, you can give them that until their negative feelings have passed.

6) Don't presume that all the negative things in their lives originate from anxiety. Because anxiety is a major issue in

your partner's life, it can be normal to conclude that all the negative things originate from their mental state.

This just is not the case.

The fact is, we're all human, and all of us have our struggles.

It is easy to conclude that everything stems from anxiety but that does little to help your partner cope with what they are going through.

Know it's important to reach out. Take the time to consider what happens to your friend. Believe them.

7) Don't try to justify to them why they shouldn't be afraid of anything. Anxious people realize their fear is not logical. They know that what they are thinking about probably will not happen.

One thing to try is just thinking over what the worst-case scenario could be. This puts it out there and may even help them to know it's not that bad, really.

The most important thing is, don't make them fun for it. They know it how it sounds.

8) Understand that your partner might be nervous about the relationship for various reasons. This is not the case with everyone, but your partner might spend more time than other people thinking about things that may go wrong in the connection.

This is simply called "anxiety about relationships."

Here are some cases of what could be of interest to them:

"What if my anxiety breaks the relationship?"

"What if they cheat?"

"What if he / she's not going to reply to the text?"

"What if someone else likes them more?"

Now, don't get me mistaken: from time to time, most people have these feelings. That is natural. But nervous people may have certain thoughts or doubts more often than normal.

It can lead to greater physical discomfort and anxiety symptoms.

These troubling thoughts could lead an anxious partner to try to find out if their thoughts are real.

For instance, if they believe they are always the one who initiates a meeting first, they may ghost you for a couple of days to see if that is true.

They question their religions to see whether they are wrong or not. This increased stress may also lead to angry or irritable moods or evasive or passive behavior.

9) Do not take it personally.

Because anxiety is a harmful emotion, it can be normal for nervous people to take it out on other people sometimes.

If this turns into violence, then you will have a conversation about it with them.

But if you notice that they are often a little moody and have a go at you, don't take it personally. It is not about you. It is just about the fear they experience.

When you take it personally, then it will turn into an argument or a fight, and it will not do anything for anybody.

Know their bad mood is just temporary. They will be back to being their nice and fun-loving self in no time.

13) Do not look down on your partner.

Yes, it is necessary to show respect and compassion. But you're not meant to look down on your friend, and hate them.

It doesn't make them feel good, nor does it do anything for you. For example, if you're dating a chubby girl, make sure that you give her respect.

Yeah, they're nervous, but that doesn't make them worse than you are. We all have our problems, and while some people have more challenging struggles than others, no one deserves to be looked down on.

It's easier to consider your partner as your equal for the partnership. This is what they would like.

Understand that they are doing their hardest to cope with their fear, and in no way do they want to be handled differently. They want to be a regular person, so treat them as one.

14) Live your life well.

Most importantly, it hurts to see your partner endure pain and suffering. That's one of the hardest things to watch.

But you must continue living your life. They don't want to be the reason you don't live life to its fullest. This adds to the pressure that they are already going through.

What they desire is for you to live life and achieve your potential.

CHAPTER 29:

How and Why to Protect Each Other

The knack to communicate well the needs and feelings of each spouse makes the marriage a good one. After all, once we understand and cherish ourselves, we are better able to express ourselves. And for this reason, happy couples stay authentic, vulnerable, as well as honest with one another, in meeting their individual needs.

So, if your marriage experienced a slump for one reason or another, you should do your best to make it great again. And this can be done by learning the communication secrets of a joyful, harmonious, and symbiotic relationship. Technically speaking, these are happiness tips that can mutually benefit couples.

Being Mindful of your Spouse at All Times

Practicing mindfulness can be instrumental in cultivating and sustaining a healthy bond with your loved one. This can strengthen your ability to become present with your partner, which increases your mutual feelings of love and joy. Also, it enables you to be extra aware of the suffering your partner may be going through.

This awareness makes you less prone to overreact whenever the spouse acts from an area of suffering. When you can maintain mindfulness during those moments your partner is hurting, you will be far more inclined and capable of supporting them when they need it most. Ensuring your partner feels supported and loved is important for the harmony within your relationship.

Effectively and Regularly Communicating

This is quite obvious and its importance is impossible to exaggerate in relationships. Completely disclosing and paying attention to the reasons for the suffering of each other is the solitary way to fix the differences among couples. Listening is vital because over and over again we spend so much time attempting to show our opinion that we neglect to recognize, besides eliminate, the behaviors that perpetuate the suffering of our partner.

Also, effective communication allows us to make sure that we hold a firm picture of reality. And this will cause our decisions not to be founded on the false-negative tales that we tell ourselves from time to time.

Willingness to Adapt as Needed

Change and growth are inevitable within healthy relationships. While people all understand that growth cannot occur without facing the unknown, the majority are deathly uneasy with adjusting. This discomfort leads people to react with only two choices: either fight the partner or run away. When we react by this mode, we lose our chance to bring accord into our bond. Hence, we must admit that relationships change. By staying mindful, we can remain calm and find out the best mode to adjust to change.

Sustaining Perspective

Maintaining an outlook on the meaning of our disparities is important. Once we lack this attitude, an insignificant distinction has the makings to turn into something very significant. To avoid this from happening, we must ask ourselves all the time if the problem is sufficiently important to cause a conflict. Often, we are better off taking our spouse as himself or herself than making a case over anything superfluous to the wellbeing of our marriage. It is far easier to sustain agreement in our relations when we skip arguing over the small stuff.

Fostering Freedom

When single, we have the full direction of our existence. Upon deciding to share your life with someone, however, both parties need to give up this concept of control. After all, when one person commands all features of the relations, the other will feel browbeaten. Oppression is untenable over the long run because people in due course resent their deficiency of freedom. When we commit to share our life with someone, each spouse must give the other a choice to respect the wishes of the other.

Love Rituals

This is an important process for successful relations. I am not mentioning here to the use of love spells, as I believe they are unethical. Instead, I am presenting to you a custom of connection that you can count on to focus yourself on your other half regularly. In the end, couples observing traditions and rituals create shared values in life. And this is because daily rituals modify our existence positively.

Just like any aspect is our life, habits are fundamental to success. Overall, they render us healthier and more productive. In relationships, these love habits can help them thrive.

1. Bestowing your partner a brief kiss daily

A daily kiss that lasts for less than a minute will boost your physical and emotional intimacy. Studies revealed that physical contact releases oxytocin, a bonding hormone, which can improve your disposition for days, besides helping you stay serene.

You can also hold hands, hug, touch, whisper little nothings, and make love that trims down cortisol, the stress hormones, as well as increase your feeling of satisfaction in the relationship.

2. Eating meals together devoid of barriers

Away from the cellphone, newspaper, and the broadcasting TV, share your meals with your beloved. Talk about your plans for the day, whatever happened the day before, or your children. During this period, everything else can wait.

3. Having stress-reducing conversations

Each day, spend half an hour to chat with your other half. This can be during mealtimes, but I suggest this be done as an addition to that. The goal of this chat is to talk about external stress and not to take up issues concerning your relationship. Pairs who actively pay attention, take turns revealing their feelings, and show concern to one another will harvest the gifts of more open linking in their bond.

4. Take trips together without the kids

Do this each year to places you both like. If your funds are limited, try looking for reasonably priced accommodations close by for an extended weekend holiday. When you do this regularly, you are also teaching your children the need to maintain the quality of relationships.

5. Working out together

Go hiking together each Saturday late afternoon or enjoy a daily stroll after dinner with your other half. Add a bit of excitement and novelty by trying boating in midsummer or cross skiing in winter. Research has disclosed that having exciting experiences can bring loving pairs closer together.

Never take too lightly the potency of intentional moments with your spouse. Doing fun stuff together like biking or singing can bring laughter and joy. Telling jokes, going to church as a family, watching funny movies, attending parties as a couple, having a body massage together, or anything new can bring you both happiness that ignites passion and keeps you connected.

Raising Unconditional Love

The theory of unconditional affection is a complex one. People hold various beliefs on this topic that ranges from unabashedly taking it to passionately snubbing it. The veracity about unconditional affection is anywhere in between. People who flatly reject the idea of unconditional affection may be looking at it as a too severe definition. They may be thinking of loving someone without boundaries and ignoring themself.

This would entail changing oneself just to continue loving the person irrespective of what that person does to them. So, the beloved can treat them horribly while still being there for that person. If this is your definition of loving unconditionally, then it is unhealthy. Unconditional love denotes that the couple focuses on whatever keeps them together.

It is not ignoring the existence of the relationship and disregarding neglect or abuse. It is not staying together even when both partners exist unhappy. Now, if you are looking to care for your partner unconditionally, you can do it in healthy ways, such as:

1. Working through the rough times.

This means that you both have to endure unfavorable conditions throughout the relationship. You should mutually not let the disappointing and dark times trick you into doubting your bond. Instead, believe with all your hearts that the love you share is worth waging wars for and working through obstacles as one.

2. Believe that both of you deserve happiness.

Actually, this is foremost of all, as one would not ever suggest remaining in a marriage wherein you are displeased. If you really love your partner, you can decide to exert extra effort to work things out. And believing that each of you deserves happiness in life can put you on the right course.

3. Do not surrender at the initial site of failure.

Accept your other half as a human who makes errors as you do. Each of you has obsessions, flaws, opinions, and particularities. After all, even people with the best easy-going attitudes possess quirks. And if your partner is imperfect, this does not mean that he is not suitable for you.

Also, it does not mean that he is a bad person. So, when you understand that nobody is perfect, it really is okay. All you need is to learn effective communication to help both of you work things out.

4. Embrace each moment together.

Keeping Love Alive Long-Term

Loving someone is, foremost of all, a decision. To keep love alive for a lifetime is a matter of will. Love can fade away and die, if not cultivated or intensified. On the other hand, it can grow, blossom, mature, and evolve into a stronger one over time. In long-term relationships that succeed, romantic affection tends to change into companionship.

Romantic love stays increasingly viewed by way of an essential element of matrimony, with 91% of women, besides 86% of men in America, stating that they prefer to marry someone they love even when they may lack the quality they desire in a spouse. This kind of love, left off the hook of the obsessions and craving of the initial phases of loving, frequently remains in long-term relationships.

In fact, some research found that it is correlated with satisfaction in marriage, and individual self-esteem and well-being. Although science gives us some awareness on the description of romantic relationships and love, this fundamental realm of human life remains a mystery. Affection, particularly the enduring kind, has been even considered as among the most researched, but least fathomed, in psychology.

Life-long romance exists, despite great rates of cheating, divorce, and sadness in married life. Scientific research has proven that strong tender love could last a lifespan, besides the published statements of many old couples who have remained in love with their spouses.

Studies even brought forth that carrying on tender love over many years has a helpful function within the brain that knows and lingers to pursue fervent love by way of an action that reaps mental rewards. And these rewards include a decline in stress and fear while boosting the feeling of safety and calmness, as well as accord with another.

MICHELLE MILLER

CHAPTER 30:

Love

Use Affirmations

While displaying love in your marriage, you should also learn the use of affirmations. Affirmations are words or acts that affirm your love for each other. When last did you tell your spouse that you love him or her? When was the last time you bought him a gift to show how you appreciate and love him? Marriage is like a flower that you water every day for it to bloom and grow.

In the same way, you should affirm for each other regularly. It is not enough that your spouse knows that you love him. You should also make him or her feel it. Fortunately, there are more than a thousand ways to express one's love for another. Over the years that you will spend together as a couple, you will definitely not run out of ways to show your love and make your spouse feel it more deeply.

Affirming one's love is done by continuously loving your spouse. There are many ways to affirm your love, whether through your words or deeds. Never forget to tell your spouse that he or she is important to you.

Avoid saying "I love you." as a mere habit. Those are three sacred and powerful words that deserve attention and respect. Say "I love you" because you mean it and say it as you look straight into your beloved's eyes.

Affirming one's love should not be seen as a duty or obligation. After all, if you are truly in love with your spouse, then affirming your love for him or her would be a natural expression of yourself. Also, you will never run out of ways to affirm your love. It can be as easy as cooking his favorite dishes, buying a surprise gift, among many others. It can also be a surprise dinner date at some luxurious restaurant, a special trip for a vacation, etc. There is no boundary to how you can affirm your love for your spouse because love is infinite.

The use of kind words when you give compliments is one of the best ways to express love. When you do this, be sure that you also use the right tone of voice. Words alone are nothing — you also need to be sincere. If you are sincere enough, and if you express your message the right way, then your spouse would feel it.

Affirming your love to your spouse is something that you should continuously do without an end. If you truly love your spouse, then this is something that is very easy and natural to do. People who are in love usually affirm their love even without thinking about it. Unfortunately, during the long course of a marriage and because of the demands of modern life, you may have to remind yourself every now and then to do some positive action to affirm your love to your spouse. This is good, and you should turn this into a habit. Make sure to affirm your love at least once every week.

Make Your Spouse Feel Important

Right now it should be clear to you that your spouse is one of the most important person in the world for you. It is only right that you let him or her know how important he or she is in your life. There are several ways to do this. You can use words and tell him or her just how important he or she is to you and you can also express it through your actions. You can get him a gift, write him a letter, give him a message, or simply treat him in a special way.

If you think that your spouse might not completely understand your kind gesture of love, then use words to make it very clear to him or her. The important thing is to make sure that him or her knows and feels that he or she is important in your life.

When a person is treated in a special way, it makes him feel important. It makes him feel loved. Hence, making your spouse feel important can do wonders for a relationship. Now, if it is your spouse who makes a move to make you feel just how important you are, make sure to express your appreciation. Although this is not related directly to communication, take note that improving the relationship can also improve the level of communication.

Another way to show your spouse just how important he is to you is by listening to him when he talks. A simple example of this is to stop whatever it is that you are doing when he talks to you. Of course, if you are the man, you should also do the same. These days, many couples do not talk properly. It is not uncommon to find couples who talk while the other person is watching a movie or reading a book.

They fail to give 100% of their attention to each other. Yes, you can still engage in conversation and be responsive even while doing something else, but the point here is that you are not giving your spouse your full attention, and this does not make your spouse feel important. You should treat your spouse in a special way.

When you communicate with your spouse, it is always worth reminding yourself that you are talking to the most significant person in your life. Unfortunately, many people fail to realize the value of their spouse and take every moment that they share together for granted. Make every moment count. Focus on your spouse and always treat him or her in a very special way. Now, it is not uncommon for people to feel that they are probably no longer important to their spouse. This is true, especially when your spouse is so busy with work and other obligations that he or she has no time to enjoy life with you — and this is also wrong. Unfortunately, this has become common in many marriages these days. However, you should not let something like this to continue. If you feel like you are in this situation, then you should talk to your spouse about it. Another effective way is to be the one to show to your spouse just how important he is to you. You don't have to make things difficult or suffer in silence. Do not forget that your spouse is there for you. If you are not happy about something in your relationship, then face it together as a team.

It is noteworthy that making your spouse feel important takes positive actions on your part. Do not be content with just knowing that he or she is important to you, but you should communicate this message through your actions and in a way that will make him or her feel just how truly important he or she is in your life.

RELATIONSHIP THERAPY

MICHELLE MILLER

Conclusion

Romantic relationships require hard work; we all know it well. Like cars, they need some regular maintenance to maintain their performance. If a problem happens, it should be fixed immediately to avoid further complications.

We can often do some essential maintenance and repair ourselves. Other times, we have to rely on a specialist to look and to give us a hand, given our efforts.

It is interesting that we take such steps easily and quickly to repair or prevent further damage to our vehicles. But we often avoid acting in our relationships until the situation gets much severe.

Unfortunately, many couples have tried couple therapy when considerable damage has been done already. Maladaptive relationship patterns have become strong, the emotional bonds between partners have severely weakened, and the unresolved past conflicts cause a high level of resentment. The list can continue.

Research supports couples' therapy as an effective way to strengthen their partnership. While there are few reasons to support therapy, many marriage therapy activities help people develop their communication skills, minimize disruptive conduct habits, and enhance their capabilities to be emotionally receptive and attentive to their partners.

If you consider counselling people but don't know if your effort would be worth it, you are not alone. Perhaps you learned about a friend's lack of success or attempted it yourself without much profit.

Good results are more likely when couples who undergo therapy are eager to learn practical skills and become both more self-aware and emotionally insecure. Only fundamental communication skills, such as "feeling" words are required. Most people find it challenging to distinguish between emotions and thoughts. This ability can also be acquired and enhanced during the therapy process.

A second most important feature of successful couples is their ability to avoid treating each other as a foe, but rather as a member of the team, collaborating to enhance mutual happiness, seeing you as "in the same team" increases collaboration and the ability of each person to be emotionally sensitive.

Thirdly, the partner's ability to feel empathy is essential. Every person must have compassion for the feelings of insecurity of others and past emotional traumas.

Finally, the willingness of each person to play their part in the problems and to make a positive change is a prerequisite for successful couples' work. Most people undergo relationship therapy with a list of the other person's grievances and want to see a therapist confirm the grievances and then alter the other person's actions. Although complaints are often valid, nothing can be resolved unless both people are ready to change some element of their conduct.

I hope that the ideas I shared can help you strengthen your relationship with your partner. Expect that there are stormy days in your relationship but facing them together is a sure way to overcome the difficulties. It is significant to have an open line of communication to be able to resolve whatever problems you may encounter in your relationship.

Keep the passion alive and sizzling because it brings pleasure and happiness. Cultivate the relationship with love, trust and commitment. It will steer you away from temptations, heartaches and tears. Make it a habit to rekindle your passion every day by showing how much you mean to each other.

Remember that it always takes two persons to build a relationship and also two to make it lasts. It is in your hands.

If you enjoyed this guide, take the time to share your thoughts and post a review. It'd be greatly appreciated!

Thank you and good luck!